Poultry Meat Hygiene and Inspection

Poultry Meat Hygiene and Inspection

Alan Bremner BVMS MRCVS DVSM FRSH
Formerly Veterinary Head of Poultry Meat Section, The State Veterinary Service, The Ministry of Agriculture, Fisheries and Food, London, UK

Mac Johnston BVM&S DVet Med MRCVS
Senior Lecturer in Veterinary Public Health and Senior Clinical Tutor at Royal Veterinary College, University of London, UK

WB Saunders Company Ltd
London   Philadelphia   Toronto   Sydney   Tokyo

W.B. Saunders Company Ltd
An imprint of Elsevier Science Limited

© 1996 W.B. Saunders Company Ltd
© 2002 Elsevier Science Limited

This book is printed on acid free paper

A catalogue record for this book is available from the British Library

ISBN 0-7020-1893-7

Typeset by Phoenix Photosetting, Chatham, Kent
Printed in Great Britain by The University Press, Cambridge

Contents

List of Contributors

AS Bremner BVMS MRCVS DVSM FRSH, *Formerly Veterinary Head of Poultry Meat Section, The State Veterinary Service, The Ministry of Agriculture, Fisheries and Food, London, UK.*

KR Gooderham BVSc DPMP MRCVS, *Chief Veterinarian, Hillsdown Veterinary Services, Marsh Lane, Hemingford Grey, Huntingdon, Cambridgeshire, UK.*

NG Gregory BSc PhD, *Incumbent for the Agmardt Chair in Animal Welfare Science at the Veterinary Faculty, Massey University, Palmerston North, New Zealand.*

AM Johnston BVM&S DVet Med MRCVS, *Senior Lecturer in Veterinary Public Health and Senior Clinical Tutor, Royal Veterinary College, University of London, Hawkshead Lane, North Mymms, Hatfield, Hertfordshire, UK.*

AW Kedward MCIEH FRSH, *Retired Environment Health Officer (Food Safety Consultant, Lynnika, Grafton Lane, Hereford, UK.*

GC Mead BSc PhD FIFST, *Professor of Food Safety and Veterinary Public Health, Royal Veterinary College, (University of London), Department of Farm Animal and Equine Medicine and Surgery, Boltons Park, Hawkshead Road, Potters Bar, Hertfordshire, UK.*

J McLelland BVMS MVSc PhD MRCVS, *Reader in Veterinary Anatomy, Department of Preclinical Veterinary Sciences, Royal (Dick) School of Veterinary Studies, University of Edinburgh, Summerhall, Edinburgh, UK.*

WJ Reilly BVMS BSc MRCVS DVSM, *Honorary Senior Clinical Lecturer at University of Glasgow, Assistant Director at Scottish Centre for Infection and Environmental Health, Hospital Bilsland Drive, Glasgow, UK.*

G Shearer BSc PhD MIFST, *Central Science Laboratory, Food Science Laboratory, Norwich Research Park, Colney, Norwich, UK.*

WJ Williams MBE, *Chairman of British Poultry Meat Federation Ltd, Blackbirds, Nettleton, Lincoln, UK.*

E Wright, *The Ashes, Common Road, East Tuddenham, Dereham, Norfolk, UK.*

Preface

The safety of food of animal origin has emerged in the 1990s as a major issue of international concern. Consumers are increasingly conscious not only of the quality of foods, but also of the foodborne hazards that can affect the safety and wholesomeness of the food. This book has been written to take account of the changes which have taken place, and those which are anticipated, in approaches to the maintenance of high standards in poultry meat hygiene and inspection. As a multi-author text, there is inevitable variation in writing style between the chapters and there may appear to be some repetition, but great efforts have been made to restrict this to that necessary to deal comprehensively with the subject of each chapter.

The poultry meat supply chain from the primary breeding flock to the table is complex, and the opportunities for contamination by microbiological organisms, and the pathways involved, are many and varied. An effective programme at all stages from farm to table is therefore necessary to safeguard public health and to assure the quality of poultry meat. As an introduction to the subject, the poultry meat industry, its development and the current situation is reviewed in Chapter 1. The poultry farm, including bird husbandry, veterinary supervision and health control, record keeping, preslaughter planning and ante-mortem health inspection are described in Chapter 2. Chapter 3 deals with the design and construction of slaughterhouses and cutting premises, with emphasis on the provision of premises which enable high hygienic standards of operation to be achieved.

Protection of the welfare of birds at all stages in the production chain, until they are rendered insensible to pain, is crucial. In Chapter 4, the welfare of birds at catching, transport, and stunning is considered. The methods of slaughter and dressing of domestic fowl, turkeys and ducks are described in Chapter 5, where the specific differences between the species and the processing problems which result from such differences are also discussed. Chapter 6 reviews anatomy, based on the chicken, with other species and interspecies differences considered. A topographical/regional approach is taken rather than the more usual systematic approach used in poultry anatomy texts, which is more appropriate to the requirements of meat inspection and enables an easier understanding of the hygienic processing of the birds.

Today's meat hygiene agencies are faced with the challenge of delivering a service which is scientific, risk-based and cost efficient and, above all, effective in consumer protection. Greater emphasis is being placed on systems to produce healthy, microbiologically and chemically clean birds rather than reliance on old-fashioned abattoir-based inspection. An integral part of the new system is application of a risk-based approach. This requires identification and characterization of a hazard before a decision can be made as to the management of the risk. Control of microbiological hazards in poultry processing is discussed in Chapter 7, including comment on decontamination of the end-product. The organisms described in this chapter concern the live bird and processing stages, whereas in Chapter 8, which deals with food poisoning associated with poultry meat, the organisms are considered as food-borne pathogens as they affect human health. The surveillance of food-borne disease and comment on prevention of food-borne disease associated with poultry meat are also included in this chapter. Despite this risk-based approach, there remains a need for judgement of fitness for human consumption following a physical inspection of birds in the processing plant, which is detailed in Chapter 9.

While much of the production takes place in the larger units, there is a significant involvement by small producers. This section of the industry, with its specific problems and its own market, is described in Chapter 10, which includes comment on the production of carcases in a traditional way.

Proper use of drugs, in particular antimicrobial and antiparasitic drugs, by farmers is most important. Chapter 11 describes the control and the supply of drugs for use with poultry. Modern meat inspection systems must check for the presence of antimicrobial and chemical residues. The surveillance requirements and the screening/monitoring systems to detect possible breaches are discussed.

The text ends with consideration of the production of poultry meat products. There is a wide range currently available and many new products will be developed in years to come. The very specific requirements of the design, construction and operating practice in plants involved in such production are described in Chapter 12.

CHAPTER 1

The Poultry Meat Industry

Introduction

Farmers have kept poultry for many centuries, with some evidence that fowl were domesticated as long ago as 2000 BC. Traditionally, poultry were kept in the farmyard to supply eggs, while the males and end-of-lay hens were used as a supply of meat and feathers. These products were sold in the local market or taken to special markets further afield. Birds were allowed to wander at will, foraging for themselves in the farmyard, although many would have been shut up in houses for the night, principally to protect them from predators. Threshing time was considered a good period at which to slaughter the birds, which would have fattened on the corn dropped on the ground.

The poultry meat industry has been and remains one of the most successful growth industries in agriculture in the world. This has been achieved through many changes from the small farmyard flocks to the industry which now produces nearly 50 million tonnes of poultry meat every year worldwide. This growth has taken place principally in America (both North and South), Europe and Asia, and until recently in the former eastern bloc countries.

The many changes to the industry since the 1930s have led to a reduction in the expense of rearing birds for meat production and hence have played a large part in reducing the cost and increasing the consumption of poultry meat. Over a 10-year period it is estimated that there has been an increase in consumption of poultry meat in the countries of the European Union from 13.8 kilograms per person in 1980 to 18.4 kg in 1990. In 1993, average consumption per person in the UK was 21.5 kg, compared with 43 kg in the USA (this was amongst the highest consumption rates per person in the world).

One of the most significant changes has been the genetic improvement to poultry stock as a result of selective breeding. The aim of the industry for many years prior to the 1950s in Europe had been the maintenance of pure-bred stock. Birds were commonly sold on their appearance rather than their production performance. However, the science of poultry breeding became more complex as it became apparent that cross-breeding could introduce hybrid vigour, the resulting offspring demonstrating food conversion rates and daily weight gain exceeding those of either parent.

As knowledge of heritable traits increased, selective breeding became more sophisticated. The fact that growth rate and body size are inherited characteristics can be used to increase the efficiency of food conversion, although there is also increased fat content of the carcase. In broilers, for example, the food conversion rate has improved from about 2.76 units of food to produce 1 unit of poultry meat in 1960 to about 1.8 units in 1995, and it is hoped that improvements will continue for some time to come. Birds now reach slaughter weight at a younger age, which means that houses can be used to produce more birds in a given period. Obviously there must be limits to the improvements which are possible, although these do not seem to have been reached yet.

There are some disadvantages to rapid growth rates, especially if rapid growth continues up to maturity. For example, artificial insemination is necessary in some modern breeds of turkey since the large breast muscle mass of the birds prevents natural mating. Some excessively fat birds, both male and female, may have reduced fertility. In some breeds it is possible for the birds to have an initial period of fast growth, followed by slower growth later on so that the breeding birds do not become too big.

Housing and rearing

Most fattening birds are reared in intensive housing, and the improvements to houses and equipment have been important in increasing productivity. Better ventilation and heating have been introduced and better facilities for cleaning and disinfecting houses have played their part. The sizes of the flocks on the farms have also increased. Some of the first houses were used for 200 birds, with about a thousand on the farm in total. Modern farms have more than 100 000 birds on the premises, with some houses holding over 40 000 birds. Feedstuffs and feeding patterns have also become better suited to the requirements of the birds, and equipment is less wasteful than the early troughs and drinkers.

Disease prevention is very important, particularly on the bigger farms, and monitoring mortality and food consumption is very important. Experienced farm workers can detect slight changes in a flock and can suspect disease at an early stage which may allow the disease to be contained or the flock to be sent early to the slaughterhouse. While veterinary science is constantly improving preventative disease measures such as vaccination and routine feeding of medicinal products, new diseases or variations of existing diseases are always likely to cause more problems. One advantage of smaller farms is in the control of disease, because it may be necessary to isolate an infected farm to prevent disease spreading.

Welfare

Welfare of poultry both during loading at the farm and in the slaughter-house has been a problem, but recent improvements in handling have pleased both animal welfare groups and the poultry industry. The possibility that gas stunning of poultry will be introduced into some slaughter-houses in the future is likely to be an advance as it will remove the present need for hanging the birds in shackles before they are stunned.

Improved catching procedures on the farm and transporting equipment reduces catching damage and the number of birds that are dead on arrival at the slaughterhouse.

Environmental pollution

One problem for the poultry industry which is likely to increase in the future is that of pollution. The release of ammonia into the air from large farm units can lead to environmental pollution, while the disposal of manure from poultry houses can also cause problems with smell and pollution of the land on which the manure is spread with nitrates and phosphates. The disposal of waste feathers, blood and offal from slaughterhouses can also be difficult, as public opinion is now turning against the feeding of these materials to poultry or other animals, even after heat treatment, which has been one of the ways of recycling these materials in the past.

The changing industry

Customer requirements and attitudes to poultry meat have changed, particularly since the 1970s, with a significant increase in the market for value-added product. There remains a small, but significant, production of traditional poultry. This includes regional specialities such as *effilé* and delayed evisceration poultry, and seasonal production of birds for special festivals, e.g. turkey for Christmas and Thanksgiving.

There are marked differences in the way the poultry industry has developed in the countries of the European Union. For example, France, Holland, Belgium and Denmark are big exporters of poultry meat, whereas Germany is a big importer. Other countries including the UK seek to supply mainly the home market, importing relatively small quantities when the price is right on the world market or when there is a shortage of home-produced poultry, and exporting mainly further processed poultry meat products. The European Union, however, is a net exporter of a small percentage of its poultry meat production.

Integration of the poultry meat industry as elsewhere in the world is fairly common in Europe. The integrated companies buy in parent stock from specialist breeders, although some companies also have their own breeding programme. The parent stock are reared on farms that are either owned or supervised by the company, which can also own the hatchery, the fattening farms, the slaughterhouse, the cutting premises and further processing factories.

Poultry meat production continued to grow during the 1980s in Europe. In the early 1990s there was a drop in production owing to the changes in the eastern bloc countries and the worldwide recession, although some evidence of recovery was seen by the mid-1990s.

The future of the poultry meat industry must depend on increasing efficiency (with more hygienic and automatic equipment) and continued diversification into value-added foods. On the farm there has to be better disease control, while in the processing plants procedures must become more hygienic with the aim of reducing the prevalence of bacteria that can cause food-borne disease in humans.

There is a need for uniform standards of public and animal health for all poultry meat production. The *Codex Alimentarius* Commission of the Food and Agriculture Organization and the World Health Organization is working towards universally agreed standards, and the General Agreement on Tariffs and Trade (GATT) seeks to remove the various restrictions and subsidies that inhibit free trade in the world market. Animal health requirements are an important consideration, as imported live birds or products can be a vector of disease.

Poultry meat hygiene and inspection must be developed within a framework which gives traders and consumers confidence. This should take account of cultural and climatic circumstances and traditions. There must, however, continue to be an awareness by food handlers and consumers that no matter how good the production systems, uncooked foods can harbour pathogens.

CHAPTER 2

The Poultry Farm and Ante-mortem

Introduction

The vast majority of poultry, of whichever species, are hatched and reared specifically for slaughter. The farms on which they are reared are usually designed for this purpose, as a high standard of husbandry is the first step in the production of clean meat. An exception to this is the specialist farm designed to house breeding stock or flocks which lay eggs for culinary use; these flocks are, however, slaughtered at the end of their reproductive or egg-laying period. This chapter is mainly concerned with poultry reared for slaughter.

The farms on which poultry are reared, even though designed for the purpose, vary greatly. Many poultry houses predate the improvements in design introduced since the 1960s. These improvements include changes such as concrete floors in place of compacted earth, better ventilation and insulation, larger houses, and more automation of feeding and environmental control. Some of the newer features have been added to the old poultry houses, but they remain old houses.

The poultry farm comprises one or more houses, but rarely more than twelve. The houses are usually timber-framed, concrete-floored buildings clad with composition boarding or timber and roofed with corrugated aluminium or asbestos. The houses are usually 12–18 metres (40–60 feet) wide and 30–90 metres (100–300 feet) long, with insulated walls and roofs. Houses are windowless so that light levels can be controlled. Lighting is electric, using tungsten filament bulbs or fluorescent bulbs or tubes.

Heating is usually by gas, either by whole-house heating or by the use of canopy brooders. Ventilation is by electric fans mounted in the ridge or in the sides of the building and controlled by one or more thermostats. A control panel offers a range of settings enabling the environment to be controlled automatically both for temperature and ventilation. Modern computer-controlled equipment can be programmed to provide the desired environment of temperature, humidity and ventilation. A print-out of the environment actually achieved is also produced.

Automatic systems for supplying feed and water are present in most houses. Feed is usually offered in a continuous trough supplied by a moving chain, or in a series of pans filled by an auger which provides feeding points throughout the house. Water is supplied in hanging, bell-shaped drinkers which are self-filling or through bird-operated nipples in a drinker line.

Bird husbandry

Rearing of poultry, whether for meat, eggs or breeding purposes, involves caring for the bird and its needs. With intensively reared poultry raised in detailed production programmes it is essential that strong emphasis is placed on correct husbandry. The biological requirements of the bird may be listed as follows.

- Adequate warmth.
- Adequate ventilation.
- A comfortable environment.
- Adequate food.
- Adequate water.
- Protection from disease.
- Protection from predators.
- Protection from excessive competition.

Success in rearing the chicks, poults or ducklings depends on their quality on arrival at the farm. For the best quality, action should be taken well in advance of the hatch date, going back to the flocks which produced the hatching eggs. Correct nutrition of the parent flock will not only prevent specific nutritional deficiencies, but ensure that chicks are lively and have a good start to life. The parent flock should be free from disease organisms which can be transmitted through eggs, such as *Mycoplasma* and *Salmonella*. Also important is the presence of maternally transmitted antibody to specific diseases. The diseases of concern are those that are likely to challenge the bird early in its life: such diseases in the chicken are infectious bursal disease, avian encephalomyelitis and possibly Newcastle disease. Thus, the correct parent flock vaccinations and a serological monitoring programme are important to the young bird.

Other factors that affect day-old quality before the birds are placed in their brooding environment are egg hygiene, the storage and age of the eggs, hatchery hygiene and correct incubation. Of particular importance is the length of hatching time and the correct time of 'take-off'.

The length of time in boxes and in transit to the farm should be minimized to ensure the chicks' best start in life. The preparation of the farm in readiness to receive the chicks is equally important. The houses should have been cleaned and disinfected after removal of the previous flock, as should all equipment such as feeders and drinkers. Lines carrying drinking water should have been flushed through with a non-toxic disinfectant. The environment should be prepared with good-quality dry litter and the temperature brought up to the brooding requirement. Adequate supplies of food and water should be available in close proximity to the brooders.

Once the birds have arrived and been placed on the floor, continuous attention is important. The group size under each brooder will influence mortality and performance; reducing the number of birds in a group reduces competition. There should be about 1000 chicks in a group – never more than 2000. For turkey poults and ducklings 500–700 birds is a better number. The effects of stunting and runting disease in broiler chicks are more severe the greater the brooding population, even within a single broiler house.

Once the birds are placed under the brooders, they should be allowed to settle. Extinguishing lights apart from the light from the brooder and a small spotlight or brooder light near to and just lower than the brooder will discourage birds from wandering into the darker, less warm areas of the house. Some houses are heated by a single source of heat, giving a whole-house brooding arrangement, but this is more difficult to manage, and close attention to bird requirements is essential.

Both food and water (particularly water) must be freely available within the lighted area. Food in crumble form is frequently scattered on corrugated paper placed in the brooder area. This has the effect of increasing the spread of the food and also encourages the birds towards the food by the sound made by others walking on and pecking at the paper.

When the birds have had a few hours to settle, a visit will indicate whether all is well. They should be grouped under the brooder in a ring, the central area being too hot for them. A break in the ring will indicate an uncomfortable area, perhaps a draughty place. The undisturbed birds will be eating or drinking, and no birds should be outside the lighted area.

During the first few days of life, bird behaviour should be observed during frequent visits. All the biological needs mentioned earlier must be checked on each visit. Warmth is assessed by the pattern of the birds in each brooding area. There should always be areas warmer than they require and also areas cooler than they require. In this way they can tell you their choice. Only when the correct temperature is achieved should the thermometer be read such that a record may be kept.

Very little ventilation is required early in life, but it is important not to let the atmosphere become too humid. Some ventilation must be given to maintain oxygen levels and remove carbon gases created mainly by the brooders. For the first few days, supplementary feeding trays or papers should be used and also supplementary drinkers. Drinkers must not be allowed to become empty. Any automatic drinkers are lowered once the litter has become trampled down. If nipple and cup drinkers are used, check regularly that water is available at each drinker.

The adequacy of this early environment can be assessed by recording the mortality, a visual assessment of the birds and by the weighing of a sample, at, say, 7 days of age. The spread of weights should be small, and normally distributed.

Over the first week, the temperature of the house and under the brooder is gradually reduced for the benefit of the growing bird. From the cost aspect, the less artificial heat applied the better, but this is often overdone. Some farmers attempt to conserve heat by not ventilating, by reducing the heat applied more than is desirable, and by using just part of the house to brood. This last practice is acceptable provided that competition for space, food and water is not increased. Ventilation should be increased gradually, and is a balance between the temperature of the incoming air and the need to remove foul air. Ventilation at night is just as important as in the day; it may be necessary to apply extra heat in order to achieve this. When the flock is about 5–7 days old, supplementary feeders and drinkers should be removed and the permanent drinkers spread out a little more to encourage the birds to use more of the house. A few days later the crumbled starter feed is changed to a lower-protein pelleted feed. In controlled environment housing, heating and ventilation requirements can be programmed auto-matically to adjust the environment to that considered appropriate to the flock.

Stocking density considerations are important. The number of birds placed in a house depends usually on the intended weight at slaughter. The maximum weight advised for chickens is 34 kilograms of live weight per square metre of available floor area. For turkeys it is about $39 \, kg/m^2$. There are, however, other aspects of stocking density which can restrict bird wel-fare and performance. Such aspects include feeder space per bird, drinker space per bird, ventilation capacity per unit of bird weight, number of birds per work-hour of supervision and other factors of lesser, but still recogniz-able, importance.

For the best attention to the flock's needs, it should be visited at least three times daily and a routine followed. The following programme is sug-gested.

- Walk round the complete house, picking up any dead birds and culling others as necessary. This should be done once a day. The culling may be done on a separate visit from dead bird collection.
- At the same time view the live birds and assess their health and any indi-cations of discomfort or lack of food or water.
- Check the environment and make any adjustments necessary.
- Check that all automatic equipment is working.

- Check that feed is available throughout the house and in all feeders.
- Check that every drinker or drinker line contains water and is not leaking.
- Check that litter condition is acceptable.
- Observe any other abnormal features and correct them.
- Record all events as required on the house record card.
- Report any serious problems to the overall manager or veterinarian as appropriate.

At least once weekly, a sample of birds should be weighed and their average weight calculated and recorded. Attention should be drawn to abnormal average weights or abnormal spread of weights to determine why this might be.

Following such a programme, and incorporating the advice offered later in this chapter on biosecurity, farm hygiene and record keeping, there should be few problems. Incorporated into the programme will be the advice on specific and general disease control offered by the farm's veterinarian.

Biosecurity

Biosecurity is a term that encompasses the measures used to protect a population of animals from disease. Such measures may also be referred to as a 'microbiological barrier'. If an infectious disease agent does not exist in the flocks of birds on a premises, it can only affect the birds by being brought in from outside the premises. The ideal biosecurity programme can be described, but few farms achieve it in practice. Breeding companies with valuable elite genetic stock and grandparent populations have very thorough biosecurity programmes. These are expensive, but have the value of allowing the buyers of parent generation chicks to receive clean, healthy stock.

Maintenance of the high health status is achieved by placing the new flock on a clean farm empty of all other stock. Ideally, the farm should be sited well away from other poultry farms, and the site should be securely protected by stockproof fencing and a stockproof, lockable gate. No farm livestock or pet animals should be allowed within the perimeter fence, and houses should be inaccessible to wild birds and wild or feral animals.

Staff working on the farm should have no contact with other poultry or other avian species such as game birds and pigeons. On arrival at the farm they should change into clean protective clothing, and foot-dipping and hand-washing must be enforced prior to entering any livestock house.

Similar precautions are essential for those people required to visit the farm, such as senior managers, veterinarians, vaccinators, maintenance personnel, etc. An active rodent control programme is necessary; if this is provided by a contractor, the employees must observe all the biosecurity procedures. Visitors with no rôle to play on the farm should not be allowed.

Feed deliveries should preferably be arranged by blowing feed from the delivery vehicle from outside the perimeter fence. Where this cannot be arranged, the cleanliness of vehicle and driver should be ensured. In any event, the driver will not enter the livestock houses. The feed itself represents a hazard (e.g. possible *Salmonella* contamination) and must be obtained from a reliable source to minimize this. Other deliveries such as gas and litter must undergo similar planned hygiene programmes. Any equipment that may be delivered to the farm, such as egg trays and trolleys to a breeding farm, must be thoroughly cleaned and disinfected beforehand. It is an additional security to spray such equipment with disinfectant solution on its arrival at the farm and to ensure it is not used within the livestock houses.

The farm's biosecurity programme should be well designed, and all the procedures written down in a manual for all staff to use. The precautions should be given in full detail, and the reason for the detail explained. Also explained should be the serious consequences which could result from failure to implement any part of the biosecurity programme.

Growing farms tend to have more activity and are less able to enforce all aspects of a biosecurity programme. They should, nevertheless, enforce as many points as possible. Recent examples of the way a disease can spread from farm to farm have been seen in Great Britain. An example of epidemic spread has been that of Gumboro disease (infectious bursal disease), which rapidly spread over the whole country. In every farm affected, the disease entered through a breach in biosecurity.

Farm hygiene

Within the farm there are certain practices which, if followed, will reduce the effects of endemic disease and the build-up of potentially pathogenic organisms. In modern poultry farming, particularly in the production of large numbers of birds for meat, the 'all in, all out' stocking procedure is strongly advised. This procedure is one in which the farm is stocked entirely with birds of the same or similar age. Not until all birds have been slaughtered and the whole farm has been emptied, cleaned and disinfected, will any more birds be introduced.

Not all birds will be killed at the same time, however, as birds are frequently slaughtered at different ages. In the case of broiler chickens this process is usually called 'thinning'. Some birds are slaughtered from each house, while the remainder are allowed to grow to heavier weights. In the case of turkeys it is usual to separate males and females by a fence across the house. The females are slaughtered first (e.g. at 10 or 11 weeks); the males then occupying the whole house are kept until 16 weeks old or more.

Unfortunately, at the time of thinning or the earlier slaughter of some birds, there is a risk of disease introduction by the catching team and the equipment used in catching (lorries, crates or modules, and fork-lift trucks). Precautions must be taken to minimize this risk, but experience has shown these precautions often to be inadequate. Infection with *Campylobacter* and *Salmonella* has been linked with the practice of thinning.

The farm hygiene programme between placements is more efficient if it is well planned in stages. Before birds are slaughtered it will be known when each house is likely to be caught. This should be anticipated not only by the correct withdrawal of medicated feed, but also by ensuring that as little feed as possible remains in the feed bin after the house has been emptied. Any necessary repairs or maintenance of the house and equipment should be planned in advance and the work scheduled for the empty period. This is preferable both for disease control and ease of working. Rubbish disposal from the site should be arranged during the empty period, and any dead birds remaining on the site must be removed. Arrangements in advance should be made for any other work required during this time, such as a visit from the rodent controller.

CLEANING AND DISINFECTION

When the house is emptied of birds a programme of cleaning and disinfection is followed. This may vary in detail for each type of house and for each farming operation, but the principles are the same:

1. Loose equipment is removed from the house for cleaning outside. This may include feeders and drinkers, although many of these are now on winches and are raised to the roof; this applies particularly to nipple-type drinkers.
2. Beams and ledges, particularly those above head height, are 'blown down'. Using a hand-held electric blower, accumulations of dry dust are blown down onto the litter. This dust inevitably accumulates in poultry houses and it is preferable to remove it while dry rather than in the wet state.
3. The litter bedding is then removed. This is usually done mechanically with a small readily manoeuvrable, for example a 'Bob-cat', type vehicle equipped with a fore-end loader, aided by shovelling and sweeping litter away from walls, support posts and other obstacles.

4. The litter is loaded onto lorries and removed completely from the poultry farm. Although it is commonly used for spreading on agricultural land, it does represent a hazard to poultry in that it will contain avian pathogens such as infectious bursal disease virus, avian rhinotracheitis virus, *Pasteurella*, *Salmonella*, *Escherichia coli*, etc. Poultry in houses downwind of any litter spreading may easily become infected. Some farms have now contracted for their poultry litter to be burned for power generation, a preferable option as risks of disease spread are reduced.

5. With the house empty of litter, a check should be made whether there is a need to sweep and shovel any residues of litter. Any feed remaining in the feed bin should be bagged off and removed, preferably to the next house to be slaughtered.

6. After this the house is washed. A power washer using water containing a combined disinfectant and wetting agent is used. All surfaces, ceilings, walls, support structures, air inlets and air extraction trunking are washed. Any equipment remaining in the house is also washed. Care should be taken not to splash any dirty material onto already washed surfaces. Finally, the floor is washed. It is best if the floor slopes to drain this wash water away rather than leaving puddles of dirty water. The bacterial count of this water is usually extremely high. After this, all washed surfaces are sprayed with water containing an approved disinfectant. The concentration used should be that recommended by the supplier, but recognition should be made of the fact that many surfaces are wet, and the diluting effect of this should be allowed for in calculating the strength of disinfectant to apply. It is common to use an insecticide incorporated with the disinfectant when litter beetles, flies or other insects have been a problem. These insects are capable of carrying infectious agents over from one flock to the next. Equipment which was taken out of the house will have been cleaned and disinfected. This may now be reintroduced to the house.

7. Any area of the house which has not been cleaned and disinfected must now be dealt with. This includes particularly electric panels which could not be pressure washed. Ideally these should be situated in part of the house separated from the main livestock area. This area, too, has to be cleaned nevertheless. Brushing down the electric panels with a soft hand-brush followed by wiping with a disinfectant-dampened cloth is recommended.

8. Particular attention should be directed to the water system. The header tank should be emptied and cleaned, then filled with a non-toxic disinfectant solution such as an iodophor. This solution is then run through the drinker lines to disinfect them. Sometimes solid material is released from the drinker lines which could block the automatic drinkers. This is

one reason for a regular programme of drinker-line cleaning. At this stage, the placing of rodent bait or setting of traps should be carried out. With no poultry feed available it is more likely the bait will be taken.

9. All houses on the farm should be approached in this same way. Afterwards, any equipment used in the cleaning process should also be cleaned and disinfected. This may include brushes, shovels, stepladders and wheelbarrows. The area outside the houses should then receive attention. The area in front of the houses should be hosed down. Places frequently missed are any on-farm offices or canteens. In addition, protective clothing such as boots, caps and overalls should be disinfected or laundered at this time. Attention should be directed at any other place where dirt or contamination is evident. Equipment used for young chicks may have been stored elsewhere and should be disinfected in readiness for use. This could include supplementary feeders and drinkers and watering cans.

10. Once the farm is clean, all houses should receive a final fogging or fumigation. Where a fumigant is used, it is advisable to heat the house to a suitable temperature before fumigating. Finally, the bedding may be introduced and the equipment assembled ready to receive the birds. When chopped straw is used as bedding, it is useful to ventilate the house as soon as the bedding has been introduced. In this way, some of the fungal spores which are inevitably present in the straw can be removed while they are still airborne.

The period of time taken for this 'turn-round' programme will vary. Sometimes, on large farms, chicks are introduced into the first cleaned house before the litter has been removed from the last house to be emptied. This is poor hygiene and disease-control practice. There should be a period of rest between the time when the farm is totally cleaned and reassembled and the receipt of chicks. The longer this period is, the better the results achieved. That is, one week is better than one day.

In order to obtain the best value from these procedures, a post-cleaning audit is recommended. A checklist should be prepared and filled in during the audit, carried out either by the farm manager or an independent member of staff. The audit might include, on an occasional or regular basis, microbiological screening of the cleaned equipment and housing.

Most of the description above pertains to a farm practising 'all in, all out' placement of birds. If a farm has multi-aged flocks and is thus continuously stocked, a suitable hygiene programme must be devised. It is usually possible for each house to be populated with a single-aged flock, and subsequently totally depopulated. Subdividing a continuously stocked farm into several 'all in, all out' units will improve bird health and performance. Some farms operate one or more brooding facilities. This entails the moving of birds to a finishing house when they are 'off heat'. Whichever practice is followed, it is usually possible for single houses or single rooms of houses to be treated as separate 'all in, all out' entities. An effective hygiene programme should follow the steps described above.

Care is necessary not to spread contamination or infection from the stocked houses to the newly cleaned houses. Separate equipment should be available for each house, including those small items used when rearing birds, such as watering cans, weighing scales, stepladders and catching frames. It is to be preferred if separate staff care for each house, but this is rarely possible. Great care, therefore, must be taken when moving between houses. Regularly replenished foot dips should be outside or just inside each house and should be used whenever entering or leaving a house. Staff should wash their hands when moving between houses. Spread of infection between houses can take place owing to air extracted from one house being taken into another. This should be minimized by planning the house ventilation systems with this problem in mind.

In addition to the end-of-crop farm hygiene programme, a daily hygiene programme should be followed during the time when birds are on the farm. The farm and the houses should always be kept clean and tidy. Only farm staff should enter the livestock houses as a rule; other visitors are by prior arrangement only. Staff members should be presentable, always wearing overalls which are regularly laundered. Boots should be worn which are clean and always dipped before and after entering a livestock house; foot dips should be replenished regularly. Hand-washing and toilet facilities on the farm must be adequate and properly maintained, with hand-washing practised regularly when handling livestock and also before break times.

Dead birds should be picked up as a first procedure every day. They should be removed from the house and held in a closed container or compound at the entrance to the farm pending collection. Vermin and feral cats should not be able to gain access to the dead birds. Neither the transport used for collecting dead birds nor the driver should come onto the premises, hence the birds being held at the farm entrance.

Planning

It is usual nowadays for anyone producing large numbers of birds to do so according to a planned programme. Planning proceeds in the reverse direction from production. Starting with the proposed sales or processing profile, the number, size and timing of birds to be delivered to the slaughterhouse are specified. This allows the farm placement programme to be calculated which will take into account the stocking densities which will pertain at the time of slaughter. The length of time taken to grow to the desired weight is then calculated. These calculations together determine the date of placement, the mix of sexes and the number of birds to be placed in each house. Allowing for a period for each farm to be emptied, cleaned and disinfected, the optimal use of farming space and facilities can be planned. Once this is done, the hatchery incubation programme, the breeder flocks' egg production programme and the day-old parent flock purchasing programme are calculated and then put into action.

Inevitably changes will be made, dependent on changes in the sales profile or accidents in production such as egg production drops, hatchability problems or growing bird mortality. The smoother the plan, however, the more likely it is that good performance will be achieved. Once the programme has been described, it is necessary regularly to monitor actual events against planned events. The growth rate of birds on the farms must be continually checked, and action taken when growth rates differ from the target weights.

Veterinary supervision and health control

All major producers of poultry retain the services of a veterinarian who is usually a poultry specialist or who has considerable poultry veterinary knowledge. These veterinarians may be company employees or in private practice. It is usual, however, for the veterinarian to be, loosely or otherwise, part of the management team. In this way, he or she is able to receive performance details, to assess problems and to advise on programmes of preventive husbandry and preventive medicine.

In this chapter the term 'disease' is used to describe any cause or failure of birds to perform normally. For the meat bird, whether chicken, turkey or duck, this can be mortality, poor growth rate, poor feed efficiency, meat inspection rejects, carcase downgrading or trimming or poor carcase conformation. For breeding stock (but not for further discussion here) it can mean in addition suboptimal egg production, fertility or hatchability, or poor egg quality. The veterinarian has interest in all these areas and is involved in determining their causes and their prevention.

As described earlier, close attention to biosecurity, farm hygiene and bird husbandry is of prime importance in disease control and optimal biological performance. Monitoring bird performance against expectation will allow problems to be identified at an early stage. Mortality and clinical disease are monitored daily. When there is an increase in either of these an investigation may include a farm visit by a veterinarian or examination of birds post-mortem. Reaching a diagnosis of the problem may require further tests involving microbiological culture, histopathology and serology.

There are two avenues of response: how to overcome the problem in the affected flock, and what measures to take to prevent a similar problem in future flocks placed on this or other farms. For the benefit of the producer and of the livestock the preventive approach should be adopted wherever possible. The disease history will indicate which specific measures to take.

Infectious diseases

A major problem in rearing birds for meat is infection with the bacterium *Escherichia coli*. It will cause clinical disease and mortality, usually as a respiratory infection or septicaemia. Recovered birds may be rejected at meat inspection due to lesions such as air sacculitis, pneumonia, pericarditis, peritonitis or congested 'fevered' carcases. This bacterium usually invades the tissues as a secondary infection to an earlier viral challenge.

Viruses may be detected by serological testing of blood samples taken at time of slaughter. Once the virus is identified a control programme can be introduced. This will, where possible, include vaccinating against the virus during the early growing period or even in the parent flocks which supply the chicks.

Programmes of vaccination and other measures are commonly used to reduce the effects of such viruses. Sometimes the vaccination programme is directed at infections which are subclinical in their effects, but can nevertheless cause production losses or, more seriously, precipitate other clinical infections. One such disease in the UK is Marek's disease. This is uncommonly seen causing clinical disease in broiler chickens, but vaccination of day-old chicks often leads to improved performance. This is more likely to be true in the older, less well-maintained farms. Marek's disease virus (MDV) is an immunosuppressive virus such that a subclinical challenge will render a bird less able to mount an immune protection against other diseases. Other immunosuppressive viruses common in chickens are chick anaemia virus (CAV) and infectious bursal disease virus (IBDV).

Some infectious diseases are capable of being transmitted from parent to chick through the egg. Monitoring of the parent flocks coupled with hygiene and biosecurity programmes keeps such infections to a minimum in the parent flocks. The monitoring programme alerts the veterinarian to any change in the flock's health status, enabling specific action to be taken as appropriate. Infectious agents in this category are the mycoplasmas of chickens and turkeys, salmonellae and, in certain circumstances, chick anaemia virus.

Other measures taken in the parent flock to ensure a healthy, good-quality chick are maintenance of good health; correct nutrition; avoidance of poor husbandry practices; and ensuring the desired antibodies are present for transmission to the chick. A good-quality, healthy chick is far more likely to rear well than a poor chick from parents lacking the attention described above.

Problems due to litter

Some infectious diseases which occur in the growing bird, or incorrect nutrition, can result in an enteric upset. This may be an enteritis or increased gut motility, or perhaps an increased thirst. The net effect is to increase the amount of fluid which is voided onto the litter. This makes the litter wet and sticky and the microbial action in the litter is reduced. Unless corrected by the timely addition of fresh litter, this can lead to problems damaging both to the bird and to its carcase when processed. The wet litter does not absorb faeces, which remain on the surface and are caustic to the birds' feet. Plantar pododermatitis may ensue which appears uncomfortable to the bird and reduces its performance. Resting on wet litter may result in black scabs developing on the hocks (hock burn) and an enlargement of the sternal bursa (breast blister). Scabbing or pressure necrosis of the sternal bursa may also be seen.

These lesions can also develop in birds on dry litter. Under these circumstances the chemistry of the litter may be at fault, for example owing to high nitrogen or high fat levels. Whatever the cause, both hock burn and breast blisters can result in trimming in the slaughterhouse and subsequent downgrading of the trimmed carcase.

Leg problems

Leg problems include a number of conditions which can result in lameness and leg abnormalities. Lame birds may spend much time resting on the litter, resulting in the development of breast blisters. If seriously lame, as in chickens with femoral head necrosis, birds will be reluctant to drink adequately and will soon dehydrate. Such birds are quickly culled, but if the condition develops just prior to planned slaughter, the bird may reach the slaughterhouse. Its carcase will be dehydrated and thus appear redder in colour, and will be rejected. Arthritis and tenosynovitis are infectious conditions which occur regularly but at a low level in the various poultry species. These again will be detected at slaughter unless the bird is culled earlier.

The primary cause of these leg problems is not well understood. Observations in the poultry house point towards early fast growth and lack of exercise as being contributory factors. Increasing the level of light intensity and modifying the early feeding programme seem to lead to fewer leg problems. High brooding temperatures and low early ventilation rates seem adversely to affect the legs of turkeys grown to heavier weights.

Ascites

Ascites is a condition seen in all species of poultry. The abdominal cavity is found to contain fluid which has developed as a result of right-sided heart failure. The causes may be several, but in the broiler chicken inadequate ventilation coupled with a high oxygen demand (fast growth rate, high feed intake) are major factors. Ascites is seen more in males than females and has a higher incidence in winter than summer. While sometimes it has a high incidence in a flock, it is seen to a certain level in most flocks. Ascites is probably responsible for 10% of all broiler chicken mortality. Some birds will survive long enough to reach the slaughterhouse, where they will readily be detected.

Tainted flesh

Tainted flesh of poultry can occur. Most recorded cases are due to feed ingredients, particularly marine fish oil. This problem is sufficiently well known that high levels of such ingredients are avoided and care is taken to reduce related ingredients such as fish meal in the pre-slaughter diets. A musty taint has been associated with wood shavings litter derived from timber treated against sap stain. This is the result of microbial action on these chemicals and the problem is usually resolved by the time birds are slaughtered. The trend for killing birds at younger ages and the rebedding of birds due to wet litter are practices which could lead to musty taint in carcases. Other causes of taint are rare, and its association with some vegetable protein meals is not proved.

A similar problem can occur if birds fall into a disinfectant foot dip. Coaltar compounds or other strong-smelling disinfectants can easily be transferred from contaminated feathers to the scalding tank water, resulting in carcase taint. For this reason it is advisable, when catching birds for slaughter, to move the foot dips well away from the house.

Many of the conditions which are seen in the slaughterhouse and result in carcase rejection, trimming or downgrading reflect on the disease incidence and husbandry conditions on the farm. For this reason the collection and examination of slaughterhouse data allow the field veterinarian more readily to identify the problems and to propose preventive action.

Zoonoses and their control

The two important zoonotic bacteria which may be implicated in food poisoning episodes associated with poultry meat are *Salmonella* and *Campylobacter*. In order to control the incidence of these organisms on poultry meat, measures must be taken at a number of stages of both production and processing. *Salmonella* and *Campylobacter* vary considerably in their epidemiology, such that different control measures are appropriate for each. What they do have in common is that they are carried in the intestines of poultry without causing clinical disease. (This statement is not entirely true, in that some serotypes of *Salmonella* may cause clinical disease in young birds and may cause tissue lesions to develop, some of which may be observed on post-mortem inspection of carcases. In addition, intestinal changes may occur in chickens challenged with *Campylobacter*. The important point is, however, that most commonly poultry carrying *Salmonella* or *Campylobacter* are clinically healthy.)

Salmonella

There are many serotypes of *Salmonella* which may be found in poultry or in their environment. Some of these will readily establish themselves in poultry populations, others tend to be transient in nature. Of particular importance are the invasive serotypes, which are not restricted to the intestine. The two most common invasive serotypes are *Salmonella enteritidis* and *S. typhimurium*. These are important as they may readily be transmitted either in or on the egg from the breeding flock to the meat generation. The invasive salmonellae are the more difficult to control, so that concentration on the control of these should result coincidentally in the control of the other serotypes.

SOURCES OF *SALMONELLA*

A bird may become infected with *Salmonella* from a variety of sources. In practice these tend to be:

- Feed.
- Water.
- The breeding flock.
- Other livestock.
- The general environment.
- Rodents, wild birds, etc.

Feed

Feed ingredients are commonly contaminated with *Salmonella*, some more commonly than others. In Great Britain, for example, animal proteins sampled by the Ministry of Agriculture, Fisheries and Food (MAFF) in 1994 were positive for *Salmonella* in over 15% of imported proteins but in only 2.2% of home-produced protein. Vegetable protein meals were more likely to yield *Salmonella* (almost 5%) than other vegetable ingredients (2%). These figures are from the returns of laboratories registered under the Processed Animal Protein Order in Great Britain.

There are codes of practice for the control of salmonellae in feed mills in the UK. Mills operating to these codes check samples of their feed ingredients and are supplied from sources operating to the best standards. In addition, the mills sample their finished feeds to determine the incidence of *Salmonella* supplied to the farm. Despite these controls, the incidence found in samples of finished feed is over 2%. It is recommended that feed be heat-treated in some way (through an expander or by pelleting) to reduce this level. Post-production contamination of feed in the coolers or in transport is a further risk which must be addressed. Some mills incorporate organic acids in the feed in an attempt to reduce these risks. Improved cooler design to facilitate cleaning further reduces cross-contamination of the end product. The on-farm storage of cereal grains (wheat, barley) is not always ideal and care must be taken by feed mills to check both the supplier and the delivery transport used.

Water

Most farms use a mains water supply which should therefore be uncontaminated by *Salmonella*. Where borehole or well water is used, care must be taken to ensure it is uncontaminated or that it is adequately treated before use. Water may become contaminated in the header tank in the poultry house, or in the drinkers themselves. These are merely routes of spread within a contaminated environment and are discussed later.

Breeding flock

A breeding flock may become infected with *Salmonella* by any of the routes mentioned. Once a breeding flock is infected, it may transmit the infection on or in its eggs to its progeny. In this way, birds on many farms may be infected and the farms remain contaminated. A contaminated hatchery may be instrumental in spreading this contamination back to other supply flocks.

In order to monitor and to control the invasive salmonellae in the UK, the Poultry Breeding Flocks and Hatcheries Order (1993), based on European Union Directive 92/117/EEC, has been brought into force. Under this order, all grandparent and elite flocks and hatcheries are monitored, as are all broiler chicken parent flocks. At broiler parent level, samples for microbiological screening are taken when the birds are 1 day old, 4 weeks old, and before onset of lay. During lay, samples of cull chicks or meconium are screened from each supply flock every 2 weeks. To assist in reducing the incidence of *Salmonella* in flocks and hatcheries, a code of practice has been prepared, containing detailed advice on farming practice and biosecurity (1).

Broiler parent flocks have been a common source of infection in broiler chickens over recent years. Efforts to monitor and control these flocks have included serological monitoring and more recently vaccination. It has become clear that the infection of 'clean' parent flocks tends to occur on the laying farm rather than the rearing farm, and that the source of infection remains on the farm from flock to flock. This is in spite of total depletion of birds at the end of lay and the thorough cleaning and disinfection of the farm prior to the introduction of the next flock. It is thought that a major player in the carry-over of infection is the rodent population, particularly mice.

Other livestock
As discussed above, the modern poultry farm should, ideally, operate an 'all in, all out' stocking procedure. No poultry should remain on the premises after depletion or slaughter of a flock. Where this is not practised, any infection on the farm can be perpetuated by bird-to-bird spread in a continuous production system. Other livestock on or adjacent to the premises might be free-ranging or farmyard poultry, pet animals such as dogs and cats, or farm animals: no such livestock should be present on the poultry farm premises for correct *Salmonella* and other disease control.

General environment
The inside of the poultry houses and the poultry premises in general should be kept clean and tidy and in a good state of repair. The premises should be well drained, with drainage ditches kept clean of vegetation and silt. The site should be kept free from overgrowth of vegetation. Rubbish and used poultry litter should not be allowed to accumulate. Houses should be in good repair and proofed, as far as is reasonable, against wild birds and rodents. After the removal of each flock, the houses should be emptied totally, thoroughly cleaned and disinfected, and all equipment similarly cleaned and disinfected. Water tanks and water lines should be flushed through with a non-toxic disinfectant. Water tanks should always be lidded; they should be positioned for both easy inspection and cleaning, preferably at ground level in an anteroom to the livestock area.

Rodents, wild birds and feral animals
Rodents have been shown to be carriers of *Salmonella* and are probably involved in perpetuating infection from flock to flock on a premises.

Trapping and baiting are important, particularly when the premises are empty and feed is scarce. Holes in the house, particularly at ground level, should be cemented up with a soft cement mixture. This should include all drainage holes, cracks, and the bottoms of doors which are only used at stocking and emptying the house. For emptying and cleaning purposes, this cement is easily broken away.

Covers should prevent wild bird ingress through ventilation areas, and feral animals such as cats should be discouraged.

MONITORING

There is no legal requirement in the UK to monitor the meat generation of poultry for *Salmonella*; there is, however, a code of practice for the monitoring of broiler chickens and their premises, which should be the minimum level for good practice.

Routine faecal or litter samples should be taken for culture during the life of each placement of birds. In addition, the standards of empty house cleaning and disinfection should be monitored. This latter programme is better carried out by measuring total bacteria in a given location rather than by screening for *Salmonella*: the results give an indication of the degree of cleaning, and can be used in discussion with cleaning teams.

Medication of birds as a method of *Salmonella* control is not advised other than in the first few days of life when it is known that egg transmission is likely to have occurred.

Campylobacter

Poultry meat is commonly contaminated with *Campylobacter*, mainly *Campylobacter jejuni*. Knowledge of the sources of infection, its spread and measures for its control are limited in comparison with *Salmonella*. It is known that the two organisms differ in many respects in their epidemiology. Vertical transmission from breeder flocks has not been shown to occur and broiler chickens are seldom found to be carriers of *Campylobacter* below 2 weeks of age. Feed is not considered to be a source of infection, but water may transmit the disease. This can be difficult to prove, as viable *Campylobacter* in water are often not readily cultured which makes screening of water supplies difficult. Most poultry farms are, however, supplied with mains (potable) water. When water from other sources such as boreholes is used, then on-site chlorination or other water treatment is advised.

Water is known to facilitate rapid spread between birds once infection has been introduced.

Although the most likely source of infection in a flock has yet to be determined, it is known that there can be carry-over of infection on the farm from one flock to the next, despite an 'all in, all out' farming practice. The standard of cleaning and disinfection between flocks is probably important, as is the length of time allowed between depopulation and repopulation (turn-round time). Strict hygiene practices on the farm such as foot dipping and hand-washing between houses by farm staff are other important factors. The introduction of *Campylobacter* onto a site may be by wild birds or rodents. Control of these and the maintenance of houses in good repair should help to keep infection off the site.

Once a flock becomes infected, spread between birds is usually rapid. Clinical disease does not occur but large numbers of *Campylobacter* are excreted in the faeces. At the time of rapid spread of infection between birds and a high level of excretion there is often described a serious deterioration of house litter quality. It may become wet and sticky. It can be debated whether high levels of *Campylobacter* in the gut are the cause of wetter than usual faeces or whether the wet litter conditions (caused by other factors) facilitate the rapid spread of *Campylobacter*. Whichever the explanation, it is important for other aspects of bird health and welfare and carcase quality to maintain good litter quality.

Catching teams, their equipment and the transport crates or modules are likely to cause considerable and rapid spread between farms. Contamination will have a greater impact when thinning flocks for slaughter than when whole houses are emptied of birds.

Other zoonoses

Other zoonoses may occur in poultry. Perhaps the only one to cause serious problems is ornithosis; the clinical disease is relatively uncommon, but subclinical carriers of infection may occur. The first knowledge of any infection in poultry has at times been due to infection being diagnosed in workers at poultry slaughterhouses. This has been more important in some countries than others. Ducks and turkeys are more likely to be infected than chickens, including on those occasions when clinical disease occurs. Infection on a premises is readily controlled by the operation of the good hygiene practices already described. Particular emphasis should be placed on 'all in, all out' stocking programmes and the elimination of wild birds from houses. Employing staff who have no contact with other avian species (particularly psittacines and pigeons) is also an important stipulation.

Record keeping

Record keeping is an important part of the livestock manager's routine. Records form a diary of events by which the manager communicates facts and opinion to others having responsibility for the birds' production.

Each house (or other unit) of birds should have its own record card which will be readily accessible. On it will be recorded the number, type and origin of the birds, as well as the date and age of placement. Daily records will be kept of water consumption (including water meter readings), house temperature (minimum and maximum), mortality and culling, as well as any clinical observations. Where appropriate, daily feed consumption will be recorded, and (with adult stock) egg production.

Less regularly, other events are recorded as they occur. Dates of feed deliveries, their quantity and type, and whether they contain medication, should be noted. A sample of each feed delivery is retained for later examination if required. Any other samples taken for examination will be recorded, such as birds submitted for post-mortem examination, blood samples for serology, and litter for microbiological screening or chemical analysis. The results of these tests should also be available. Any medication given in the drinking water, in the feed or by any other route will also show the necessary withdrawal periods prior to slaughter or prior to taking eggs for culinary use. Dates and types of vaccination will also be shown, as will bird check weights and any similar records. Housekeeping or maintenance events to be recorded include power failures and their duration, feeder breakdown, flooding and any similar happenings. All these programmes and events should be entered on a single house record card. A visitors' book will record all visitors who enter the livestock houses; it will contain the date of the visit and the visitor's signature.

In preparation for the intended slaughter of a flock it is important that the records show which medicaments and other products have been administered during the life of the flock. The dates of administration should be shown so that the period of withdrawal prior to slaughter may readily be calculated. This includes drugs not requiring a veterinary prescription such as anticoccidials and antihistomonads, for which there is a required withdrawal period. The Veterinary Written Direction accompanying the food will describe the withdrawal period required for any in-feed medication prescribed. Any water-soluble medication provided should always be accompanied by a signed record or prescription which indicates the withdrawal period.

The manager must be particularly alert to the above requirements when just part of a flock is to be slaughtered. The common practice of 'thinning' removes some birds at a lighter weight, allowing the remainder to grow to heavier weights. There is frequently difficulty in planning such programmes.

Prior to slaughter, a production report is prepared. This is furnished to the slaughterhouse veterinary inspector at least 72 hours before intended slaughter of the birds. The report will include the farm of origin, the intended date of slaughter, the number of birds to be slaughtered, flock mortality data, any diseases diagnosed and the results of any laboratory examination. Also included will be the details of any medication given. Other information should be provided if required, and a pre-slaughter veterinary inspection of the birds on the farm may also be requested.

Ante-mortem or pre-slaughter health inspection

If a satisfactory production report is furnished to the official veterinary surgeon (OVS) 72 hours prior to intended slaughter, on-farm ante-mortem inspection is not required. There may, however, be reasons for inspecting birds on the farm to observe and record aspects relating to slaughter and carcase quality. The visit may be carried out by the OVS or by the farm's supervising veterinarian.

The preparation for the visit will take account of the need for good hygiene and biosecurity discussed in other sections of this chapter. The visit should not increase the risk of disease spread. Clean overalls and substantial clean, disinfected boots should be used during the inspection. These will be the veterinarian's own protective clothes or will be provided by the farm. The aim should be to avoid introduction of infection to the farm or removal of infection from it to another farm. The risk relates to the person, the vehicle and any equipment.

The inspection should attempt to assess all aspects of health and welfare of the birds, their environment, their suitability for slaughter, record keeping, and farm hygiene and biosecurity.

The kind of premises involved will become apparent when the veterinarian first arrives at the farm; whether it is neat and tidy, and the houses in good repair. Records should be inspected. The overall attention to detail in the records will give a general view of the standard of management. Specifically, a check should be made of the feeding programme with respect to drug withdrawal times and any water-soluble, injectable or other medicaments used.

The pattern of mortality may highlight problems that have occurred. Any post-mortem or other samples recorded can be questioned. It is a frequent error that the farm manager may not have been told the results of any examinations carried out. Copies of these should be available at the time of the ante-mortem inspection. Check weights and water consumption figures may indicate whether the flock has performed normally.

The birds themselves should be viewed in their normal surroundings and, in the first instance, examined as a total flock. A checklist is useful to assist observation. The veterinarian should begin by entering the house gently in order not to disturb the birds. The normal flock will be well spread through the house; movement will be unhurried, but usually purposeful, to eat, drink, scratch, etc. Birds should be relatively uniform in size and feathering. There will be a certain amount of 'chatter' but no extreme calls nor respiratory noises. There will be a normal 'bird' smell.

The abnormal flock may show a lack of movement, possible locomotory disturbance. There may be huddling of birds in groups. Birds may be uneven in size and feathering, and the feathers may be dirty. A noisy flock indicates discomfort or disturbance. There may be respiratory noises (coughing, sneezing or râles). A sick flock may give off a foul, diarrhoeic smell.

After the flock has been checked, the environment should be inspected. Light intensity should be bright, illuminating the whole house. Dim lighting leads to less activity, and reduced exercise may result in leg problems. Additionally, dim lighting will hide problems and lead to poor husbandry. Excessively bright light can lead to cannibalism (feather and vent pecking) although this is less likely in the docile broiler strains of chicken.

The litter should be dry and friable. Wet or spongy litter can indicate an enteric problem or poor drinker management. The temperature should be comfortably warm. Birds should not be gasping from the heat nor inactive because of the cold. The humidity should be moderate, not steamy with excessive condensation on cool surfaces such as walls and drinker lines. A dry, dusty atmosphere is also wrong. Ventilation should be sufficient to keep the air fresh and free from a smell of ammonia. It should be possible easily to see the end of the house without its being obscured by a dusty haze. The ventilation should not be increased to the point of causing draughts, although this may be desirable in very hot weather. The floor space should be evenly occupied by the flock. Empty spaces usually indicate a problem (draught or wet litter). Any factors likely to cause tainted carcases must be considered.

Consideration can then be given to the individual bird. Not every individual will be viewed, but attention should be directed to certain birds as one glances round the flock. Is the bird behaving normally? Is it well grown or stunted? Is it well feathered? Is is clean? Droppings from individual birds should be examined for colour and consistency. Respiratory signs and sounds should be observed, such as coughing, sneezing, râles, gaping, gasping, head shaking, swollen head, swollen eyes, and nasal or aural discharge. Nervous signs may be observed such as trembling, ataxia, falling, paralysis, circling or blindness. Locomotor inadequacy may include crooked toes, enlarged hocks or other joints, slipped tendons, straddled legs, paralysis, abnormal bone conformation, leg weakness, abnormal posture or wing drooping. External signs may include feathering, skin lesions, eye lesions or signs of parasites.

In a large flock there will always be some abnormal or possibly sick individuals. By far the greatest majority of birds are normal. It will be rare to consider that a flock is not suitable for slaughter when a judgement is being made. The most likely reason is failure to observe medication withdrawal periods rather than sickness of the birds. It may, however, be appropriate to advise the culling of obviously sick individuals before the flock is slaughtered. This would be on the grounds both of reducing levels of contamination in the plant and of welfare of the individual birds. It is unnecessary to subject a bird to catching, transport and slaughter if it will obviously be rejected at post-mortem inspection.

No bird may be slaughtered for human consumption if it is showing clinical signs of ornithosis or salmonellosis. When some other clinical disease is evident and recent mortality rates indicate there may be a requirement for a greater than usual post-mortem judgement time or trimming of carcases, then adequate warning should be given to the slaughterhouse veterinarian.

Where it is thought that birds are suffering from a condition that may affect their suitability for slaughter for human consumption, it may be necessary to arrange for additional tests. These may involve post-mortem examinations on the farm or culture tests at a laboratory. There will always be some urgency over arranging this — if there is a delay in slaughtering, the welfare of the birds may be compromised, as may the total farm hygiene programme.

Perhaps the greatest value which can be gained from pre-slaughter inspection occurs when a particular farm has provided diseased or poor-quality birds over a period of time. It may be helpful for the OVS to explain this to the farm's veterinarian and to request a visit to assess the next flock due to be slaughtered. Such an approach can be of benefit to both producer and meat inspector.

Ante-mortem or pre-slaughter inspection at the slaughterhouse is less readily carried out for a variety of reasons:

- Birds are not being observed in their normal surroundings and thus may not exhibit the behaviour which would have been seen.
- Inspection of birds in crates is difficult; the closest observations that can be made are when the bird is in the shackle.
- Only a few birds can be inspected at any one time in this way.

There are certain advantages, however, to checking live birds on the line. Some indication of possible damage in catching or transporting can be gained. Feet can be inspected for incidence of plantar pododermatitis.

Catching and loading birds for slaughter

The arrangements for catching and transport of birds for slaughter are part of the planning programme described earlier in this chapter. Modifications are made to the overall plan depending on particular requirements. The purchasers of the poultry carcases or portions of carcases usually demand particular weights. Part of the rearing programme on the farm demands check weighing of the birds to determine their growth rate. Growth can be at greater or lesser rates than anticipated, so that changing the order in which houses of birds are slaughtered may be necessary. These changes notwithstanding, it is usual to plan the slaughter programme a week in advance. This is important not only in preparing the production reports, but in managing feed deliveries and feed withdrawal programmes. Planning the slaughter programme also takes into account the continuous flow of birds at the slaughter plant and the utilization of transport.

When birds are caught for slaughter they are placed in various forms of container. These may be loose or fixed crates, or modules which have several compartments or drawers into which the birds are placed. These transport containers must be of non-corrodible material and be easy to clean and disinfect. Cleaning and disinfection must be carried out after each use. Inspection of these containers and of the lorries used for live bird transport is best carried out routinely at the slaughterhouse. The cleaning and disinfecting procedures can readily be observed, as can the result of these procedures. Microbiological checks on the crates are of value. Although similar checks can be made when the lorries arrive at the farm, this is not always easy. Much of the loading is done during the hours of darkness, making inspection difficult. Further, there is frequently no-one of authority on the farm at this time.

The method of catching and loading varies depending on the type of crate used. The more common method is to have a module comprising several compartments which is delivered into the poultry house by a fork-lift truck. Birds are caught and counted into each compartment according to an agreed density. This density will have taken into account the size of the birds and the weather conditions. When full, the fork-lift truck will remove the module and place it on the lorry. With loose or fixed crates it is usual to carry the birds to the lorry. This involves more walking by the catching team and is thus a slower programme. The actual method of catching and carrying poultry will differ with the species of bird concerned and its size (see Chapter 5).

Reference

1. MAFF. Code of practice for the prevention and control of Salmonella in breeding flocks and hatcheries. PB 1564. MAFF Publications: London, 1993.

Further reading

1. Jordan FTW, Pattison M. (eds) *Poultry diseases*. 4th ed. London: WB Saunders, 1996.
2. Pattison M. (ed.) *The health of poultry*. Harlow: Longman, 1993.

CHAPTER 3

Design and Construction of Slaughterhouses and Cutting Premises

Introduction

Before a slaughterhouse or cutting premises is designed and constructed, many aspects have to be considered. The first is that there must be some assurance that there will be a market for the poultry meat produced at the premises. Secondly, for efficient use of labour, equipment and buildings, a slaughterhouse has to keep working at full production or as near as possible to full production, for as many hours as possible. There need to be, therefore, guaranteed sources of live poultry and a supply of labour, as well as a market for the product.

The poultry for slaughter will come from several farms, which should be as near as possible to the slaughterhouse, so that the journey for the birds is not too long. While this is the ideal, sometimes domestic hens at the end of lay have to be transported long distances because there are not many slaughterhouses that slaughter these birds, and those that do have to go some distance to obtain enough birds to keep the slaughterhouses working effectively.

Many companies that sell poultry meat are vertically integrated, which means that they supply the day-old birds to the farms that rear the poultry for slaughter, as well as running or supervising these farms. These companies have breeding farms where the parent stock (purchased from specialist breeding companies) are kept, and a hatchery where the eggs are incubated and hatched. The day-old poultry are then supplied to the rearing farms. Careful planning and disease control are required, but it is relatively easy for these companies to ensure the supply of birds of the required age and weight, for the slaughterhouse to maintain production. The alternatives are to have contracts with independent farmers or to buy birds ready for slaughter on the market; the latter has advantages when birds are plentiful, but there can be problems when birds are in short supply. The management of poultry meat cutting premises also requires a continuous supply of carcases, although carcases may be kept in cold stores to provide a buffer stock for times of shortage.

Once the supply of poultry to the slaughterhouse is assured, the maximum throughput of poultry per hour and per day has to be decided.

Whether this throughput justifies buying automatic equipment which increasingly can carry out much of the processing, or whether some of the functions that can be carried out by automatic equipment should be done manually to save capital costs, is also relevant to the design. Although line speeds for automatic equipment are constantly being increased, some staff and meat inspectors are required to carry out duties on the poultry and poultry carcases which are conveyed within the premises on shackle lines. It is important that these people have sufficient space, the right equipment, and time in which to work with the individual carcases, so that they are able to carry out their duties efficiently. Some countries lay down the maximum speed of the line where the carcases are to be examined by meat inspectors. Hanging-on the live birds is still a manual activity and the staff carrying out these duties must also be given the right conditions and time in which to carry out their work. The throughput therefore has to be considered not only in relation to the supply of birds, but also in relation to the working conditions for the staff and meat inspectors.

The traditional way to lay out the conveyor lines, which transport the poultry within the slaughterhouse, is for there to be one killing line, which transports the birds from the hanging-on of the live birds until the completion of slaughter and defeathering, followed by two to four evisceration lines where the evisceration and inspection of the carcases is carried out. The size of the various rooms depends, to some extent, on the number of lines, so this is also relevant to the size of the premises (Figure 3.1).

Most major plants now work at least 16 hours in 24 hours on poultry or carcases, with a thorough cleansing and disinfection of the premises in the early morning before the first shift of the day arrives. The number of birds slaughtered each hour and the number of hours during which carcases are produced and processed will affect the size of the work rooms as well as the chilling and freezing equipment and the refrigerated holding and storage rooms. The refrigeration equipment in the chilling and freezing rooms must be capable of dealing with the carcases and meat as these are produced, so that cooling can begin immediately after the completion of processing.

The types of products leaving the premises will also affect the size and design of the plant. Very few premises are now built for the production of carcases only, so that at least a cutting room will have to be provided, enabling portions and deboned meat to be marketed. There is a greater variety of portions and deboned meat now being produced than was the case several years ago, so modern cutting premises are designed to be bigger than before. Space has to be provided for the different activities that are required in cutting, deboning, wrapping and packaging. Further processing by cooking or smoking, where the product can be eaten by the consumer without further processing, should be carried out in completely separate premises, although they could be on the same site, provided there is effective

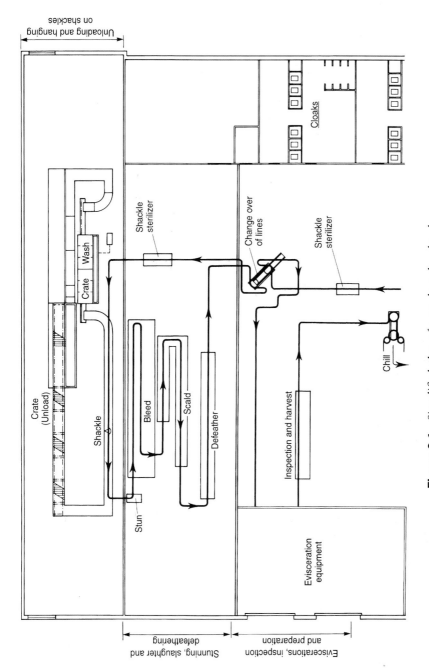

Figure 3.1 Simplified plan of a poultry slaughterhouse.

separation. The manufacture of meat preparations, where other foodstuffs are added to the raw meat, should normally take place in separate premises, although some processes may be allowed in a separate part of the cutting room if it is big enough to ensure there is no hygiene risk.

Many managers consider that it is difficult to manage a plant employing large numbers of people. This is less common now that automatic equipment has reduced the need for staff to carry out some of the tasks, but in some countries, particularly where labour is relatively cheap, over a thousand staff can work in the same premises. It is difficult to supervise all these people and to ensure that they carry out their tasks correctly and hygienically, so where many staff are required, it is better to split the premises into completely separate units, e.g. the slaughterhouse and the cutting premises, for easier management supervision.

The requirements for the site

The site for a slaughterhouse or cutting premises will have to be carefully selected, and be big enough not only to cater for the proposed premises but also to permit enlargement of the buildings if the business expands in the future. There should be a good road system to the premises and a reasonable source of labour. The site must have an adequate supply of water and electricity as well as facilities for removing waste, including waste water.

The whole site on which the buildings are constructed must have a surrounding wall or fence and be large enough to permit the separation of the 'clean' side of the premises from the 'dirty' side. It is preferable for two entrances to be provided from the road, one for the dispatch of the product, the 'clean' side, and the other for the reception of poultry and the dispatch of the waste products, the 'dirtier' side. Two entrances to the site are not always possible, in which case there may be one shared entrance provided the lorries entering the site are immediately separated into those going to the clean side and those going to the dirtier side. There has to be sufficient space for the lorries to manoeuvre and be able to reach their loading and unloading bays. It should not be necessary for any loading or unloading of lorries to involve the movement of crates of live poultry, materials, or edible or inedible products, across an open yard. The roadways used by the lorries, the surround to the premises and the pathways used by pedestrians should be constructed of concrete, with falls to drains to remove surface water.

Other buildings will be required on the site to hold poultry on arrival on the lorry, as well as facilities where lorries can be cleansed and disinfected. Separate washing facilities will be required for the meat lorries and the lorries that carry birds. There should be a drained base to the lorry wash areas with a supply of water and disinfectant. Where there is a risk of frost which might freeze the water, a supply of warm water should be available. A gate-house at the entrance to the premises to control the movement of vehicles and people onto and off the site is usually required, and car parking space is also necessary.

There should be no live animals on the site nor poultry in the immediate neighbourhood, because of the risk of the spread of diseases. Other businesses near to the proposed site should be investigated to see if they present a risk of contamination, for example aerial contamination by smoke or dust, or by providing a suitable environment for vermin to live and feed. If there is a serious risk, then the site should not be used for the production of food for human consumption.

Water

The water supply has to be potable, although the legal requirements for this standard vary between countries. Normally there are physical, chemical and bacteriological standards laid down for potable water. Premises producing meat that may be exported should be provided with water that complies with the requirements of the importing country. If there are any doubts about the standard of the water supply or the supply is from a source which is not potable, then provision should be made for a water treatment plant. Depending on the source, the water may need to undergo a variety of different treatments, e.g. filtration, flocculation, sedimentation and chlorination. Chlorine needs a contact time of 20 minutes in water to ensure that visibly clean water is bacteriologically safe. If a water treatment plant is necessary, it will occupy considerable space and should be catered for in the design of the site. An alarm system should be included in the water treatment equipment so that if any of the processing ceases to work properly the management can be alerted quickly. The amount of water required in the premises varies, depending on throughput and the type of equipment used. Some premises use water to convey the offal once it has been removed from the carcase, and waste feathers can be also conveyed by water. Frequent washing of the carcases, the cooling of carcases in water, and processing larger carcases which requires more water, also increase the amount of water which is necessary and which has to be disposed of as waste water. Estimates suggest that 30–60 litres are required per bird in a poultry slaughterhouse. A water storage tank or tanks will be necessary if there is not a guaranteed continuous supply of water to the site, and the tanks must be covered and be capable of being cleaned. An electricity generator may also be required if there is a possibility of the electricity supply failing. A supply of hot water is required for the premises for cleaning the rooms and equipment and for wash-hand basins; this supply should come from a boiler which is heated by gas, oil, electricity or solid fuel.

Waste water

The easiest way of removing waste water from the premises after screening to remove feathers and offal, is for it to go directly into the sewerage system of the local authority. However, this is not always possible, as the sewerage system may not be capable of handling the large amount of dirty water which comes from a slaughterhouse, in which case some preliminary treatment of the waste water will be necessary. A fine screen which removes much of the solid organic materials still left in the water, a fat trap and a final water treatment plant may be needed and should be sited as far away from the slaughterhouse as possible, to prevent any risk of contamination. There should also be a surrounding wall or fence to this area to prevent unauthorized entry. Some waste water treatments consist of aeration of the water: these aeration processes may cause turbulence and water droplet formation, and in this case there should be a wind screen to prevent the spray being blown onto the food processing premises.

Waste products

Occasionally the waste products, e.g. feathers and offal, are heat-treated on the site for use in animal feedstuff or as fertilizer. This processing can cause problems of cross-contamination unless the plant is constructed and situated so that there is no risk of contamination to the food factory from people who work in the waste processing premises, from the raw materials or the products and from mobile equipment which may go between different buildings on the site. Evidence suggests that the heat processing of waste should not be carried out on the site where food for human consumption is also being produced, as the risk of cross-contamination is too great. Feathers and waste should be collected in a bay which can be closed to the outside and has its own drainage. A skip is usually housed in this bay and is taken away daily or more often if necessary. Duck and goose feathers for use in clothing or bedding, can be processed in a separate building, and this factory should also be sited so that there is no risk of cross-contamination of the food premises.

Planning consent

Once the site of the premises has been decided it may be necessary, in some countries, to consult with the planning authorities to ensure that the site is acceptable. The planners will consider the access to the premises by road and whether the large lorries used in transporting both the live birds and the final product can enter and leave the plant without causing problems such as an increase in traffic congestion. Another aspect the planners will wish to consider is the pollution problems of noise, smell, the movement of lorries and cars, and the disposal of waste water and waste products. People living near to the proposed site may object if they suspect it will affect their quality of life, particularly if the premises will be operational both day and night. Frequently it is considered easier to build the premises some distance from human habitation and to transport the staff to the premises by bus.

The design of the premises

The workrooms must be designed so that there is a flow of product from the reception area to the dispatch bay with no crossing or back-tracking of conveyor lines when they are carrying live poultry, carcasses or further processed poultry meat. The removal of the waste products within the workrooms should be in the opposite direction to the flow of the birds, carcases or the product, and waste should be removed as rapidly as possible from the workrooms directly to the waste storage areas. The route taken by the staff and visitors to enter the various workrooms must also be considered so that they enter at the cleaner end of each room without going through other workrooms or storage areas. Corridors should be constructed so that staff may reach their workrooms from the changing rooms and toilets without the risk of contaminating the product.

The control of vermin or elimination of places where they can live, has to be considered both in relation to the construction of the premises and the whole site, during the design stage.

The first phase of the design should be to consider the size, position and the number of rooms required to contain the equipment and the staff, rather than to start with a building and try to fit the equipment into that building.

The slaughterhouse

The environment in all workrooms must be light, spacious, at a suitable temperature and humidity, with good ventilation and with no excessive noise, particularly in rooms where people are working for any length of time.

Hanging-on room or bay

Most countries have legislation which requires that the different procedures of slaughter and dressing are carried out in separate rooms to ensure hygienic production. The first procedure is the removal of the birds from the container in which they were transported from the farm and hanging them into shackles suspended from a conveyor which takes the birds to the next section. This first part of the process, which tends to be dusty, should take place either in a room or in a covered bay (Figure 3.2). This area should have walls, floors and ceilings that are smooth so that they can be kept clean, and there should be no ledges where dust or water can accumulate. The floor should be laid with falls to drains; because of the movement of lorries or fork-lift trucks in this area, the number of drainage channels should be kept to a minimum and those that are necessary should be protected by strong grids which may be removed to clean the channels. The crates may be washed and disinfected in this room or bay, after emptying and before being put back on a clean lorry; however, the cleaning and disinfection should be in a completely separately drained area and the clean crates must leave the cleaning equipment and be stored in such a way that the live birds do not recontaminate them.

Some countries have a maximum time that the birds can be suspended in shackles before they are killed. The time, however, must be long enough to allow the birds to quieten down before they go into the stunner. The shackle line should not take the birds around sharp corners before entering the stunner as this can make the birds excited and likely to rear up in the shackles, which may mean their heads do not go into the stunner.

Ante-mortem inspection

It is possible for the ante-mortem inspection to be carried out in the hanging-on area providing special facilities to permit inspection are provided. Lighting in this inspection area may be a problem because bright lights can excite the suspended birds. Normally low intensity or coloured lighting is provided in this area which helps to quieten the birds. Although the inspector may need bright light for examination of suspect poultry, it should be possible to inspect most of the poultry under dimmed lighting. A separate room, equipped for ante-mortem inspection, may be provided, through which the birds pass on their way to slaughter. Facilities should be available for live birds which are detained by the inspectors, either for a more detailed inspection or for hanging-on for slaughter at the end of the shift. The birds should be detained in a separately drained area capable of holding small numbers of birds, held in crates, and protected from adverse weather conditions. In consultation with the inspection service, the management of the premises may decide that it is not worthwhile holding individual sick birds, which instead should be killed and treated as unfit for human consumption; in this case this detained area may not be necessary, unless required by legislation. However, the inspection service may wish to hold a lorry-load of poultry for further inspection or a report from the farm of origin. A covered and ventilated holding bay, with fine water-sprays to cool the environment in hot weather, should be provided at all slaughterhouses to protect the birds from adverse weather on arrival and while awaiting slaughter. The

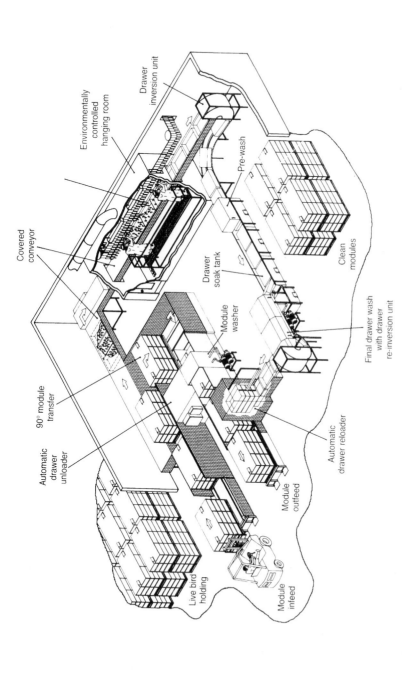

Figure 3.2 Layout of unloading bay for the system devised by Anglia Autoflow Ltd. This is a modular system using open-top drawers. The module and drawers are washed prior to automatic reassembly. (With kind permission of Anglia Autoflow Ltd.)

ventilation should be fan-assisted and should be provided to all crates or modules on the lorry. A part of this building may be separated and used to hold the detained birds, when it is necessary. The detained area should have separate drainage and a partition between the detained birds and other poultry to minimize cross-contamination.

Slaughter and defeathering room

The birds, once hung into the shackles, pass into a room to be slaughtered and defeathered. Slaughter consists of stunning, unless this is not allowed by a religious requirement, and the cutting of the blood vessels of the neck. In some countries legislation requires a certain bleeding time, and the bleeding trough, which is placed beneath the shackled birds and collects the blood, should be large enough to allow the birds to bleed out before entering the scalding tank. The cutting of the blood vessels can either be done manually or by automatic equipment. If automatic equipment is provided there also has to be a person present who can ensure that the blood vessels have been cut or make any necessary cuts in birds that have not been cut correctly by the automatic machinery. Adequate working conditions for these workers must be provided in this area with hand-washing facilities, a sterilizer and an apron wash. If there is a risk of blood splashing from the bleeding area onto the scalding or the defeathering area, a partition should be constructed to prevent this. Blood is normally collected, removed and stored separately from the rest of the waste produced at the premises, so the bleeding trough requires its own drainage for the removal of blood.

The defeathering is a two-stage process: the birds are first immersed in warm water in one or more scalding tanks, and then pass on to plucking machines which drag the feathers from the skin by means of rotating rubber fingers. Several plucking machines are required in sequence in modern processing premises. Waste feathers are removed either by a dry belt or by water in a drain under the defeathering machine. Frequently the water used to transport the feathers is recirculated, in which case the water, after screening to remove feathers in the waste products room or bay, is taken in pipes which must not pass through any other workrooms before discharging directly, without any splashing, into the drain along which the waste feathers are to be transported. The pipe through which the recirculated water passes must be clearly identified as carrying non-potable water. The drainage within the waste products room or enclosed bay must ensure that the waste water does not contaminate other parts of the premises, and the walls and floor must be finished to ensure they are capable of being kept clean.

Ventilation in this slaughtering and defeathering room must be carefully controlled to minimize condensation. Scalding tanks should be provided with a hood and a fan-assisted system for extracting steam. The intake of air must also be controlled to ensure it is not polluted, and screening to remove dust and insects is necessary.

Evisceration and preparation room

A further room is required for the evisceration and dressing of the poultry carcases. Evisceration, meat inspection, carcase washing and water chilling of the carcases can take place in this room provided these functions are separated by sufficient space to allow good working conditions with no risk of contamination from one procedure to the other. Automatic equipment used in the evisceration of the carcases is frequently placed in a separate room to reduce the risk of injury to the staff and to remove the noise this equipment makes from the working environment (Figure 3.3). Wrapping and packaging of carcases normally takes place in a separate room although it can take place in the same air space as evisceration provided it is well separated by distance.

Edible offal can be washed and cooled in this same evisceration room, but it is more hygienic if the offal is transported to separate rooms to be washed and then chilled, either by water or air chilling. The giblets are normally

Figure 3.3 Automatic equipment for eviscerating broilers, with permission from Stork PMT BV.

then placed in a sealed, waterproof wrapping before removal to a refrigerated storage room.

After completion of evisceration and carcase washing, the first-stage chilling of the carcase has to take place. Carcases can be chilled in water immersion chillers (Figure 3.4) or in chillers where refrigerated air is blown around the carcases in a room. Some air chillers have fine water sprays which are directed onto the carcases. This water prevents the carcases drying out and cools the meat by evaporation. The chillers must have adequate capacity and be situated so that the carcases can be moved directly into the chillers as soon as the post-evisceration washing has been completed.

Occasionally carcases, having passed through a water immersion chiller, are held in tanks of ice and iced water overnight. These tanks should be held in refrigerated rooms, and in some countries the tanks have to be continuously drained of water through a hole in the tank. If this is required, extra drains should be provided in the chill rooms.

Adequate space must be provided for the selection of carcases, their wrapping and packaging, and to permit easy movement of the packaged carcases to the refrigerated storage rooms. Blast freezers will be required if frozen poultry is to be produced on the premises and these must be capable of freezing the wrapped carcases, normally prior to boxing and as they are pro-

Figure 3.4   Counter-flow water immersion chillers, with permission from Stork PMT BV.

duced so that there is no undue delay before entering the freezers. Turkey carcases are sometimes frozen in supercooled brine. The brine is likely to attack structural finishes – particularly metal – in the premises so the tanks are usually placed in a separate room where resistant finishes are provided.

Storage rooms

A number of refrigerated stores must be provided, to hold the wrapped and packaged carcases at the required temperatures; the rooms should be large enough to permit the selection of carcases when they are wanted for sale or for further processing. If chilled carcases are stored there should be a sufficient number of chilled storage rooms to ensure that they can be cleaned out each time they are emptied and left to dry before being used again. Boxed meat or boxed carcases must be stored in separate rooms from products or carcases that are not boxed. One of these storage rooms must be lockable and designated for holding detained carcases, when required. These detained carcases could come from a flock where the inspection service require further tests to be carried out before the meat can be released for human consumption.

Dispatch

A sealed docking bay for dispatch is required. A refrigerated air lock at the dispatch bay will help to maintain the temperature of this area and of the box of the lorry, and so maintaining the temperature of the poultry carcases.

Cutting and deboning

If cutting or deboning of the carcase takes place on the slaughtering premises, a separate room must be provided for these processes. The wrapping of the products may also take place in this room. The processes carried out in the cutting room should be arranged so that the carcases or meat do not have to remain in the room any longer than is necessary. Some products require more than one process during cutting and deboning, in which case there must be refrigerated storage available to hold the meat between processes. The carcases should not be brought into the cutting room until they are at a temperature of 4° Celsius or lower, and a refrigerated storage room should be available in case of a breakdown during processing when the carcases and meat can be stored at the correct temperature until the processing starts again. Cutting or deboning can be done either by automatic equipment (Figure 3.5, page 44) or manually when the carcase is either hanging from a moving shackle, held on a moving cone or placed on a cutting board. Throughout the processes the meat temperature must not be

(a)

(b)

Figure 3.5 (a) Automatic equipment for cutting portions of broilers. (b) Automatic equipment for cutting and manual wrapping and packing. With permission from Stork PMT BV.

allowed to rise above 4 °C, and in hot climates it will be necessary to have air conditioning to maintain the temperature of the room at about 12 °C. Placing the wrapped product into boxes may take place in the same room provided the boxes were over-wrapped for delivery and then stored in a clean room prior to being brought (already made up) into the cutting room. The boxing process should be sufficiently far away from the cutting or deboning process to ensure that there is no hygiene risk. The design of the cutting room will depend on the method of cutting, wrapping and packaging which is used, and the throughput.

If the cut meat is to be frozen, one or more blast freezers should be provided, depending on the amount to be frozen. The blast freezers must have the capacity to ensure that the freezing is carried out without any delay. The blast freezers may be either spiral chillers or rooms. If rooms are provided, they should not open directly into a workroom to ensure that the temperature of the workrooms is not affected. Deboned meat or portions may also be frozen using tunnels of liquid nitrogen or carbon dioxide. Rooms where these gases are used must be well ventilated to ensure that pockets of gas do not build up where people are working.

There must be sufficient refrigerated storage space for the final products, allowing for the separation of boxed and unboxed products. In most premises it is preferable to include at the design stage separate storerooms for boxed and unboxed products, so that the premises has the versatility to deal with both types of packaging. The temperature at which the products are stored should be 4 °C or lower: most poultry meat is now stored below this temperature.

Separate cutting and boning premises

Separate cutting premises are frequently constructed. The requirements for the site, waste disposal, cutting rooms and storage are similar to those for cutting rooms combined with a slaughterhouse. In addition, sealed reception bays with associated refrigerated storage rooms are required to receive the carcases. The storage should be near to the cutting and deboning room. Some cutting premises receive some carcases which are boxed and some carcases which are not, in which case separate storage rooms are required for these two types of packaging. If the carcases arrive in cardboard boxes then a special deboxing area or room is required. The hygienic removal of empty used boxes from this area must be ensured.

Occasionally frozen carcases are thawed before cutting. This thawing should take place in a temperature-controlled room which ensures that the temperature of the meat does not rise above 4 °C . Dry goods storage and at least one dispatch chill or cold store will also be required, depending on whether the final products are frozen or chilled and whether they are packed in cardboard boxes or not. The final presentation of the product depends to some extent on the purchaser. Some purchasers may require boxed products and others require the product to be placed in plastic crates. When designing premises it is worth considering that both types of packaging may be required and provide dual storage accordingly. It is very difficult to adapt premises once they have been constructed and this can limit the sales from the premises. A sealed dispatch bay must be provided.

Other aspects of site should be similar to those required for slaughterhouses.

Poultry meat preparations

Poultry meat preparations are defined as fresh meat to which other foodstuff has been added or which has been submitted to some other process such as heating, but where the meat is not fully cooked. These preparations may be manufactured in separate premises or in association with a slaughterhouse or cutting premises. Normally the manufacture of meat preparations should take place in separate rooms, although in exceptional circumstances, where there is no hygiene risk, the process may take place in a cutting room, but separated by space from other poultry meat. If the process includes heating, or the addition of spices or other foodstuffs which could taint other products, these processes must be carried out in separate rooms and only when the preparations are wrapped and packaged can they join any other products produced on the premises.

Some flash-fried preparations may also be produced, which consists of conveying cut and shaped poultry meat, perhaps breaded as well, through a hot fat for a short time to cook the outer layers of the product. Where this occurs it is important that the fryers are placed in a separate ventilated room and that the flash-fried preparations are immediately conveyed out of the fryer to be cooled. Frequently a nitrogen freezing tunnel is used and it is preferable that this cooling takes place in another room, to avoid condensation problems. Once wrapped and packaged the product may join the other products from the premises and they should be stored under the same conditions of temperature and separation required for all the products.

Mechanically recovered meat

Mechanically recovered meat can be produced in separate premises or, more usually, in the cutting premises. Bones that have already had the meat removed manually are placed in machines which separate the remaining meat from the bones, producing a purée of meat and the waste crushed bones. The temperature of the bones as well as of the final product has to be precisely controlled. The process should be carried out in a separate air-conditioned room, capable of maintaining an ambient temperature of 12 °C or lower. Unless the bones are to be processed immediately after completion of the removal of the meat, there must be refrigerated rooms for the storage of the bones awaiting processing. Occasionally these bones may be frozen for storage. If frozen bones are used as raw material, a chiller will be required that can be used for thawing the bones before processing. Facilities for the quick freezing of the product must be provided and this can be plate, blast or spiral freezers. Wrapping may take place before or after freezing and the product should be packaged in a separate room and then placed immediately into refrigerated storage.

Ancillary rooms for all premises

Changing rooms for both men and women must be provided in all premises. The access from the changing rooms to the workrooms must be through corridors and not across open spaces where protective clothing can become dirty. The changing rooms should be equipped with lockers for clothing, showers and toilets, and there should be wash-hand basins placed near to the toilets. Toilets must not open directly into workrooms. Facilities should be provided to supply staff with clean protective clothing and for the disposal of their used clothing. The taps for the wash-hand basins must not be capable of being operated by hand; normally they are operated by foot or knee, although photoelectric cells are also used. Disinfectant soap dispensers and disposable towels should be provided for the wash-hand basins, with a container for the collection of dirty towels. Hot-air hand dryers which operate automatically without the need to press a button may be used, although there is some dispute about the hygiene of operation of this equipment. In slaughterhouses a separate changing room should be provided for staff working in the hanging-on bay and in the killing area. Canteen facilities should also be provided. Either separate canteens for the staff working in the dirtier area should be provided, or the staff must change out of their working clothes before entering the canteen. If there are windows in these rooms, they should be fly-proofed if it is intended to open them. Rooms should also be provided for the inspectorate with changing facilities, lockers for clothing and facilities for the necessary office work.

Clean storage for boxes must be provided as well as separate storage for the other dry goods. Storage space is often underestimated when planning a new premises, with the consequent problems once the premises are in operation.

A room where moveable equipment can be taken to be cleansed and disinfected is also required. During the design stage the siting of this room or rooms must be planned. The access of the used equipment and the route taken by the washed and cleaned equipment must be considered so that recontamination of the equipment is prevented. Within the washroom there must be two separate areas – one for equipment waiting to be cleaned and one for the cleaned equipment.

A laboratory and engineers' workroom are also necessary. Although the work carried out in these two rooms is different, access from these rooms is required to processing areas. The staff are normally working in rooms where clothing can become contaminated and therefore before they go into processing areas they should pass through a hygiene area where they can wash their hands and put on protective clothing. Culturing specific bacteria that can cause human illness should not be done in a laboratory within the buildings where food is prepared or stored, because of the risk of contamination of the product.

In all premises, waste materials are produced and must be stored pending removal from the premises. The waste should be stored in a room or a bay with external doors. There is a variety of ways in which waste can be moved to the storage areas. It can be blown, moved by a vacuum, or transported through drains in the floor, or on belts or in bins. Whatever method of transporting the waste is used, it is important that there is no risk of spreading contamination within the premises and the waste should be moved to the storage area as directly as possible. The storage area must have its own drainage to ensure that no waste water will seep out into other areas, and it must be constructed so that it is capable of being cleansed and disinfected. The exit from this waste area must be directly into the yard, and separate from the areas where food for human consumption is being unloaded or dispatched. Any bins from this area must be cleansed and disinfected before returning to the workrooms.

Finishes within workrooms and food storage rooms

The walls, posts and partitions within workrooms and storage rooms where poultry meat or poultry carcases are processed or stored must be smooth, impervious and light in colour, with rounded corners and angles. The top of partitions should also be rounded. Coving is required between the walls and the floors. Areas or corners of walls, which may get knocked, should be protected with inset stainless steel sheets. It is preferable to have no windows in working rooms, but if these are required, they should be high up in the wall, with a smooth, impervious finish and a sloped sill, and must not be capable of being opened. Doors and door frames must have a smooth, light-coloured, impervious finish, and the doors between workrooms or entrances from outside or into corridors must be self-closing and tightly fitting. Small gaps in the walls may be necessary to permit movements of shackle lines from one room to another. Care must be taken to ensure that carcases or birds suspended from the shackles do not drag against the sides or bottom of the gap. Fire doors may be required from workrooms to the outside. These must remain closed except in an emergency. Plastic strip curtains must not be used in rooms unless the product is wrapped and boxed, as the strips tend to drag over any items that are pushed through the curtain and this leads to contamination.

Before the floor can be planned, the position of the equipment must be known so that drainage for waste water can be correctly placed in the floor. The equipment will include the hand-washing and sterilizer facilities for the use of the staff, as well as larger processing equipment and refrigeration units, and the waste water from all this equipment must be positively ducted to drains. Some equipment such as the plucking machines produces waste water along the length of the machine, and this waste can be collected in a channel under the equipment. The drainage channels must be designed so that they can be kept clean and they should be covered with a grating in areas where people or equipment are likely to cross the channel. Drains must be fitted with gratings and be trapped to prevent odours and vermin from entering the workrooms. There is also, unfortunately, splashing of water onto the floor from some equipment at present used in slaughter-houses and the floor must be sloped to direct this water to drains.

The floor must be impervious, smooth, easy to clean and disinfect, rot-proof and strong enough to be able to stand the wear and tear of equipment and people and the hostile environment of fat, blood and hot and cold water. It should be laid in such a way that the waste water flows to a drain or to a channel which removes the water to a drain. There must be a slope to ensure that there is no pooling of water on the floor. Waste water in the drainage channels in workrooms should flow in the reverse direction to the flow of the product and not go from one room to another but directly into a sewerage pipe. The fall within the channels must ensure that the water flows away and pools of water are not present in the drain. Although the floor has to be smooth to permit drainage of water it must not be slippery and dangerous for the staff. Drainage should not be provided in a room which is used for the storage of frozen products.

The ceilings must be smooth and capable of being cleaned, with the minimum number of ledges or other areas where dirt can lodge. The ceiling or roof should be insulated to reduce condensation. False ceilings can be constructed, although in areas where there is a damp atmosphere, unless the false ceiling can be properly sealed, it is better to line a sloping roof. Most services going to the equipment should be brought into the rooms as near as possible to the place where they are required, and may be brought in through the ceiling.

Lighting

In some countries light levels throughout the premises (both for the staff and the meat inspectors) are laid down by law; but in all cases it must be adequate to permit the staff to see clearly. In workrooms the light should be at an intensity of 220 lux at the working surface and brighter for inspection stations. The light should be placed so that no shadows are cast onto the carcases or products, and it must not distort the colour of the meat. In other areas such as corridors and storage rooms the light intensity should be around 110 lux. The tubes or light bulbs must be of shatterproof glass or there must be a suitable cover of shatterproof material.

Ventilation

Ventilation must be provided in all workrooms. There must be both outlets and inlets to ensure that the pressure in the room is balanced and air is not drawn from one workroom into another. The ventilation system must also be designed to ensure good working conditions. Areas such as the hanging-on bay need a system that keeps the dust away from the staff working there. The ventilation must be adequate to cope with all the temperatures likely to be experienced in the workrooms taking into account the climate of the country concerned, and air conditioning may be required. Ventilation must not depend on outer doors being opened, when dust and vermin can also get in.

Most cutting rooms will require some air conditioning as the temperature of the carcases and meat must not rise above 4 °C in the cutting premises. Care must be taken to ensure that the air conditioning does not cause cold air to blow onto the staff working in the rooms as this causes discomfort.

Equipment in working rooms

The design of equipment is important to ensure that it is safe to use, can be cleansed and disinfected, and that the parts in contact with the birds, the carcases or the meat products are made of material that does not corrode, preferably food-grade stainless steel or plastic. Any joints between surfaces must be made smooth and level. Unfortunately not all machines can, at present, be manufactured to this standard; for instance, the plucking fingers in plucking machines are not easy to keep clean because the fingers are made of rubber or rubber substitute which becomes worn and cracked with use. Other parts of certain equipment cannot be easily cleaned, e.g. electric motors, and these parts should be positioned to ensure that there is no risk of contamination of the product from this equipment. Parts of machinery in contact with carcases or the product must be capable of being regularly cleaned – preferably between each bird or carcase in a way that does not cause cross-contamination to other carcases or products. During breaks in work the whole machine must be capable of being cleansed and disinfected and this has to be considered during the design stage of the equipment.

Hand-washing facilities must be provided at the entrance to workrooms, and adjacent to staff who cannot easily leave their work stations. The sinks should be provided with hot and cold water, or warm water at a temperature of about 30 °C. Taps must not be capable of being operated by hand or elbow; there must be a dispenser of disinfectant soap and a supply of disposable towels, with a container for used towels. At some work stations constant running warm water can be provided over a sink and this permits a rapid rinse of hands between carcases. Sterilizers, operating by means of water at a temperature of a minimum of 82 °C will be required in the workrooms or in an adjacent room, where staff use implements. Sterilizers can be heated by an electric element or by circulating hot water or steam. There should be an overflow from the sterilizer to wash away accumulations of dirt and fat. The sterilizer must be designed to accommodate the equipment which it is to clean. A sterilizer for knives, for instance, should be capable of disinfecting only the blade and the join between the blade and the handle, so that during work times the knife can be quickly selected. A sterilizer that can take the whole knife will also be required at break times.

Facilities for washing aprons and boots should be provided, preferably in a hygiene area outside the workrooms. This should be either a spray cubicle or a trough, with an area where the aprons can be hung to dry, situated near to the wash area. The pipes bringing the water into the workrooms must be exposed for as small a distance as possible within the work rooms, to prevent any areas where dust can collect. Hot-water pipes may be insulated and the insulation material should be completely covered with a material that can be kept clean. If there is a possibility of back siphonage of water, then vacuum breakers must be included in the water system. There should be no dead-ends in the pipework for water, as bacteria can multiply in these and contaminate the water in the system.

Provision must be made for washing, cleaning and disinfecting the rooms and equipment during breaks in production and at the end of the working day. Hose connections for cleaning fluids and for hot and cold water should be provided in all workrooms and in waste collection rooms or areas. A room should be provided for the storage of cleaning materials and cleaning equipment.

The conveyor systems for the shackles should be designed so that the number of surfaces that the birds or carcases touch as they are dragged round the plant are kept to a minimum. Birds must not drag over crates, and carcases must not rub against walls or equipment. Some conveyors are designed to transfer carcases from one area to another, e.g. the belts used in cutting rooms or when dropping birds from the killing line to be conveyed to an area where they are hung on the evisceration lines. The contact surfaces in this equipment must be kept clean and a method of continuous cleaning should be designed into the equipment. Shackles, particularly those on the killing line, must pass through a wash once they have been emptied and before they are used again. Rotating brushes can be used to clean the shackles. However, these brushes must also be kept clean and if water sprays are used to do this the waste water must be collected and piped into a drain.

Implements used manually by the staff must also be manufactured of material that does not corrode. The handles must be comfortable to use and the design must ensure that the implement can be cleansed and disinfected by washing under running water and then placing in a suitable sterilizer. Care must be taken to ensure that the sterilizer is insulated so that it is not a safety hazard. Some countries do not insist on sterilizers on the line provided the implements can be sterilized by other acceptable means.

Electrical switches should normally be placed outside workrooms, although for safety reasons they sometimes have to be placed inside the room. Where this is a requirement the switch must have a waterproof cover which allows the area around the equipment to be properly cleaned. Temperature probes and thermometers are required in areas where temperatures have to be controlled, and these instruments should also be capable of being cleaned and made of impervious material. The ambient temperatures in storage rooms should be recorded at regular intervals and appropriate recording equipment should be available, with an alarm which signals when the temperature is not within the acceptable range.

Containers in which meat is moved should be made of plastic or food-grade stainless steel and should be designed to ensure that they can be cleansed and disinfected.

Meat inspection stations should be provided with space and a stand on the line to permit the inspector to carry out the inspection of the carcases. Also required are a directed light which will not cast shadows and which allows the inspector to see inside the cavity of the carcases, a hang-back rail, a sterilizer, a hand-wash basin, and containers which can be locked to prevent unauthorized access, and which can hold the carcases or poultry meat considered unfit for human consumption.

CHAPTER 4

Welfare of Poultry at Slaughter

Introduction

This chapter considers the welfare of poultry at catching, transport, stunning and slaughter. It draws on information reviewed in references 1–6, and puts it into a practical context.

Pre-slaughter handling and transport

Pre-slaughter handling can affect the welfare of the bird and the quality of the carcase. Bird welfare can be compromised in eight ways (Table 4.1), all of which have some bearing on carcase quality or value.

Table 4.1 Welfare problems associated with catching, transporting and unloading poultry.

Death
Bruising
Broken bones
Torn skin
Metabolic exhaustion
Dehydration
Emotional stress
Temperature stress

Death

Although death *per se* is not necessarily a welfare insult, the events leading to death can be. The prevalence of deaths during transport is low when expressed in relative terms (e.g. 0.2%), but high when considered on an absolute basis (e.g. 120 birds per plant per day). Warriss *et al.* (7) found in a survey of 1113 journeys involving 3.2 million broilers in the UK that the longer the journey time the higher the incidence of deaths. When journeys lasted less than 4 hours the incidence of birds dead on arrival (DOA) at the processing plant was 0.156%; for longer journeys it was 0.283%. The relationship between death rate and journey duration was not linear, but instead it accelerated with time. This feature is probably common to other poultry species, and it indicates that the condition of the birds deteriorates as the journey progresses. In the case of broilers two situations could be occurring. Firstly, there could be a progressive rise in temperature leading to a rise in mortality; however, work in the UK has shown that as long as the vehicle is moving the temperature in the transport crates is usually held within acceptable limits. It was only when the vehicle came to a halt, such as traffic jams, that the temperature rose markedly. The second situation applies to flocks with a history of congestive heart failure (CHF). If there is a progressive oxygen deficit due to crowding, trampling or inadequate ventilation, birds which are prone to CHF will be compromised and some may die.

In another survey, in which the DOA rate in broilers was 0.19%, it was found that the major cause of mortality was in fact CHF. This accounted for 47% of the deaths, and 35% of these birds had ascites. Besides an oxygen deficit, the stress of catching, loading and transport itself could be precipitating heart failure in those birds with an underlying CHF condition, by affecting the heart rate and stroke volume. Acute heart failure, on the other hand, was relatively uncommon (4% of all deaths). Congestive heart failure can be recognized in DOA birds from an engorged, massive heart plus congestion of the lungs with blood.

Occasionally there are times when the DOA rate for a lorry exceeds 3%. This usually coincides with hot weather, and instances of approximately 50% mortality have been reported in end-of-lay hens which were transported from Spain to the Netherlands. An innovation which could help to reduce heavy losses would be the installation of temperature monitoring systems within the transport crates. These would include a display of the temperature on the driver's dashboard plus an audible warning system; the driver could then adjust the ventilation hatches remotely to regulate the temperature to the required level. The siting of the temperature sensor may prove to be problematic as well as being critical.

Trauma accounts for about 35% of the catching and transport deaths, and the main causes of fatal trauma in the UK are shown in Table 4.2. Hip dislocation is thought to occur when the birds are carried in the broiler sheds and loaded into the transport crates. It occurs usually in heavy birds (3 kg or more), especially when they start flapping their wings while several are held in a bunch by one leg. There is torsion at the hip joint, and the femur comes away. Quite often the proximal end of the femur is forced into the abdominal cavity where it can rupture an air sac and allow blood to enter the lungs. So, when the DOA carcases are examined it is common to

Table 4.2 Causes of fatal trauma in broilers dead on arrival.

Trauma	%
Dislocated or broken hip	76
Haemorrhage from the liver	11
Head trauma	8
Intraperitoneal haemorrhage other than from the liver	3
Other (including damage to keel, tibia, ilium, neck)	2

find a combination of blood in the mouth and a dislocated hip joint. Sometimes this damage is caused by too much haste on the part of the catchers. For example, one particular broiler company had a problem with dislocated hips in the 1980s. At that time the catchers were paid for completing the job instead of at an hourly rate, and they rushed the job in order to get home early. When this was changed to payment on an hourly basis and they were not allowed to leave early, there was less incentive to work fast and the prevalence of deaths from hip dislocation fell.

Bruising, broken bones and torn skin

Bruising and broken bones are usually acquired as the birds are being handled, but there are anecdotal reports from some countries of breast bruising occurring during transport, especially where the roads are rough and truck suspension inadequate. The prevalence of broken bones varies between bird types. One survey of end-of-lay hens showed that the rate was 29% by the time the birds had reached the water-bath stunner, but more recent assessments have produced a lower estimate of 16%. Much of this damage is to the ventrocaudal protuberance of the keel and the rear margin of the ischium, i.e. those parts of the body which protrude and are unprotected when a hen is pulled by a leg backwards out of its cage. Various methods are used for catching and removing hens from battery cages, and the general recommendation is to reduce the level of lighting and to catch and remove each bird individually while holding it by both legs. Catching by one leg and pulling more than one bird out at a time can lead to more damage. At some units a piece of wood is placed over the feed trough before the birds are removed and this acts as a breast support slide. Research has shown that there is no advantage in terms of broken bones from using the slide, and it can be a hindrance if it reduces the size of the cage entrance. If cage entrance size is too small the keel hits the trough and the ischium strikes the upper lip. Where the cage entrance is less than about 17 cm the bird has to be rotated on to its side as it is drawn through the entrance.

In broilers one study estimated the prevalence of broken bones in the live birds at the processing plant at 3%. The fractures were in the femur, radius, ulna, furculum and ischium. By the time the birds had reached the end of the processing line, 96% of the carcases had broken bones, principally the pubis, ischium and furculum. From the processor's point of view catching damage plays only a minor part in the overall problem of broken bones, but unlike processing damage it is more often associated with a haemorrhage. In those birds that arrived at the plant dead, 27% had dislocated or broken femurs.

Crushed skulls can be a problem where plastic drawers in modules are used. The catchers should ensure that no heads are sticking up when the drawers are being closed. Although some birds with broken necks get trapped in this way, it is difficult to distinguish this cause from manual neck dislocation simply by examining the carcase.

It is also difficult to monitor the prevalence of broken bones in the live birds as they arrive at the processing plant. The simplest and probably best procedure is to examine the birds which arrive dead as they are being discarded by the hanging-on staff. If the level of broken bones in the DOAs for a flock looks as though it is going to be high, it can be instructive to examine (by palpation) the live birds once they have been hung on the line, and to look at the plucked carcases for dislocated hips which carry a large haemorrhage. Examining the pectoral girdle in birds after they have been stunned does not necessarily give an accurate picture of the ante-mortem level of broken bones, because stunning itself causes fractures in the furculum, coracoid and scapula.

The level of ante-mortem wing bruising should be assessed before the birds are plucked. This is because plucking does induce some post-mortem wing bruising, especially in poorly bled carcases. When making an ante-mortem examination it can be helpful to use a wet cloth to part the feathers and allow a better view of the skin. Red wing-tips can be particularly common in turkeys. They are caused by violent wing flapping, and it is important to ensure that the wings do not flap against any metal stanchions in the hanging-on area. Wing flapping, in general, can be controlled by using breast comforters (plastic strips which are parallel to the line and against which the birds rub as they are conveyed to the stunner), by making sure the line runs smoothly and evenly (e.g. joints in the line are level), dimming lighting in the hanging-on area, and ensuring there are no sharp contrasts in lighting (e.g. as the birds are conveyed past the entrance of the hanging-on bay).

Breast bruising can be a problem in turkeys if they are loaded roughly on the farm, and leg bruising can occur in all types of bird if the hanging-on staff hold the birds roughly by the drumsticks.

Occasionally a flock may be delivered which has some yellow or green

Table 4.3 *In vivo* colour changes in bruises.

Approximate age of bruise	Colour of bruise
2 minutes	Red
12 hours	Dark red-purple
24 hours	Light green-purple
36 hours	Yellow-green-purple
48 hours	Yellow-green
72 hours	Yellow-orange
96 hours	Slightly yellow
120 hours	Normal

bruising. The approximate age of the bruise can be determined from Table 4.3, provided the assessment is made on the fresh carcase (yellow bruising fades as the carcase ages). The 'green leg' condition is caused by an old haemorrhage which occurred when a gastrocnemius tendon ruptured. This damage does not necessarily occur during handling. Typically the prevalence would be less than 0.1% but in some flocks the prevalence has been as high as 27%.

Torn skin can be serious in ducks, which are apt to climb on top of one another when they are being caught.

Metabolic exhaustion and dehydration

Ante-mortem stress can have profound effects on meat quality in the red meat species. For instance, stress-induced glycogen depletion in the muscle can result in a high ultimate pH, and very dark, dry meat. Acute exercise stress before slaughter can lead to hyperthermia and a paler, unduly wet meat. The incidence of high ultimate pH in meat has been observed to increase with journey duration in broilers, but no analogous poor-quality conditions are recognized in the poultry industry. What is more common is the phenomenon known as stress-induced heat shortening. When birds are stressed, particularly when this involves considerable wing flapping, the breast muscle becomes acidotic and its temperature is raised at the time of slaughter. The combination of low muscle pH and high temperature leads to tough meat. It is in the processor's interest therefore to minimize physical struggling and to ensure that the birds are not hyperthermic when they are slaughtered.

Dehydration is most commonly seen in sick, lame or undersized birds. These birds may not be able to reach the elevated drinkers in the growing shed. In broiler carcases dehydration can be recognized from the skin being tough and difficult to tear by hand, and the muscle is sticky in texture. In extreme cases there may be visceral gout.

Emotional and temperature stress

Emotional and temperature stress are not easy to recognize in crated birds on a lorry, and so it is important to consider the environmental conditions as well as the state and behaviour of the birds.

From a welfare point of view the optimum ambient temperature for chickens that are reared in temperate climates is 22–24 °C. Prolonged temperatures above 38 °C are dangerous. Normally the rectal temperature is 41 °C but when it exceeds 42.5 °C the birds begin to pant. Beyond 45 °C panting declines and may cease altogether, so as to conserve body water. Besides panting, the other means of losing heat are vasodilation in the shanks and comb, and increasing the body surface area to encourage convective heat loss. Panting and vasodilatation are the relevant mechanisms in crated birds, but the heat exchange through panting can be compromised if the humidity is high (greater than 70% relative humidity). In tropical climates it is advisable to transport the birds during the cooler periods of the day, and tall crates should be used which allow air movement over the birds' heads. If the crates are stacked on top of each other they should be spaced on the truck in rows with wide aisles. The object is to allow adequate air flow over and around the birds (in particular around their heads) to encourage convective and evaporative cooling. There is bound to be some sacrifice in the weight of birds that can be carried when wide crate spacing is used, but this will be offset by a lower mortality.

At the other extreme, the lower critical temperature for chickens is about 16 °C. This corresponds to the ambient temperature at which the bird will increase its rate of heat production in order to maintain body temperature. The lower lethal body temperature, at which 50% of a lorry load would be expected to die, is between 19 °C and 24 °C. The only obvious symptom of cold stress in crated birds is feather erection. In countries with cold climates such as Finland, birds are transported during the winter in insulated, mechanically ventilated vehicles which are similar in appearance to chilled meat transporters. Whatever the climate, whether it be hot, temperate or cold, it is advisable to alter the stocking density of birds in the crates according to the anticipated weather conditions.

In some countries it is a legal requirement that the birds are protected from all adverse weather. Cold stress is aggravated considerably if the birds are wet, because additional heat is lost through evaporation of the water. Besides protecting the birds from rain, it can be important to ensure that the crates are reasonably dry and in particular that they are free of ice before the birds are loaded.

An obvious source of unnecessary emotional stress for the birds is abuse by the catching staff. Where cases have come to light, they have often been partly caused by difficult working conditions. For instance, if the nest boxes cannot be cleared from broiler breeder sheds prior to depopulation the staff sometimes use unorthodox methods of removing and herding those birds which are hiding under the boxes. Similarly, catching end-of-lay hens in some of the alternative housing systems can be a difficult job leading to impatience and mishandling.

Research on hens has shown that removing birds three at a time from battery cages is more stressful than removing them one at a time, as determined from the plasma corticosterone levels. Fear, as indicated by the tonic immobility reaction, increases as the journey duration increases.

In broilers there is considerable variation in the thickness of the birds' shanks, particularly between males and females. The size of the gap in the shackle where the bird's leg is held also varies (range between broiler plants is 0.95 cm to 1.4 cm), but in general there is greater variation in the birds. This means that birds with thick shanks require some force when inserting their legs into a shackle. Compression of the periosteum of the bone in this situation is potentially painful for the bird. The tightness of the restraint is important in two other respects. Firstly, the fit should be sufficiently tight to ensure good electrical contact between the shackle and bird (when using constant voltage stunners), otherwise there is a risk of inadequate current flow. Secondly, the grip must ensure that the bird does not become dislodged from the shackle during plucking. Clearly, there is a compromise between the need to provide a low electrical resistance at the shackle electrode thus ensuring an adequate stun, and not hurting the bird through compression of the shank. Some broiler plants and most turkey plants use shackles of the double W (Churkey) design, as distinct from the single W type. The double W design gives a choice of shackle gap widths. It is also possible to provide wider gaps in the shackles for the males if they are killed on a separate line to the females.

Besides being potentially painful, it is likely that suspending a bird upside down from a shackle causes it some distress. For this reason it is advisable to minimize the time between shackling and stunning. However, it is also important that the wing flapping that occurs at shackling has subsided by the time the birds reach the waterbath. Survey work has shown that the minimum hang-on period which would allow this activity to subside is 12 seconds for broilers and 25 seconds for turkeys.

Ante-mortem inspection procedures

Ante-mortem welfare inspection procedures should be undertaken on a routine basis at all poultry processing plants. These include:

- Examining the birds waiting to be slaughtered for thermal and physical comfort.
- Monitoring the prevalence of DOA carcases as each flock is being unloaded, and examining the DOA carcases for causes of death, prevalence and types of trauma, and prevalence of dehydration. If necessary, the inspection should be extended to live birds where a serious problem is evident.
- Assessing whether the birds are being handled unnecessarily roughly by the hanging-on team.
- Assessing disturbance in the birds as they are conveyed to the stunner.
- Checking that runts are not being hung on the line.

When a problem occurs it may not be possible to solve it straight away. If so, the cause of the problem should be investigated and steps taken to ensure that it does not happen again.

Stunning and slaughter

Stunning before slaughter is a legal requirement in many countries, but there are nominated exceptions such as Jewish and Moslem slaughter, neck dislocation and decapitation which do not always require pre-slaughter stunning. There are four reasons why stunning is performed:

- To minimize the chance of the birds feeling pain during and after neck cutting.
- To minimize distress that could occur during bleeding out.
- To immobilize the bird to allow neck cutting to be performed easily and accurately.
- To prevent the convulsions which occur during bleeding out in unstunned birds.

There are three ways in which the procedure can go wrong. The birds may be mispresented to the stunner or the current may be misapplied; secondly, the current may be insufficient to stun all the birds instantaneously; and lastly, the birds may regain consciousness before they die. The general principles of electrical stunning will be considered first as this allows a clearer explanation of the reasons and solutions for these faults.

Electrical stunning

The most common devices used for electrically stunning poultry are the water-bath stunner and the hand-held head-only stunner. The water-bath stunner consists of an open tank of water through which the birds are drawn as they are conveyed along the overhead line. The water acts as the live electrode, and a metal bar which makes contact with the shackle usually acts as the earth electrode. Thus, current flows through the whole of the bird (except for its feet) when it is being stunned. In order to stun the bird, some of the current has to pass through the brain. For simple electric circuits, current flow is determined by Ohm's law: $V = IR$, where V is the voltage, I is the current and R is the resistance. The circuit for a four-bird water-bath is shown in Figure 4.1. Resistance exists between the bird's legs and the shackle, in the water of the stunning bath and within the body of the bird. The resistance within the bird varies between different tissues, and the routes of least resistance determine the distribution of current through the bird and hence the amount of current that passes through the brain.

The resistance provided by the water can make a significant contribution to the total resistance in the circuit. Its exact value can be influenced by the depth of water between the bird and the metal plate supplying the current. In Figure 4.1 the resistance provided by the water is shown as being common and equal in all birds. This is true provided the metal plate spans the whole length of the bath. If instead it is shorter than the length of the bath, and it is positioned (say) in the middle of the bath, the distance between the

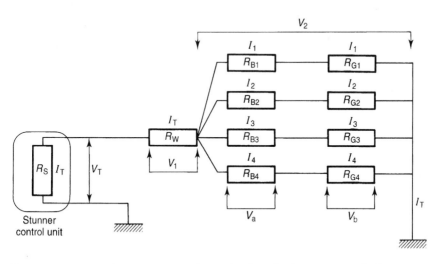

Figure 4.1 Equivalent resistive pathway for four birds in a water-bath stunner. $V_T = V_1 + V_2$ and $V_2 = V_a + V_b$; $I_T = I_1 + I_2 + I_3 + I_4$, where R_s is the inherent resistance of the stunner, R_w is the resistance of the water or brine, R_{B1-4} is the resistance of the birds, R_{G1-4} is the resistance between each bird and earth, V_T is the total voltage output of the stunner control unit and I_T is the current flow.

bird and the plate (and hence the resistance provided by the water) will be greater for a bird at the entry of the bath than for one in the middle. In this situation there is a danger that the bird entering the bath will not be instantaneously stunned, but it may receive sufficient current to tetanize it. As it is conveyed to the middle it receives a higher current and so when it leaves the bath it may appear to have been adequately stunned. Some direct current (DC) water-bath stunners are fitted with a metal plate just below the surface of the water. This is provided for hygiene reasons but it will also reduce if not eliminate the resistance provided by the water. However, it is important to ensure that the birds do not experience electric shocks with this system, and bounce off the plate before being stunned.

The resistance of the shackle depends on whether the contact is wet and on the pressure with which the shanks are gripped. Some authorities recommend that the shackles should be sprayed with water immediately before the water-bath to help lower this resistance. Most water-baths have an earthed bar against which the shackle makes contact. If the contact is interrupted and if the overhead line is not perfectly earthed, the resistance for that particular bird could rise and so current flow will fall. The shackles should make continuous contact with the rubbing bar throughout the stunning procedure.

The average resistance per bird provided by all the components in the circuit varies considerably between processing plants. For example, in one study on six plants in the UK the range was 1153 ohms to 1965 ohms. Owing to this wide variation it is difficult to recommend standard stunning voltages, and instead the recommendation has to be in terms of average current per bird.

Present stunners supply the current at a constant voltage. The voltage can be regulated with a dial or switch and the required average current per bird is titrated into the circuit using the current displayed on an ammeter. Some ammeter displays are unreliable and it is advisable to calibrate them periodically. Constant current stunners should not be used, except where they supply current separately to each bird. Otherwise, current will take the route of least resistance and low resistance birds will be overstunned while the high resistance birds will be understunned.

An important question is, what is the minimum current that should be used? Most authorities agree that from the welfare standpoint it is desirable to induce a cardiac arrest at stunning in at least 90% of the birds. This can be achieved using the currents shown in Table 4.4. However, it could be argued that lower currents are acceptable provided neck cutting is performed adequately and there is no chance of the birds regaining consciousness. In this situation it is important to know what the minimum current is which induces an effective stun independently of inducing a cardiac arrest. Various methods have been used to answer this. In the Netherlands work on pigs and sheep has looked at the effect of electrical stunning on the induction of epilepsy in the electroencephalogram (EEG). It is widely accepted that if a *grand mal* epilepsy is produced in the EEG, the animal is unconscious. Using this criterion the minimum current which induces epilepsy (unconsciousness) in 98% of the animals has been proposed as the recommended minimum current for commercial practice.

In the case of poultry, however, electrical stunning does not usually produce a *grand mal* epilepsy. Instead the EEG shows a *petit mal* epilepsy, and this is not necessarily diagnostic of unconsciousness. So for bird species the recommendation has been based on other criteria. Two approaches have been used. One was to assess the minimum current which produced an acceptable duration of overt behavioural unconsciousness. A current of 105 mA per bird was found to produce at least 52 seconds of apparent insensibility before broilers showed a return of head righting behaviour and co-ordinated neck movement. Another approach was to examine responsiveness in the EEG to sensory stimuli. If the brain failed to show any somatosensory evoked responses it lacked the neural integrity which was a prerequisite for perception of that stimulus. In other words absence of the evoked response was an indicator of unequivocal unconsciousness in that sensory modality. The current necessary to induce loss of somatosensory evoked responses in broilers is over 120 mA per bird. So, the minimum current that guarantees an effective stun is approximately the same as that which induces a ventricular fibrillation in 90% of the birds (Table 4.4). Nevertheless, 105 mA per bird should be adequate provided neck cutting is performed promptly and properly.

An important criticism of some water-bath stunners concerns pre-stun shocks. The problem is, however, peculiar to particular plants rather than being widespread in the industry. There are four ways in which it occurs. Firstly, in water-baths that do not have an entry or exit ramp, water is continuously fed into the bath and it overflows either from the entry or the exit lip. There should in fact be no overflow at the entry lip otherwise the birds will get an electric shock from this water which will be electrically live.

Table 4.4 Average current per bird necessary to induce a ventricular fibrillation in 90% of birds.

Species	*Average current per bird (mA)*
Chicken	120
Duck	130
Goose	130
Turkey	150

Secondly, in water-baths that are fitted with an entry ramp, the ramp becomes wet from water which splashes out of the bath. If the ramp is not electrically isolated from the rest of the tank (e.g. by an air space), it will be live wherever there is a wet route to the water in the bath. Thus birds will get an electric shock when their heads make contact with and are drawn up the ramp. The third way is for the wing of the bird to dip into the water-bath before the head. This is only a problem for slow line speeds, but it is a common feature in turkey plants because this species has a large wingspan and the wings hang below the head. It can be avoided by redesigning the entry ramp such that it holds the body of the bird back and allows the head, body and wings to be drawn together over the edge of the ramp into the bath. Alternatively, where birds are stunned singly in a water-bath, a sensing device can be installed which detects the bird's body and switches the current on for a fixed duration. The relay is activated only when the bird is in a position where the neck or crop region is going to be making contact with the water. The tonic extension at the onset of current flow causes the head to plunge immediately into the water. A fourth way in which broilers can get pre-stun shocks is if the rate at which their heads are immersed in the water is slow and they recoil before being immersed. This might be a feature of stunners which use particular electrical waveforms.

Pre-stun shocks are recognized from the abrupt recoil the birds make on contact with the entry ramp or relevant part of the water-bath stunner. Electrical leaks can be tested quite simply with a voltmeter by measuring the voltage of the surface which is suspected of being live relative to earth. It is important to make sure that personnel are electrically isolated from that surface when the test is carried out.

Another fault at some killing lines is that some birds miss the stunner altogether, either because they are runts and do not reach the water level, or because they are flapping their wings and raise their bodies as they pass over the bath. These features are relatively uncommon. For instance, one study showed that on average 0.4% of the broilers were undersized and escaped the stunner, and that 0.6% missed the stunner because they were 'fliers'. The problem of runts missing the water-bath can be avoided by not hanging them on the line with the other birds, but keeping them back and treating them separately. Occasionally, staff indifference at hanging-on results in some birds not being placed at the base of the shackles. This causes the birds to be held above the water level and so they miss being stunned. In addition, a bird may miss being stunned if its head is held up by the wing of an adjacent bird.

At one time it was thought that if birds were immersed into the water-bath too deeply, then current would enter the body of the bird and flow to the shackle while bypassing the brain. Subsequently, research has shown that immersing birds to the base of the wing has a comparable effect on brain function to immersing the head only.

Waterfowl often pass through water-bath stunners with only their bills and crop region in contact with the water. The cranium is above water. When ducks were stunned this way with 105 mA per bird it was found that there was less disturbance in brain function than when the whole head was submerged. It is not possible to state categorically that incomplete immersion of the head is unacceptable, but it is a cause for concern.

It has been suggested that the effectiveness of stunning could be compromised if the bird is wet. The water in the bird's plumage could act as a conductor and so direct the current away from the brain. This concern is justified to some extent when low currents are used. For example, it has been found that when broilers received 81 mA per bird (33 mA per kg live weight) they recovered coordinated muscular activity more quickly than similarly treated dry birds. Thus the duration of unconsciousness appeared to be shorter. With higher currents (120 mA per bird) there was no appreciable difference.

Some birds urinate or defaecate during stunning and hence foul the water of the waterbath. This is more pronounced where high stunning currents are used. In some countries there is a hygiene requirement that waterbath stunners should be fitted with a metal plate or perforated sheet just below the surface of the water. The intention is that birds should be stunned with their heads incompletely immersed in the water of the waterbath, as this will discourage them from inhaling water during the spasm at the onset of current flow. Research has shown that about one-third of chickens inhale water into their lungs during stunning when such a device is not used, and so if the device is effective it is justifiable on hygiene grounds.

Electrical stunning can cause broken bones, particularly in the pectoral girdle. It has been argued that because of this and because end-of-lay hens have fragile bones, the stunning voltage used for hens should be kept as low as is reasonably possible. This view, however, assumes that high voltages are associated with a higher prevalence of broken bones than low voltages. In hens this is not the case; low voltages induce high levels of damage which are not exceeded when the voltage is increased. There is no sound argument for compromising the welfare of the birds by using low voltages.

There is no doubt that electrical stunning can cause breast meat haemorrhages in broilers and turkeys. This has been demonstrated by comparing electrical stunning with gas stunning for which the prevalence of these haemorrhages can be as low as 3%. An important issue, however, is whether it is correct to assume that raising the stunning voltage within normal limits results in more breast meat haemorrhages. Laboratory trials have shown that the prevalence of breast meat haemorrhages rises when the stunning current increases beyond 130 mA per bird (when using a 50 Hz sinusoidal alternating current). At currents between 45 mA and 130 mA per bird the level of breast meat haemorrhages was about 22%. Experience at commercial processing plants shows that the prevalence of breast meat haemorrhages when using low voltages is often much higher than this (approximately 35%), and so the underlying problem is more serious than might be inferred from some of the research trials. In-plant trials have shown that increasing the current over the range of 68 mA to 115 mA had a limited effect, but the type of waveform that was used was critical. A 50 Hz clipped sinusoidal alternating current (AC) waveform was worse than an unclipped sinusoidal AC waveform when compared at the same current level, and it also caused more broken wishbones. Work in the Netherlands, however, showed that when 75 V (estimated current 50–60 mA per bird) was compared with 150 V (estimated current 100–120 mA per bird), 70% of the flocks showed an increase in the severity of breast meat haemorrhages when the stunning voltage was increased. In the remaining 30% of the flocks breast meat haemorrhages declined as voltage increased. This lack of consistency between studies and between flocks emphasizes the flock-to-flock variation in the response to electrical stunning. In addition, when a constant voltage stunner is used there is likely to be considerable variation in the current received by each bird. This in turn will result in variation in the effects of stunning between birds.

High-frequency electrical stunning has two theoretical advantages over low frequencies such as 50 Hz. Firstly, it reduces the intensity of the muscular spasm at the onset of stunning, and this in turn can result in a lower prevalence of breast meat haemorrhages and broken bones in the carcase. Secondly, beyond about 125 Hz there is a reduction in the prevalence of a ventricular fibrillation at stunning, and some sectors of the industry contend that this promotes bleeding efficiency. Research trials have not confirmed this view; the yield of blood is not influenced by cardiac arrhythmia, provided the birds are given long enough to bleed. Where there is a low incidence of ventricular fibrillation at stunning it is important to ensure that the neck is cut promptly after stunning and that both carotid arteries are completely severed. Otherwise there is a risk that the birds will regain consciousness. When a 350 Hz DC is used, the stunning current required to abolish evoked activity in the brain and hence produce an unequivocal stun, is similar to that for a 50 Hz AC – 120 mA per bird.

Hand-held stunners which apply current across the head usually operate at about 117 V and they deliver approximately 340 mA. At this current level they are effective at inducing a stun. However, the duration of apparent unconsciousness may be shorter than for water-bath stunners, possibly because there is less interference with neuromuscular transmission. This prompt recovery coupled with the fact that it is unusual for a head-only stun to induce a ventricular fibrillation, makes it important to cut the necks promptly and efficiently. It has been recommended that the stunning current should be applied for about 5 seconds (when using a 117 V, 50 Hz sinusoidal AC), and that both carotid arteries should be cut within 10 seconds of the end of stunning. This recommendation applies to turkeys as well as chickens.

The duration of unconsciousness provided by electrical stunning is quite short. For example, when water-bath stunning does not induce a ventricular fibrillation (while applying 105 mA per broiler), the time to the onset of recovery of consciousness is on average 104 seconds. In some broilers the time to recovery is as short as 52 seconds, and in hens it can be as low as 22 seconds. In the case of hand-held stunners the time to recovery of consciousness is on average 116 seconds, and in the quickest recovering bird 30 seconds. The duration of unconsciousness also depends on the current level that is used and the duration for which the current is applied.

Inducing a ventricular fibrillation at stunning is desirable from the welfare point of view because when this occurs it is no longer essential to exsanguinate the bird promptly and efficiently in order to kill it. A ventricular fibrillation also results in a prompt and punctual loss of brain function and decreases even further the likelihood of the bird regaining consciousness. Wormuth *et al.* (8) concluded that triggering heart fibrillation depends on the peak current received by the bird. Prolonging the current flow cannot be used to reduce the peak current required to achieve ventricular fibrillation. The

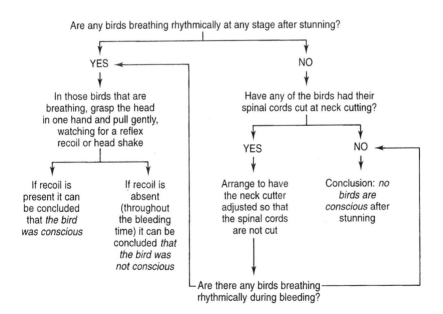

Figure 4.2 Testing for the recovery of consciousness in broiler processing lines.

prevalence of ventricular fibrillation is also influenced by whether the birds are wet or dry. If they have been allowed to get wet with rainwater or from a shackle and shank sprayer, a lower proportion of birds will experience a ventricular fibrillation when low stunning currents are used. The physical symptoms expressed during bleeding by the birds which did not have a ventricular fibrillation at stunning are sometimes wrongly diagnosed as signs of consciousness. The characteristic symptoms of the stunned state without fibrillation are an arched neck (dorsoflexion), wings held close to the body and tremoring in the wings with the legs rigidly extended. When there is a ventricular fibrillation the birds relax soon after stunning, the wings and neck drop and the pupils dilate. One of the most useful symptoms to look for is the resumption of rapid or normal rhythmic breathing during bleeding. A conscious bird is not likely to hold its breath for very long, and so the absence of breathing should indicate unconsciousness. Normal rhythmic breathing, however, is not proof of consciousness, but it indicates that further tests are required to establish whether the birds are stunned. A schedule for the appropriate tests is given in Figure 4.2.

Neck cutting

Neck cutting is performed either with a machine, or manually with a knife. The automatic neck cutters make their cut either at the front, side or back of the neck, depending on the make of machine and on the way it has been adjusted. Manual neck cutting is performed in one of three ways. For large birds, a narrow-bladed knife is sometimes inserted into the side of the neck between the trachea and backbone. A more common method is to pass the knife across the underside of the neck. This is usually done at one side of the neck and so only the blood vessels on that side are cut. The other method is to insert a knife into the mouth of the bird and cut through to the anastomosis between the two jugular veins at the base of the skull (beak cut). This method is sometimes used for the 'Traditional Farm Fresh' trade, since it does not leave a visible wound.

Some alarming cases of recovery of consciousness have occurred when only the jugular veins have been severed. Turkey farmers who use hand-held head-only stunners and then sever the jugular vein anastomosis using the beak cut run a serious risk of some birds regaining consciousness during bleeding. The same applies to chicken processors who use low stunning currents in combination with a two-bladed automatic neck cutter which is set to cut the jugular veins only.

Checking which blood vessels in the neck are severed is a simple but messy procedure. The best approach is to wear a plastic apron, place the bird on your lap and make a midline tear or incision along the ventral surface of the neck and jaw, exposing first the jugular veins and then the carotid arteries. The exact location of these is described in Chapter 6.

Studies which have examined the time to loss of brain function following a variety of neck cutting or slaughtering procedures have shown that inducing a ventricular fibrillation is the quickest method of arresting brain function, followed by decapitation and severing both carotid arteries. On this basis, it has been recommended that birds should either be subjected to a ventricular fibrillation at stunning or have both their common (or internal) carotid arteries severed at neck cutting. In order to cut both carotid arteries it is necessary to cut the whole of the ventral aspect of the neck, including the trachea and oesophagus. Some processing firms are reluctant to sever the trachea because this would result in a section of trachea being left attached to the neck flap, and it would have to be removed by hand later on in the line. However, there are a number of neck flap and residual crop removing machines available now which are claimed to remove any pieces of trachea from this region.

Turkeys are usually bled manually after cutting only one carotid artery and jugular vein. Cutting the turkey's trachea has no consequence on the efficiency of trachea removal, and so a cut that severs both carotid arteries should be used. In quail the neck is not usually cut after stunning and instead the carcase is processed as if it were a game bird. In this situation it is essential that all quails have a ventricular fibrillation at stunning. It so happens that this species is very susceptible to electrically induced ventricular fibrillation; currents as low as 45 mA are lethal.

The optimum time between stunning and neck cutting is determined by three factors. Firstly, it should not be so long that it allows the birds to regain consciousness before they die. Secondly, it should be long enough to allow the supervisor to assess whether the birds are stunned when they leave the water-bath. Thirdly, the birds should be given sufficient time to allow their necks to relax and thus feed into the guide bars of the automatic neck cutter. On average the time to neck relaxation after the end of stunning is 9 seconds in broilers, but this may be influenced by whether they experience a ventricular fibrillation.

It is general practice for a person to stand alongside the bleeding tunnel and manually cut the necks of any birds which were not cut by the automatic killer. These birds are often those that escaped being stunned by the water-bath stunner.

The Farm Animal Welfare Council in the UK has recommended that all birds should be dead by the time they enter the scalding tank. This can be tested with the corneal reflex. The head of the bird is held in one hand using the thumb to open an eyelid, and the other hand is used to place a pointed instrument (e.g. the stub of a feather shaft) onto the cornea. The eye is observed for a response in the nictitating membrane, not the eyelid. If it is absent and none of the birds are breathing, one can be confident that the birds are dead. However, it must be emphasized that the test needs to be done on a large number of birds in order to check whether *all* birds are likely to be dead. When this test was applied on 100 birds at 28 plants it was found that at 75% of the plants all the birds had no reflex, and on average 1% of the broilers had a positive corneal reflex. This test also provides an opportunity to check whether any birds are conscious when they reach the scalding tank.

Although decapitation and neck dislocation without prior stunning are permitted methods they do not necessarily cause instantaneous impairment of brain function. Evoked responses in the chicken brain take time to fail when either of these methods are used, and they do not produce any immediate changes in the amplitude or latency of the evoked responses, unlike concussion. So there is reluctance to commend these methods as being humane. Nevertheless, they are simple and so they are used for immediate euthanasia where there is no better alternative.

Gas stunning

At the time of writing (February 1996), one plant in the UK had been successfully stunning broilers for eight months using a new gas stunning system, a company in Australia was testing a gas stunning system, a UK/Danish consortium was about to launch a gas stunning unit, an equipment manufacturing company in the Netherlands was developing an alternative gas stunning system, and carbon dioxide stunning was being used on a small scale in Japan.

One of the potential welfare advantages of gas stunning is that the birds can be stunned in their transport crates. This avoids the pre-slaughter stress of removing them from the crates and hanging them on the killing line. In addition, recent research has shown that electrical stunning may not cause an instantaneous stun in all broilers, even when applied in the prescribed manner, and so gas stunning would avoid the problem of some birds experiencing electric shocks before being stunned.

Carbon dioxide is being used because it has distinct narcotic properties, it is a dense gas and so it is reasonably easy to contain, and because it is a naturally occurring gas leaving no undesirable residues in the meat. However, experience in humans has shown that it is an unpleasant gas to inhale, it is aversive in poultry, and it has been recommended that it should not be used at high concentrations. An acceptable system is to use a low concentration of carbon dioxide in combination with anoxia. A mixture of 30% carbon dioxide in less than 2% oxygen has been recommended, and this can be achieved by displacing air with argon and adding carbon dioxide to the correct final concentration. This gas mixture, and anoxia alone, do not elicit aversive behaviour in the birds, and they produce fewer breast meat haemorrhages, red wing-tips, wing vein haemorrhages and broken bones in the carcase than conventional electrical stunning.

In turkeys, neck cutting following gas stunning can be performed up to 10 minutes from the end of stunning without adversely affecting bleeding efficiency. Ante-mortem inspection of all the birds may be required to ensure that no DOA birds are inadvertently processed with the gas-stunned birds.

Fault finding

There are two approaches to enforcing welfare requirements in processing plants. Firstly, one can ensure that the equipment is performing according to technical specifications (e.g. the stunner delivers the correct current). Secondly, one can examine the behaviour and reflexes of birds and the condition of the carcases for any overt welfare problems (e.g. check that the majority are effectively stunned between the water-bath and neck cutter). For a comprehensive view it is necessary to use both approaches.

Routine inspection

The following provides a checklist for systematically assessing the welfare of the birds in the processing plant:

1. Thermal and physical comfort of the birds awaiting slaughter.
2. Acceptable level of force being used in shackling the birds.
3. No runts are being hung on the line.
4. Monitor the prevalence of DOA birds and their cause of death.
5. No disturbance in the birds as they are conveyed to the stunner.
6. No pre-stun shocks at the water-bath stunner.
7. No birds passing over the stunner without entering the water.
8. Continuous contact between the shackle and earthed rubbing bar over the water-bath.
9. Correct stunning current per bird.
10. All birds are stunned when they leave the water-bath stunner.
11. Correct neck cutting in terms of the blood vessels that are cut.
12. No birds recover consciousness after neck cutting (see Figure 4.2).
13. No birds entering the scalding tank are conscious or alive.

Common equipment faults

The following are common faults in stunning and slaughter equipment or facilities:

1. Broken transport crates are not replaced or repaired.
2. Inadequate facilities for cooling the birds waiting on the lorry to be slaughtered.
3. Water on the entry ramp of the water-bath stunner is electrically live.
4. Voltmeter and ammeter displays are inaccurate.
5. The plate or bar which supplies current in the water-bath does not span the length of the bath.
6. Neck cutter is set too shallow – the cut does not allow prompt and adequate exsanguination.
7. Neck cutter is set to sever the spinal cord and thus masks the physical expression of recovery of consciousness.
8. Where a ventricular fibrillation is not induced at stunning, the automatic neck cutter does not sever both carotid arteries.

References

1. Bayliss PA, Hinton MH. Transportation of broilers with special reference to mortality rates. *Appl Animal Behav Sci* 1990; **28**:93–118.
2. Bilgili SF. Electrical stunning of broilers – basic concepts and carcass quality implications: a review. *J Appl Poultry Res* 1992; **1**:135–46.
3. Gregory NG. Stunning and slaughter. In: Mead GC (ed.) *Processing of poultry.* London: Elsevier, 1989; 31–63.
4. Gregory NG. Stunning of broilers. In: *Proceedings of XIX World's Poultry Congress*, Amsterdam. Vol. 2. 1992; 345–9.
5. Gregory NG, Wilkins LJ. Skeletal damage and bone defects during catching and processing. In: Whitehead CC (ed.) *Bone biology and skeletal disorders.* 23rd Poultry Science Symposium of the WPSA. Carfax, 1992: 313–28.
6. Knowles TG, Broom DM. The handling and transport of broilers and spent hens. *Appl Animal Behav Sci* 1990; **28**:75–91.
7. Warriss PD, Bevis EA, Brown SN, Edwards JE. Longer journeys to processing plants are associated with higher mortality in broiler chickens. *Br Poultry Sci* 1992; 33:201–26.
8. Wormuth HJ, Knauer B, Schutt-Abraham I, Schallenberg G, Boosen, M. 1990; BMELF Forschungsvorhaben 88 HS002 Inst. Vet. BGA.

CHAPTER 5

Poultry Processing: Domestic Fowl, Turkeys and Ducks

Introduction

The UK poultry processing industry hardly existed before the Second World War, when poultry was considered to be a delicacy eaten by comparatively few, mostly on Sundays and special occasions. After the war, an increasing demand for meat and protein-rich foods saw the emergence of the poultry industry with the development in the 1950s of the broiler processing plants.

The methods of slaughtering and dressing poultry carcases changed significantly over the second half of the twentieth century in response to the rapid growth of the industry. However, the basic processes of slaughtering and dressing have not changed. These processes are breaking or cutting the vessels in the neck with (in the majority of cases) prior stunning. This is followed by defeathering which normally includes scalding in hot water and the process of evisceration with salvage of the edible offal. The carcase is then washed with water, chilled by cold air or water and prepared for sale.

Following growth of the poultry industry, automatic machinery was introduced and became financially acceptable as the throughput increased. Moving shackle lines were introduced first, followed shortly by automatic scalding and defeathering. Automatic evisceration and harvesting of the giblets were introduced widely in the 1970s, followed by automatic chilling. Wrapping and packaging remain labour-intensive, but automatic portioning is being introduced increasingly into cutting premises.

Domestic fowl

Developments in Europe were influenced by American concepts, where a poultry industry had developed some years before the Second World War. An increased supply of what had previously been a luxury commodity had wide public appeal, and growth of the industry was rapid and built on the frozen broiler. Numerous small processing plants appeared; the industry entered a brief period of overproduction followed swiftly by recession, and then swung back again.

The industry became more competitive and when the UK entered the European Union many small processors were not in a position to meet the new standards imposed and were closed or taken over by larger companies until the top eight companies controlled the majority of the UK market. Farm producer processors with low overheads, and enjoying exemptions from certain requirements, also survived and are likely to continue to do so, since they supply the more traditional and seasonal markets. Growth of the industry had been so rapid that technology had lagged behind, but with the development of larger companies the science rapidly caught up, with a continued increase in the sophistication of processing equipment and techniques. Development of value-added or further processed products has had some influence on primary processing operations. There are occasions when presentation of the whole carcase may not be so critical, and where the product is to be given an enhanced shelf-life care must be taken that this is not used to mask a lowering of standards at the primary operation stages.

A great deal has been achieved by breeding developments, producing birds with better growth performance and greater customer appeal. There was a marked difference in customer preference of carcase colour in some regions based on the historical distribution of breeds. These preferences are becoming less well defined with the passage of time and the influence of retailers.

In addition to the broiler chicken, two other types of birds must be considered:

Hens

When hens have fulfilled their function of egg production, usually when they are 12–24 months old, they are of low value and present processing problems. The small on-farm processors are usually able to accommodate disposal of their own spent hens through local outlets, whereas egg producers and breeders send their hens to processors who specialize in hen processing. The large broiler processors do not generally process hens for the following reasons:

- Hens are of a different conformation, and equipment would need to be adjusted or may not even accommodate the carcase.
- Scalding requirements may be different.
- Venting and evisceration processes would result in the discharge of considerable amounts of egg, fat and oily fluids over machinery and other

surfaces within the area, causing difficulties in maintaining cleaning processes.

- It would be necessary to separate the processed carcases of hens from the carcases of broilers.
- The need for hen processing is intermittent, which would affect the general efficiency and programming of other operations.
- The market for the hen carcase is different from the broiler market.

This has led to the great majority of hen processing being carried out by a few processors who are prepared to adapt their operations to accommodate the associated difficulties and develop appropriate outlets for the final product.

Only relatively few better-quality whole hen carcases actually reach the final consumer, despite the fact that compared with broilers there is a much fuller flavour. Many of the better carcases go to a variety of catering outlets, with the remaining carcases being deboned with the meat generally being used by the larger food manufacturing companies in canned and further processed products.

Poussins

Poussins are widely regarded as fowl of approximately 30–35 days old with a weight range of 0.2 kg to 0.7 kg. They are farm processed to satisfy a local demand or special order. Farm processing has the advantage of being able to accommodate a variation in size and conformation when employing manual or simple mechanical processing methods. Sometimes farms may be in the fortunate position of being able to select stock to accommodate order specification. On a larger scale poussin processing is very specialized, with the entire operation adapted to accommodate the smaller birds, and a successful operation depends on a constant supply of good-quality stock.

The poussin processor is dealing with a more delicate commodity, where cleanliness must have a high priority as the product has a larger surface area in proportion to weight. The notable advantage in poussin processing is that the necessary chilling is achieved more quickly.

While it is more costly to produce poussin than the larger broiler, it is a quality product with an appeal in many countries.

Technical aspects of processing

The large processors have adopted some form of a mechanical system of live bird transfer from farm to factory, while for reasons of cost and practicality smaller operators have generally continued to use fixed crates on the lorry or a loose crate system.

At the processing plant the mechanical systems allow the birds to be presented at the hanging-on stations in open trays or by means of delivery belts which leave operators free to lift the birds by both legs for placing in the shackles in front of them. These systems allow the number of staff to be reduced, but care has to be taken as too great a reduction in staff could lead to pressures resulting in rough handling.

The mechanical systems have been generally responsible for a significant reduction in injury both at the farm and at the factory by providing easier handling. Apart from the welfare advantages, the reduction in broken wings and dislocated legs has resulted in a significant reduction in mechanical damage during defeathering and evisceration operations because of the improved and more uniform presentation of carcases to processing equipment.

Smaller operators employing more conventional handling may not encounter the same level of injuries and mechanical damage with their lower operating speeds. With on-farm processing, apart from there being less handling and live bird transfer, there is often some benefit from a single management structure.

SLAUGHTER

Legislation requires that birds are rendered insensitive to pain until death supervenes in order to satisfy welfare requirements (see Chapter 4). Welfare codes of practice were successful in bringing about changes in neck cutting practices. The industry has moved away from unilateral neck cutting and systems where the spinal cord is severed. Bilateral neck cutting has become increasingly accepted, using double rotating blades or complete ventral cutting with all major blood vessels being sectioned. Slaughter at the farm may in some cases involve automatic stunning but is often carried out manually by the person who also performs the neck cutting operation.

Gas stunning trials conducted with chicken have been encouraging and could become the preferred method with large-scale operators. The birds, however, are anaesthetized to a level whereby they do not recover consciousness and therefore a means of identifying birds 'dead on arrival' has to be found. It does not appear that gas stunning has any adverse effect on the product and it may be that it can actually improve the final quality.

PLUCKING

The scalding and defeathering of chickens have often been regarded as space-consuming operations producing feathers which are a low-value byproduct. They are, nevertheless, stages that can greatly affect the success of subsequent operations, particularly during processing of broiler chickens.

The scalding operation is primarily to facilitate removal of the feathers but is also beneficial in controlling feathers during their collection. The wetting process has a softening effect on debris adhering to skin, allowing it to be detached during defeathering and enhancing the appearance of the carcases. It also considerably reduces the distribution of feather- and dust-borne bacteria.

Scalding involves immersion of the carcases in hot water for periods varying from 1.5 minutes to 4 minutes, with the length of the immersing track dictated by the line speed. The temperature is varied according to the type of bird and category of final product. It is desirable to maintain hock cover during scalding and to keep the water as clean as practicable through a system of water overflow and replacement. Birds leaving the scalding tank remove a significant amount of water in their feathers, and water replacement must not therefore be assessed by observing the overflow.

The temperatures in the scalding tank used for fresh broiler products are usually between 50 °C and 54 °C, and a temperature fluctuation of more than 2 °C is unacceptable. For processing hens and birds for the frozen market, the temperature is usually about 55 °C. There has been a tendency to reduce tank temperatures slightly with the improvement in efficiency of defeathering equipment. Wetting agents may be added to scald water to assist its penetration to the feather follicles. The development of scalding tanks producing greater water turbulence by injecting air has achieved improved penetration, and most producers choose not to use chemical additives.

When the water temperature is too high the surface layers of the skin may be removed and also the subcutaneous fats may break down, resulting in adhesion between the skin and underlying muscle during air chilling. This produces a blotchy appearance which has been referred to as 'barking'. When carcases are chilled by immersion in water these blemishes are not produced, owing to skin hydration.

The importance of good defeathering must not be underestimated, as this operation can result in some penetration of contaminants. The extent of the problem is influenced by the condition of the birds, the state of the scalding tank water and adjustment of the defeathering equipment. Feathers are removed from the carcase by the multidirectional action of serrated rubberized flails of varying length. Systems consist of several banks of equipment, each exerting a different emphasis on the area of feather removal (Figure 5.1). Improvement in quality of the flails, together with development of units providing easier adjustment, has reduced skin damage and produced a cleaner result. Well-directed water spraying at the end of the defeathering reduces cross-contamination levels and at this point the use of chlorinated water may be advantageous.

Figure 5.1 Defeathering equipment with flails rotated for cleaning and maintenance.

Feathers removed by wet mechanical operations have usually been collected in floor channels and carried by water to a screening process in a designated feather collection area. The increasing cost of water has seen the development of belt collection systems carrying feathers to a hopper from which feathers are blown through pipes to a bulk collection area.

Farm processing may use dry mechanical defeathering processes with rotating rollers with rubberized discs or flail. In these smaller operations birds may be fed between the rollers by hand. Feathers may be collected in a large sack using suction.

Normally the slaughter and defeathering line is separate from the evisceration and dressing shackle line so birds are removed from the former by cutting the hock, to remove the feet and shank, and replaced on the evisceration line. This transfer was done manually but can now take place mechanically.

EVISCERATION

Evisceration has presented manufacturers of processing equipment with their greatest challenge in developing machinery because of the complexity and diversity of the operation. There has been a measure of success but they are continually improving and modifying their equipment to give results which in some respects are better than can be achieved manually. Technology, particularly in this area, has been responsible for both increasing throughput rates and reducing labour costs. Any equipment used for these processes must also be designed to be easily cleaned.

Mechanical evisceration is achieved stage by stage and may involve six or more units of rotating equipment which accommodate the moving shackle line.

Firstly the vent is cut by a plunging cylindrical knife driven around a centring pin which locates the cloacal opening. On withdrawal both the vent and bursa of Fabricius are hung over the back of the carcase. The next part of the operation is to open the carcase to ready it for removal of the viscera; this is achieved by a cutter which plunges in to the vent opening, pushing the intestine down to prevent damage and subsequent contamination. The blades then open to make a uniform predetermined cut. Successful evisceration relies heavily on the accuracy of vent opening and cutting. The carcase passes on to the eviscerator where it is clamped by the wings and a centring bracket which rests between the thighs. The eviscerating spoon is then inserted and, with a scoop-like action, pulls the viscera from the cavity. Depending, to some extent, on the type of neck cutting, the majority of crops may also be removed by this action. This type of machine is being succeeded by an eviscerator which removes the contents of the cavity by a gripping action.

The viscera are detached from the carcase and either suspended to the side of the carcase or deposited in a tray which runs in front of the carcase (Figure 5.2, on page 80). The viscera remain identifiable with the carcase to which they belong and are presented at the inspection station with less damage and in a way which makes their examination easier. These systems have reduced the risk of microbiological contamination and the staining of the skin surface from direct contact with the internal organs being draped against the back of the carcase following their removal. This improvement has also allowed a significant saving in wash water. The detachment of viscera has facilitated the development of fully automated giblet harvesting, which has increased yields and at the same time produced considerable savings in labour costs.

The eviscerated carcases pass to a neck skin finishing machine, which involves the plunging action of a toothed, rotating metal rod through the body cavity into the neck cavity. The teeth on the rod collect any remaining pieces of the crop, oesophagus, trachea or thymus before plunging further when the debris is removed before the rod returns to its initial position. This operation facilitates the drainage of the cavity and may include a cavity wash function.

Necks are removed by a unit which first severs the cervical vertebrae at the base and then pulls the neck from the carcase. The neck skin is slit vertically; where birds are sold as whole fresh product, it is particularly important that the neck skin is not damaged. Carcases are then subjected to what the industry often refers to as a final inspection machine. This machine removes remaining lung, hearts and other debris from within the body cavity by insertion of a suction arm. The final operation within the evisceration

Figure 5.2 Maestro evisceration system. (With kind permission of Meyn Equipment, Holland.)

area is the inside/outside wash process using forceful spraying equipment. It is important that sprays are adjusted to achieve the best possible result. This is the point in poultry processing where the bacteriological standard of the raw product is at its highest. Thereafter it can only deteriorate through handling, contact and the passage of time.

At the other end of the scale are smaller units which do not enjoy the assistance of sophisticated mechanical equipment. Simplified eviscerating aids have, however, been developed with the small processor in mind. On some farms a single person will carry out the complete operation, one bird at a time. The farm processor may enjoy some benefit from being able to accommodate variations in product size and, to some degree, quantity, both of which can assist in satisfying the requirements of seasonal demand.

As chicken spoils rapidly compared with other meats, it is important that the temperature of birds is reduced as quickly as practicable to a point at which bacterial growth is minimized, in order to prolong shelf-life. Chilling facilities often provide useful physical separation between the evisceration and secondary processing areas, and may at the same time beneficially reduce the ambient temperature of the adjoining areas.

CHILLING

Automated line transfer machines have become a proved and accepted part of poultry processing, allowing the chilling process to become an integral part of a continuous flow operation with automatic weighing and grading (Figures 5.3 to 5.5). In addition to providing a continuous flow of carcases, the return shackle cleaning systems can be incorporated in the chill line. A disadvantage of this single-track chilling line is that it requires a larger floor area than multitier systems. However, increased efficiency through controlled air turbulence and humidity has reduced chilling time by up to 25% compared with multitier bar systems. Multitier systems have also been

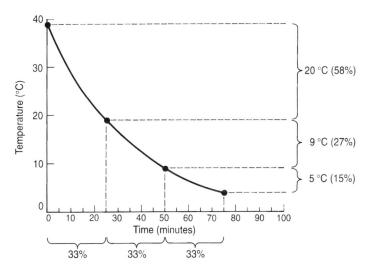

Figure 5.3 Typical time/temperature curve for chickens cooled in an air chiller, showing the proportion of heat removed at varying times.

Figure 5.4 Single track air chiller. (With kind permission of Pennine Environmental Services Ltd.)

difficult to clean and maintain, in addition to producing contamination problems from neck dripping on to lower carcases.

Weight loss during air chilling has always been of concern, averaging approximately 1.5% in many systems and increasing to more than 2% with overnight holding. The loss is slightly higher with small carcases due to the higher ratio of surface area to weight. More recent through-flow systems have significantly reduced the weight loss, and development of controlled water spraying combined with air chilling may achieve a negligible weight loss.

Immersion chilling of poultry is generally more efficient and the overall operation is normally prescribed in some detail by legislation. This is to control water temperatures and to ensure that water flow is counter to the direction of the carcases. Immersion chilling is generally employed for chicken where whole carcases are used for the frozen trade or where there is a further drip and chill process prior to further processing. Legislation requires the inside and outside washing of carcases before immersion and

Figure 5.5 Bar chiller.

stipulates the minimum amount of water to be used for each bird in order to reduce the amount of cross-contamination during chilling. Processors have often referred to immersion chilling as a washing process, as aesthetically the carcases have a more even and generally improved appearance. Birds chilled by this process are much more uniform bacteriologically than birds that are air-chilled. Chlorination of the water in the chiller to levels of between 50 p.p.m. and 100 p.p.m. improves bacteriological results.

Small processors who cannot justify the cost of through-flow equipment continue to use wheeled A-frames or bar hanging facilities in walk-in chill rooms, which can fit in well with batch processing and accommodates their need for overnight holding.

FURTHER PROCESSING

The four items known as giblets are the neck, liver, heart and gizzard. They make up approximately 9% of the edible components of the chicken, which is not inconsiderable. In the early days of the industry almost all chickens were sold with giblets which were enclosed in a pack and inserted in the body cavity. This meant giblets achieved the same market value as the carcase but required a labour-intensive operation involving harvesting, sorting, chilling and packaging. There was, in addition, difficulty in achieving a shelf-life compatible with the carcase. Larger processors are now marketing fewer whole chickens with giblets.

With the greatly increased use of chicken for portions and deboned meat there has been an increase in automation where only sorting requires people to carry out the work. These developments have suited the bulk collection and packaging of giblets for distribution to food processors (Figures 5.6 and 5.7). On-farm processors do not usually have the facility of these outlets and still look to include the giblets with the carcase, which is still popular with some customers.

The portioning and deboning of chicken was the first real move towards value-added products, and developed consumer popularity rapidly. The accuracy of cutting is important in achieving the maximum yield and profit. Where mechanical systems are employed they are usually set in favour of the higher value component to an extent determined by legal definition, presentation and acceptance by the customer.

The cooking time for portions is relatively short and some retailers expect the producers to mature carcases for up to 24 hours in order to improve the

Figure 5.6   Liver collection and sorting station.

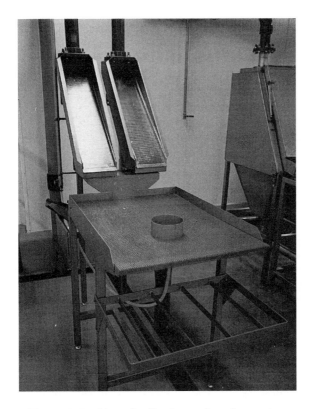

Figure 5.7   Gizzard collection and sorting station.

texture and flavour of the product. Holding carcases in a chilled environment produces a measure of inconvenience. Hanging carcases in an air chill facility is much preferred to the practice of storing chilled carcases in bins, which is likely to produce cross-contamination and cause distortion which gives rise to handling and cutting difficulties. It is essential to have complete separation between the raw and cooked sides when there is a cooking process.

Portioning was later followed by deboning operations as further processed products evolved. Both portioning and deboning operations are labour intensive, which has promoted the development of automated equipment. This has proved successful for portioning but less successful for deboning because of the presence of bone and cartilage in the meat. Some processors have therefore retained a preference for manual deboning to satisfy customer specification (Figure 5.8, page 86). Equipment has been developed which uses X-rays to detect bone and cartilage and performs

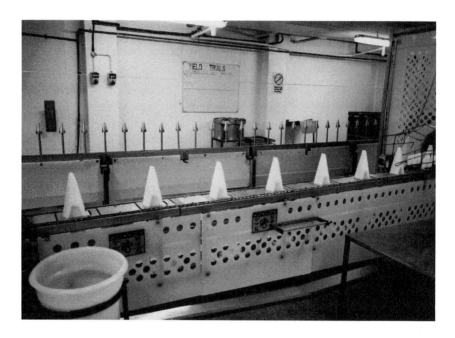

Figure 5.8   Manual deboning lines.

automatic rejection. The high cost of this equipment may not be justified at this stage, and processors may reserve the use of X-ray scanning for the final product where it can detect other categories of foreign material, including metal. Rejections may be high and show fluctuations, making it difficult and costly to fit into the programme; manual back-up is also required.

Deboned meat is easy to store at the premises prior to further processing, or alternatively conveniently lends itself to bulk packing, freezing, accumulation and disposal through the export market.

MECHANICALLY RECOVERED MEAT

Where deboning and cutting operations generate bone with residual meat in sufficient quantity it becomes financially viable to employ a mechanical recovery system for the removal of the remaining attached meat and fat. This equipment operates in one of two basic ways. The earlier system involves the feeding of skeletal tissue into a hopper, before entering a cylinder along which a ram travels pressing the content against a plate with numerous minute perforations in it. The pressure is adjusted so that the soft tissues pass through the holes while the bone and cartilage remain as a bone cake, which is pushed through an opening to the side on withdrawal of the ram. The recovered soft tissue is collected in the form of a purée. This system is intermittent and often not convenient for the large-scale operator.

In the other system the skeletal material is usually broken down into smaller pieces for convenience and passed via a hopper to a metal tube by means of a screw feed. The material for treatment is brought under pressure as a result of the tube narrowing, when again the soft tissues are forced through perforations in a paste-like form. The bone and cartilage are diverted to a separate outlet where they are collected for treatment and recycling or for use as a pet-food additive. This process has the advantage of producing a continuous flow and therefore has a larger throughput capability. It is also more easily dismantled and generally considered to be easier to clean and maintain.

The mechanically recovered meat is usually frozen down in slabs for ease of handling and the majority of processors use plate freezers for this purpose. Whatever the system of refrigeration it is important that the temperature is reduced quickly to not more than 3 °C to control microbial development, as the temperature may be considerably increased during the process.

The yield of mechanically recovered meat can be varied by raising or lowering the operating pressure, but the calcium levels increase as the pressure increases and care must be taken to remain within acceptable parameters.

The mechanically recovered meat often falls in to two categories:

- Low fat – obtained from the front half of the carcase and considered to be high grade.
- High fat – obtained from the rear half of the carcase and considered to be low grade.

A bacteriological standard for mechanically recovered meat is usually set by customers, the majority of whom accept a maximum total viable count. Customers may require testing for specific organisms. Product failing to meet a customer's specification is usually diverted to pet food manufacture, although even manufacturers of pet food may require standards similar to those for products for human consumption.

Turkeys

Technical aspects of turkey processing

With the present-day emphasis on healthy eating, turkey meat, being naturally low in fat, has become increasingly important as a basis of meals suitable for all occasions. In the UK where a whole turkey is still eaten regularly, particularly on Christmas Day by most families, turkeys are slaughtered all year round to produce portions or to provide meat for further processed products. This practice has led to turkeys being grown to their most economical weight for age, taking into account floor space and food conversion ratio. Stags are normally processed at around 17 kg and hens at 9 kg live weight. The predominant strains are the BUT T8, Big 6 and Nicholas.

This section comments on all aspects of processing from on-farm loading to despatch of the finished product, taking into account recent innovations in processing machinery normally found in the major European processing plants. Legislation is also taken into account.

CATCHING AND TRANSPORTATION

Catching is mostly carried out by hand during the night hours. Short-term feed and water withdrawal prior to loading is an advantage to the processor, as an empty crop and gut reduces the possibility of faecal contamination. For loading, birds are segregated by means of movable partitions and driven to the loading end of the shed. Birds are held by having both feet in one hand and one wing in the other and placed carefully into the crates to prevent bruising. Dismountable modules with a sliding door or modules with slide-out drawers are the most popular. These are brought into the shed or to the door. Some static module vehicles are still used, but problems arise when lifting heavier birds, resulting in damage from flapping when the birds are carried outside the sheds. It is important that the containers are thoroughly cleaned and disinfected between each load to minimize the possibility of spread of disease.

European Union legislation giving details of distances permitted, transport times, drivers and operators' responsibilities, together with other provisions, can be found in Directive 91/628/EEC on the welfare of animals during transport.

LAIRAGING AND OFF-LOADING

On arrival at the processing plant the birds are held in a lairage to protect them from adverse weather conditions, always ensuring that adequate ventilation is provided. It is considered beneficial to rest the birds for 1–2 hours after their journey to relax them and to reduce stress.

Off-loading is by hand for static and side-load modules, directly from the lorry with the operator moving up or down the side of the lorry on a hydraulic platform. The birds from the dismountable modules may be transferred into a reservoir before they are transported to the handlers by conveyor belt. Dismountable drawers are fed along an enclosed conveyor until arriving at the hanging-on point. The handler, with all methods, hangs the bird by both feet upside down onto a moving shackle conveyor, usually running at between 2000 and 4000 birds per hour. The maximum permitted hanging period for turkeys prior to stunning is 6 minutes. It is beneficial to have subdued lighting and dark-coloured walls to keep the birds calm and reduce flapping in the hanging-on area.

STUNNING AND BLEEDING

Stunning has been the subject of much debate over recent years and will vary from one plant to another. In all cases birds must be rendered unconscious prior to venesection and they must not regain consciousness before death.

The most popular type of stunner is a water-bath through which the bird's head passes so that the bird is either stunned or killed depending on the current used. Care must be taken to ensure that there is no forward overflow of water from the bath which will produce pre-stun shocks.

A carotid artery and jugular vein are severed by a cut beneath one side of the head after a stun by a current of about 180 milliamps. Residual blood in the carcase may become a problem with further processing becoming more sophisticated. Stunning with a high frequency of about 380 milliamps prior to cutting both carotid arteries has proved more successful in ensuring a satisfactory bleeding-out of the carcase.

Automatic killers are available, but not widely used because of the variation in length of turkeys at any given age.

Gas stunning, using either carbon dioxide or a mixture of carbon dioxide and other inert gases such as argon, is currently under investigation. This involves containers or modules of birds being killed in a chamber and then shackled, possibly mechanically, prior to venesection. It is claimed meat quality is improved, and the welfare aspect is fully satisfied as there is no shackling of live birds and no possibility of pre-stun shocks.

Slaughterhouse workers must be competent and efficient and have some form of approval. In the UK licensing is required.

SCALDING AND PLUCKING

Scalding and plucking are the next process and the machines are designed in most cases to complement each other, depending on the type of product to be produced. Fresh product (either whole birds or portions) which are to be air chilled are soft scalded at around 50 °C to leave the epidermal layer intact. Frozen product, usually immersion chilled, will be hard scalded at 55 °C or above. The purpose of the scalding is to loosen the feathers by opening the follicles prior to feather removal by the pluckers. The normal dwell time for small turkeys in the scalder will be around 2 minutes 15 seconds. Larger birds require a minimum time of 2 minutes 45 seconds. For soft scalding the dwell time will be increased.

The contamination washed off the birds as they are immersed in the scalding tank can lead to the water becoming highly polluted. To overcome this, sectional or multistage scalders are now available in which the water gets progressively cleaner as the birds pass through the different stages. In counterflow scalders clean water enters the same end of the scalder as the birds exit, so that the cleanest water is on the cleanest birds. Prior to scalding, foot scrubbing can take place to remove any loose debris, usually of faecal origin, which could be washed into the scalder and increase the bacterial load.

The cabinet design for a scalder should be as simple as possible to eliminate corners or dirt traps and enable the machine to be effectively cleaned. Scalders may be single or multipass and will be specifically designed for a given situation. To ensure effective plucking the feathers must be completely wet. As the birds are pulled through the water they will tend to float on the surface. To keep the birds fully immersed water is allowed to overflow from the top section of the tank and air is simultaneously injected from the bottom to produce a 'jacuzzi' effect.

Plucking should commence immediately at the exit from the scalder so that there is minimal heat loss. Some processors have a quill puller installed between the scalder and the plucking machines, which consists of two contrarotating rollers for removal of the tail feathers.

The design of the plucking system will be peculiar to the type of scalding. For hard-scalded birds there will be a pre-flighter constructed with three or four banks of domed heads to which fingers of hard rubber are attached to remove primary flight feathers and remaining tail feathers. Each adjacent plucker head contrarotates so that the birds remain hanging vertically on the shackle. One or more pluckers, usually with either discs or flails with the fingers of progressively softer rubber, are then used to complete the removal of feathers from the carcase. A horizontal bank of domed plucking heads can be fitted to a pre-flighting unit to remove the feathers of the scapula and neck area.

After soft scalding, flails will remove the feathers from the body to ensure that the epidermis remains intact on the breast and thighs. Disc pluckers with harder rubber fingers will then complete the defeathering of the wings and drumsticks. Spraying of water in the plucker at the same temperature as the scald tank to reduce heat loss is advisable.

Whichever type of scalding or plucking is used it is essential to keep adjusting profiles of the plucking machine to the size of the birds to ensure that all feathers are removed and no damage is done to the skin.

EVISCERATION

In most modern plants slaughter and evisceration take place on one continuous line. Evisceration, however, must take place in a separate room. The birds remain shackled by their feet until the evisceration is completed. This reduces the likelihood of cross-contamination during unshackling and rehanging from one line to another. The risk of birds falling off the shackles during the various evisceration processes when held in the shackles by the hocks is also eliminated.

The object of the evisceration process is to remove all the organs from the body cavity in a hygienic manner. It is important that there is no rupture of the alimentary tract which would cause contamination of the carcase by organisms that could cause food poisoning or spoilage organisms that reduce shelf-life of fresh poultry. To achieve these objectives the birds remain hung vertically and should be touched as little as possible. Where automatic machinery is used the individual pieces of equipment, which are usually of a carousel design, must be washed in potable water during each revolution, ensuring at the same time that no cross-contamination is caused by splashing the cleaning liquid onto the carcases.

Some plants may vary but for automatic evisceration it is normal to carry out the process in the following sequence.

Neck splitting is done using a helical screw to pick up the neck and hold it in position by holding the head against a retaining bar until a knife in the final groove of the screw makes a vertical incision the full length of the neck from the shoulders to the head. A hand-held knife is then inserted under the neck skin to separate the skin, which is then severed at the head leaving the neck skin intact on the carcase. This skin may be required for final presentation of the carcase or breast portion.

Venting (removal of the rectum and cloaca) is carried out by dropping a circular blade around the rectum and severing the skin. Either by mechanical means or by vacuum, the rectum is withdrawn from the cavity, together with the cloaca, and carefully draped over the back of the carcase. By regular maintenance of the machine, keeping the blades constantly sharp, this process will be carried out in a consistent and efficient manner thus ensuring the hygienic control of the remainder of the evisceration process. Regular adjustment of the machine is necessary as weights of birds vary from load to load.

A vent opening machine then makes a vertical slit from the vent opening to the tip of the keel (breast) bone to prepare the bird for evisceration. A manual back-up to these two machines may be advisable to ensure that the birds are properly presented to the eviscerator. This would not be necessary for species such as chicken where weight and size variations at a younger age are small. Variations in weights of up to 5 kg are possible in turkeys aged 20 weeks or more, which have major effects on body size and conformation.

Continuing development of eviscerating machines has produced a number of different models for horizontal evisceration. Earlier models, many of which are still in use, work vertically with a stainless steel spoon travelling down the internal surface of the backbone to a pre-set depth and lifting out the complete visceral package on its return stroke. The kidneys will remain untouched inside the bird. If the machine is correctly adjusted and the birds healthy, the lungs will be removed together with the viscera, which are then laid down the back of the bird ready for inspection.

Horizontal eviscerating machines either work on a platform system or have a parallel line to the evisceration line where the head is picked up as evisceration takes place. The bird is held horizontally so that the viscera are hanging free of the carcase for inspection instead of being in contact with the back of the birds. When evisceration and inspection have taken place the head is released and the birds return to their vertical position.

On-line inspection of the organs and body cavity then takes place during which whole birds, or some of the offal, may be rejected. The most common rejections involve livers which have lesions or are discoloured, and lungs which may show varying degrees of air sacculitis. Where air sacculitis is chronic the meat may be recovered from the carcase providing that there is no cross-contamination with other carcases in the chilling process.

Recovery of the offal can be manual or by machine. The heart and liver, from which the gallbladder is also removed, are manually removed by pulling or with scissors. In all cases care must be taken not to rupture the gallbladder. The remaining viscera are then put into a gizzard harvester. The machine will separate the gizzard from the viscera prior to defatting in a chamber using rotating rubber plucker fingers. The gizzard is then split by a rotating blade and opened to form the shape of a butterfly before thorough washing and peeling off the yellow membrane.

Following washing and cooling, the heart, liver and gizzard can be packed in an impermeable wrapper for insertion into a whole bird; otherwise they will be bulk packed for further processing or for sale.

When processing large male turkeys the gonads may be harvested and packed for human consumption after thorough cleaning.

Individual processors will decide at which point to remove the head. This is most efficiently done by locking between two bars in the shape of a V and pulling it off as the bird continues down the line. If the venesection and neck skin removal have been carried out correctly the trachea will be pulled out with the head.

Crop and trachea are removed by hand or knife, or by drilling out on a carousel. With the last method it is imperative that the crop is empty of food and is not ruptured on removal. Rupturing causes contamination of the neck skin area. This soiling is particularly difficult to remove.

Necks are removed by a neck cracker which drives a sharp piece of stainless steel through the neck, at the base of the neck in the crop area, which is located against an anvil. Damage to the neck skin can take place if the machine is not correctly positioned.

A final inspection machine removes the remainder of the lungs by vacuum and also any other loose debris in the body cavity. This is followed by an inside/outside washer. This machine will be enclosed in a cabinet, and a high-pressure spray will wash the outside of the bird with potable water. Simultaneously a lance will enter the body cavity and spray the inside of the bird. In the UK the level of chlorine in the water is increased to around 25 p.p.m. as an added antibacterial safeguard, but this practice is not allowed in most European countries.

Trimming of any damaged or diseased parts is carried out by a trained operative or inspector following a final visual inspection.

Turkeys are deshackled from a continuous line, by a machine which breaks the shank, draws the sinews and finally removes the metatarsus at the hock joint. If the birds have had their sinews pulled at the end of the killing line they will have been reshackled by the hocks on the eviscerating line and processed in the same manner.

CHILLING

The majority of turkeys are air chilled. This is carried out by hanging singly on shackles or on a 'Christmas tree' type shackle which can accommodate up to 16 birds.

Air chillers will usually consist of two chambers, the first at a temperature of 10 °C and the second at minus 5 °C to complete the process. A residence time in these chambers of 4–8 hours will be required to bring the deep muscle temperature to below legal limit of 4 °C. Air chilling dries out the skin, darkening it in colour. This can be undesirable, so air and spray chilling is used where fine sprays of water raise the humidity of the air, keeping the skin moist and accelerating the cooling process.

Water immersion chilling is practised in the UK, particularly for large turkeys. Legislation permits only contraflow chillers to be used. At entry of the chiller system the temperature of the water must be below 16 °C or below. During the passage through the chiller the water becomes progressively cleaner and cooler so that at the exit the temperature of the water does not exceed 4 °C. This is achieved by adding ice through the various stages and at the exit adding refrigerated water, thus ensuring a good contraflow.

Whole turkeys or turkey meat chilled in this manner may only be traded in frozen form throughout European countries. However, in countries where immersion chilling is practised they must permit importation of chilled meat of this type. Full details of hygiene requirements for all aspects of poultry processing are to be found in the Poultry Meat, Farmed Game and Rabbit Meat Hygiene Directive 92/116/EEC.

Ducks

Technical aspects of duck processing

This section deals with duck processing in high-speed plants. This is a relative term, because high-speed duck processing lines rarely operate at speeds above 3000 birds per hour, whereas chicken lines commonly run in excess of 6000 birds per hour.

All species of poultry are handled in a similar way with the live bird manually removed from its transporter crate and placed in a shackle. The design of shackle varies from species to species (Figure 5.9), and enables the bird's

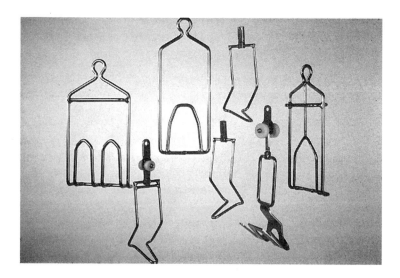

Figure 5.9   Suspension shackles. (With kind permission of Stork PMT.)

feet to be held securely while the conveyor moves it through the processing plant.

This section assumes the birds are of a Pekin type of duck (favoured in the UK, USA and the Far East) as opposed to the Barbarie or Moulard type of bird (generally favoured in France).

The processing of waterfowl differs from other domestic species in a number of significant ways. These are primarily concerned with the fact that waterfowl require more sophisticated plucking techniques. The various byproducts are more valuable and are therefore recovered. These differences, in turn, pose differing problems when hygiene and inspection techniques are being considered.

During the growing process, ducks moult their first crop of feathers at a relatively earlier age and a second feather growth takes place. This can happen at any time between 46 days and 56 days of age, depending on the type and maturity of bird, and can present problems for the high-speed processor. There is a very narrow time-span between first and second feather growth when plucking is easier, and this should be the target time for processing. Ideally, this should also be planned to coincide with the optimum weight for best profitability. Planning of processing days is therefore more critical than for other poultry species. Birds processed while the second feathering is at an advanced stage are more difficult to pluck adequately. Allowing birds to live longer, say more than 70 days, has obvious economic consequences, although at this stage the second feather growth has probably been completed and plucking again becomes easier.

STUNNING

Owing to the density of the feather cover and the fact that waterfowl feather contains down clusters which act as insulation, it is more difficult for low-voltage stunners to be effective. The down covering also means that few processors use automatic killing machines as the blades quickly become blunted.

As a general guide, ducks require a longer contact time in water-bath stunners than other species, and an electrical current of about 110 mA does not appear to produce adverse carcase effects. It has also been demonstrated by Gregory and Wooton (1993) at Bristol that stunning is more effective if ducks' heads are completely immersed in water-bath stunners, although this is not easily achievable in commercially available models. There are obvious welfare and legislative benefits in ensuring birds are rendered totally insensible.

At the time of writing, research into gas stunning of poultry is being undertaken and the results are being studied. It is possible that commercial machines will be available to the industry by the year 2000, with improved bird welfare. However, equipment to stun ducks adequately may require further research because of the ability of waterfowl species to hold their breath at will, e.g. when diving or feeding underwater. Any unfamiliar or unwelcome atmosphere may trigger this physiological reaction, thus rendering the gas stunner partially ineffective.

Venesection can take several forms, but the most common killing method is to insert the killing knife into the mouth of the bird and sever the left carotid artery, twisting the blade before withdrawal to sever the right carotid. Slaughterhouse workers must be adequately trained before being allowed to undertake this task and will have varying techniques to suit local circumstances, for instance if the worker is left-handed.

PLUCKING

As with all poultry species, birds are suspended by their feet and pass on a moving conveyor line into a scalding tank. This consists of an immersion bath of varying dimensions, depending on the operating speed of the plant, which allows the birds to be immersed for periods varying between 1.5 minutes and 4 minutes. Turbulence of the water is created by pumps and causes the carcase feather follicles to expand, facilitating feather removal at the next stage of the process.

Because of the feather and down coverage, there is a natural tendency for ducks to be waterproof. The design of the scalding tank is critical to ensure good plucking. As a general rule, ducks require more turbulence in the scald water and, in almost all high-speed waterfowl processing, high scald temperatures of 60–61 °C are common. There is a hygiene advantage in having scald water at these temperatures as few bacteria survive for any length of time, including spoilage organisms. A dwell time of about 3–4 minutes in the scalding tank should be sufficient to ensure adequate feather removal in the plucking machines.

Plucking machine designs vary in detail depending upon the manufacturer concerned. The general principle is that birds pass through banks of rotating discs, each disc holding between six and nine rubber fingers, which, with the force of their rotation, remove the loosened feather from the carcase. Plucking machines for ducks are usually similar to those used for turkeys, although experimentation with the thickness and pliability of the plucker fingers will generally produce optimum results. The number of discs and the size of the machines vary to suit the species involved and the operating speed of the plant.

The plucker fingers may require more attention in terms of hygiene or replacement to minimize cross-contamination and maintain plucking standards because of the greasy nature of ducks. The type of machine used is important, as some machines are designed to facilitate cleaning whereas others present hygiene problems.

The screening of plucking machines and the collection of feather is vitally important to a duck processor. Duck feather, and in particular its down content, is commercially valuable. The dried, purified feather and down is used in a variety of bedding, insulated clothing and fashion goods. The feather is normally collected in water troughs below the pluckers, which must not be allowed to be contaminated by the viscera or other offal, and is then pumped over screens for separation from the process water. The feather is subsequently washed, rinsed and dried and may be graded depending on the sophistication of the plant concerned.

It is likely that some signs of a second feather growth will be visible on some birds however competently the plucking machines perform their task. The outer layers of the skin are removed during plucking, because of the high temperature of the scald, and any imperfections in feather removal are very visible. Ducks are then usually subjected to a further stage in the plucking process which involves immersion in a food-quality wax to remove the remaining feather stubble. The birds may be immersed in a hot-water dip tank at 70–80 °C immediately following plucking. This causes the newly formed follicles to stand out from the carcase and facilitate wax adhesion in the next part of the process. For hygiene reasons, however, this part of the process is becoming less frequent in Europe, although it is still common in many other parts of the world.

In most European plants the ducks pass through two wax tanks, each containing a microcrystalline hydrocarbon wax of food quality held at a temperature of circa. 90 °C. Each processor may have its own wax formulation and operating practice. The general principle is that the bird passes into a hot, highly liquid wax bath which forms an initial coating around the bird. The bird then passes into a second tank where a similar wax at a slightly lower temperature covers the first and forms a laminated coat, the wax gripping the feather follicles remaining on the carcase. The bird then passes into a pre-cooled water tank which ensures the wax hardens on the carcase. This is subsequently stripped manually, or by machine, when the tiny feathers previously visible on the carcase are removed with the wax. The wax is then filtered, treated and recycled. Plant inspectors should always ensure that the wax removal is complete, and careful management of the wax process will ensure that the coated wax is removable without crumbling. Once the wax becomes fragmented during removal it is likely to be less effective in its plucking role, and complete replacement should be considered. In a high-speed plant, wax would normally be changed every 8–14 weeks, depending on the efficiency of the wax management system. Most plants devise a layout to prevent the heads from entering the wax bath to avoid the possibility of wax remaining in the mouth or trachea.

EVISCERATION

Duck feet are served in most Chinese restaurants and are considered a great delicacy in the Far East. Duck processors worldwide, therefore, utilize the duck feet for human consumption. Depending upon the layout of the plant, the feet may be removed prior to immersion in the wax, or prior to, or following, evisceration. At whichever stage this occurs, the inspection service will wish to see the carcase before the feet are removed. The separation from the carcase usually takes place at the hock joint and it would be here that the signs of synovitis would be evident if present. For birds that are passing before the inspector on the evisceration line with the feet attached, a separate inspection should not be necessary. It is normal practice to skin the feet prior to despatch and a number of foot skinners are commercially available. They will be located at varying points in the plant depending on the specific layout. The inspector may be required to certify that the feet have been processed hygienically and are fit for human consumption to satisfy the requirements of the importing country.

Duck tongues are also in demand in Chinese cuisine and at some stage in the process will be removed, washed and packed. Subject to the birds' general health, this should present no problem for the inspectors, although again, certification may be required to state that the product is fit for human consumption.

Many high-speed duck processing plants have automatic evisceration equipment which has been specifically designed for ducks. The design of the equipment must recognize the different physical characteristics of the duck compared with the turkey and the broiler chicken. As a significant proportion of processed duckling goes to Chinese restaurants some may need to be processed with heads and necks remaining attached to the carcase. This is to satisfy the requirements of the Chinese chef who will display the cooked bird in this way. This may affect the layout and type of equipment used and may prevent some plants using full automatic evisceration. Legislation normally permits birds to be packed with head and neck attached and still receive the full health mark.

The general sequence of evisceration is very similar to that for other types of poultry. One difference on automated duck evisceration lines is that gizzards are not easily capable of being split or skinned by commercially available machines. European legislation requires that the horned membrane is removed if whole gizzards are to be included in the gizzard packs. Processors therefore have the choice of manually opening the gizzard and attempting to remove the horned membrane by hand, or, alternatively, to cut the ends of the gizzards and discard the horned membrane area as inedible offal. This may change if more sophisticated equipment is developed.

As there is no outer layer of skin following the high temperature scald and immersion in hot wax, it is important to minimize handling and maximize water sprays and washing facilities to avoid cross-contamination of the carcase. Once contamination has occurred, it is more difficult to clean a hard-scalded duck carcase than other soft-scalded poultry.

As in other domestic fowl, the neck, heart, liver and gizzard ends (or gizzard without horned membrane) make up the giblet pack. These are usually washed in chlorinated water and cooled prior to packing.

Ducks are generally unaffected by the diseases which cause high mortality in broiler or turkey flocks. Duck virus hepatitis (DVH) is endemic in some areas of Europe and usually controlled by vaccines. Flock health records will accompany birds to the processing plant and the veterinary inspector will have previously been alerted to any unusual health or mortality problems at the farm of origin. The on-line inspection will usually be concerned with identifying symptoms of *Escherichia coli* infections, and occasionally ascites, although other problems may arise from time to time.

CHILLING

Following evisceration, the processor has a number of options for final presentation of the duck, generally determined by customer requirements. Until comparatively recently, most hard-scalded ducks were chilled by immersion in cold water. This was primarily due to two factors:

- By utilizing controlled chlorine levels in the chilled water, the processor was able to control the growth of *Salmonella* and other organisms which might cause food poisoning on the carcase. Research, however, has shown that spin chilling contributes to cross-contamination of the carcase. Legislative requirements governing the operation of spin chillers, together with water temperatures and water flows, have to a large extent minimized this problem.
- The duck carcase without the outer skin layer was prone to discolouration when subjected to cold air blasts during the chilling processes.

Duck processors have therefore continued to use water immersion chilling many years after the broiler industry had moved to air cooling of eviscerated carcases. Recent developments of spray cooling, which enables the moisture and humidity to be controlled during the chilling process, have largely overcome these problems and increasingly modern duck processing plants have installed spray cooling equipment. Spray cooling has the advantage of eliminating bird-to-bird contact and reducing levels of contamination, and is generally confined to fresh (i.e. chilled) product. The appearance of relatively dry spray-cooled carcases has the appeal which major supermarket customers in the UK and Europe demand.

Water immersion chilling is still a common way of cooling the carcases for frozen ducks and, given the legislation covering water content, does not adversely affect the appearance of the finished product.

Raw further processing of duck carcases is not as well developed as with other forms of poultry. The physical characteristics and the meat to bone ratio on duck carcases does not lend itself to appealing plate presentations of portioned product. Most major duck processors offer quarter and half ducks, together with leg joints, breast joints (both boneless and bone-in), presented in a variety of packing. As a general rule, however, the innovative marketing pioneered by the broiler and turkey industries has not been followed by similar success for the duck industry. There is relatively little automated processing equipment specifically designed for the cutting or portioning of duck carcases and it is therefore usually done manually. The potential cross-contamination risks will be obvious unless the process is carefully controlled, particularly in terms of carcase temperature.

In countries which produce *foie gras* it is standard practice to cut the carcase to remove the liver intact. The resulting joints, breast fillets (maigrets), duck legs and *confit de canard* also can be sold, but *foie gras* is not produced in the UK.

CHAPTER 6

Regional Anatomy of the Domestic Birds

Introduction

In contrast to the majority of the accounts of avian anatomy, the approach taken in this chapter is mainly topographical or regional rather than systematic since it is felt that this is more appropriate to the requirements of poultry meat inspection. The description is primarily that of the chicken but because of the basic uniformity of structure in birds it is applicable to the other domestic species. However, all the important interspecies differences in the anatomy are covered.

Surface features

Skin

Over most parts of the body the skin is extremely thin and relatively avascular, and unlike in mammals it is only loosely attached to the underlying musculature. Consequently, any bleeding that occurs after damage to the skin during crating and transportation to the slaughterhouse can under-run the skin some distance and may result in extensive blemishes. In birds other than ducks and geese, vascular areas of skin appear in the breast region during brooding and serve to maintain the temperature of the incubating eggs. Not all areas of skin are thin. The beak or bill, the claws and the scales covering the feet are heavily keratinized (Figure 6.1). Frequently the upper beak is cut back to prevent cannibalism. In ducks and geese the bill is formed by soft, leather-like keratin and has lamellae at the edges which interdigitate with the bristles of the tongue to form a grasping or straining organ. The front of the upper and lower bills in these species has a hard, horny, plate-like nail rich in mechanoreceptors. In pigeons the base of the upper bill is formed by the white, thickened, sensitive cere. A well-developed horny spur arises from the scaly region of the foot in the male chicken, pheasant, grouse and turkey, and in chickens may reach a length of 6 cm. It is small or absent in females. The comb, wattles and ear lobes of chickens are ornamental and

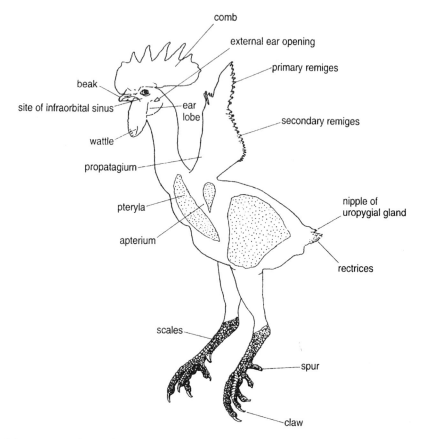

Figure 6.1 The surface features of the chicken. With permission from King and McLelland (1).

are based on a highly vascular dermis. They are especially well developed in males. The colour of these structures may indicate the health or physiological state of the bird. Dubbing or removal of the comb in day-old chicks is sometimes carried out to prevent cannibalism. The comb reflex may be tested in the slaughterhouse to ascertain if a bird is conscious or not. In place of a comb turkeys have an extensible conical snood on the top of the head which can be raised or lowered, and there is an unpaired median dewlap in place of wattles. The skin over the entire head and upper neck in turkeys is thickened and highly vascular. Birds possess a very large skin gland, the uropygial or preen gland, near the tip of the tail (Figure 6.1). This bilobed, holocrine sebaceous gland has two openings on a median nipple-like process. During preening birds transfer the fatty secretion of the gland from their bills onto the feathers, keeping them moist and water-repellent.

Feathers

The characteristic shape of birds is provided by the contour feathers which can be divided into flight feathers and general body feathers. The main flight feathers of the wing are the primary remiges attaching to the metacarpal and phalangeal bones, and the secondary remiges attaching to the ulna (Figure 6.1). Cutting the remiges on one side is sometimes carried out to make the bird unbalanced and therefore incapable of flight. The fold of skin on the leading edge of the wing opposite the flight feathers is the propatagium, which carries an elastic ligament. The propatagium in ducks may be used for tagging. The flight feathers of the tail, the rectrices, are associated with the fleshy uropygial mass. The body contour feathers are not evenly distributed over the bird but are arranged in tracts, the pterylae, between which are relatively bare areas of skin, the apteria. Below the contour feathers lie the fluffy down feathers, the partly fluffy semiplumes, the bristles, and the hair-like filoplumes which remain on the carcase after plucking and can be removed by singeing. Moulting of the feathers generally occurs annually after the breeding season; in chickens this is usually in the autumn.

Head

The large eyeball of birds is strengthened near the cornea by a ring of small bones, the scleral ossicles. The surface of the eye is protected by a transparent nictitating membrane which sweeps across the eye from the nasal side of the orbit. This corneal reflex is absent after stunning in the slaughterhouse. The eye is associated with three glands including the nasal gland dorsal to the orbit, the gland of the nictitating membrane caudomedial to the eyeball, and the lacrimal gland at the lateral canthus. The external ear opening (Figure 6.1) lies caudoventral to the eye. It is protected in place of an ear flap by a circle of specialized contour feathers. Below the eye lies the infraorbital sinus, a diverticulum of the nasal cavity. Infection of the sinus is relatively common, and since the sinus is not bounded on the outside by bone the condition is easy to diagnose. The nostrils (see Figure 6.6) lie at the base of the beak. In the chicken and turkey the nostril opening is reduced dorsally by a horny flap, the operculum, and ventrally by a vertical sheet of cartilage.

Oropharynx

The entrance to the oral cavity is called the gape. Unlike in mammals, there is no soft palate so it is difficult to determine the boundary between the oral cavity and the pharynx. Consequently the common chamber is referred to as the oropharynx. The roof of the oropharynx (Figure 6.2a) contains two slits in the midline. The rostral opening is the choana and leads to the nasal cavity. The smaller caudal opening is the infundibular cleft which is the common opening of the right and left auditory tubes. The floor of the oropharynx contains the tongue and the laryngeal mound (Figure 6.2b).

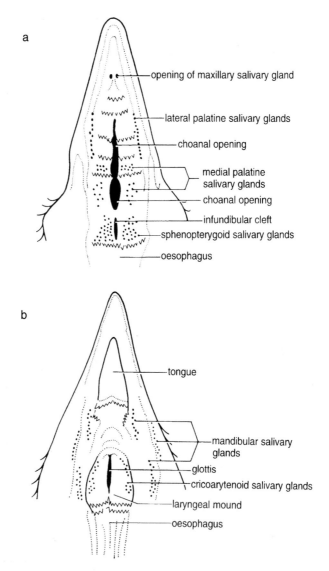

Figure 6.2 The roof (a) and floor (b) of the oropharynx of the chicken. With permission from King and McLelland (1).

The tongue in most of the domestic species is relatively simple, but in ducks and geese it is more specialized. In the duck the caudal part of the tongue has a fleshy eminence while the lateral margins have overlapping bristles and tooth-like processes. The bristles interdigitate with the lamellae of the bill. The laryngeal mound contains on the rostral surface the glottis which is the entrance to the larynx. An epiglottis is absent and there are no vocal folds. In the chicken the surface of the oropharynx carries many backward-pointing papillae. Below the mucosa lies an almost continuous layer of mucus-secreting salivary glands which have numerous openings into the lumen.

Feet

The foot in most birds has four toes, three directed forwards and one backwards (Figure 6.1). In ducks and geese the forward-pointing toes are webbed. The joints of the foot are supported on the standing surface in the chicken by pads of fatty tissue. In the slaughterhouse the feet are normally cut off in the tarsometatarsal region, although in some countries they are removed at the hock.

Skeletomuscular system

Spine

The spine is highly rigid over much of its length due to the fusion of the vertebrae forming in the chicken the notarium, synsacrum and pygostyle (Figure 6.3). The synsacrum is fused to the pelvis. A notarium is absent in ducks and geese. The fusion in the chicken starts at about 4 months in the notarium and at about 7 weeks in the synsacrum. The long cervical region of the spine, in contrast, is highly mobile, allowing the head to be used for all the tasks which would normally in mammals be carried out by the forelimb. Between the notarium and synsacrum is the fourth thoracic vertebra which because of its isolated mobility is vulnerable to a number of clinical conditions.

Thoracic cage

The sternum (Figure 6.3) is massively developed owing to the requirements of flight. Its main feature is the extensive ventral keel for the attachment of

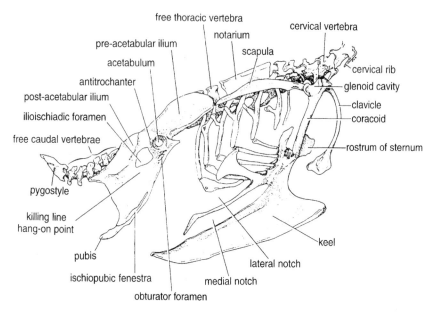

Figure 6.3 The trunk skeleton of the chicken. With permission from Raikow *et al.* (2).

the flight muscles. The caudal part in young birds is cartilaginous and flexible. The five or six pairs of ribs are entirely bony and consist of vertebral and sternal parts. The uncinate processes of the vertebral ribs strengthen the thoracic wall. In the chicken floating ribs are associated with the last few cervical vertebrae.

Thoracic girdle and wing

The thoracic girdle (Figure 6.3) consists of the scapula, coracoid and clavicle. Unlike in mammals the avian scapula moves very little, and is firmly held to the thoracic cage by ligaments and muscle. The stout coracoid holds the wing away from the sternum during flight. Right and left clavicles fuse to form the furcula (wishbone) which acts to keep the shoulder joints the correct distance apart when the wings are moving. Where the scapula, coracoid and clavicle meet is a space, the triosseal canal. Through this canal runs the tendon of the supracoracoid muscle which causes the upstroke of the wing.

The wing consists of the humerus, radius and ulna, radial and ulnar carpal bones, the carpometacarpus and three digits (Figure 6.4). The humerus provides attachments for the two flight or breast muscles. The

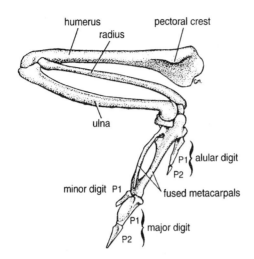

Figure 6.4 Lateral view of the bones of the right wing of the chicken. With permission from King and McLelland (1).

breast muscles lie on top of one another on the lateral surface of the sternal keel. The tendon of the superficial muscle, the pectoral, attaches to the undersurface of the humerus and causes the downstroke of the wing. The tendon of the deep muscle, the supracoracoid, runs through the triosseal canal to attach to the pectoral crest on the upper surface of the humerus. This muscle causes the upstroke of the wing. It is characterized by being tightly bound by connective tissue, and in adult turkeys and broilers is the site of Oregon muscle disease.

The ulna in the chicken is thicker than the radius. The secondary remiges attach to it by ligaments. For a short while after hatching there are two rows of carpal bones, but by about the third week the distal row has fused with the metacarpals forming the carpometacarpus. The digits include the alular digit, the major digit and the minor digit which have two, two and one phalanges respectively. The primary remiges attach to the metacarpus and digits.

Pelvic girdle and hindlimb

The pelvic girdle consists of partly fused ilium, ischium and pubis (see Figure 6.3). The ilium is also fused to the synsacral part of the spine. Ventrally the pelvis is open since the right and left bones do not meet in the midline to form a symphysis. The fusion of the bones and the arched shape of the pelvis help to support the trunk in the standing position.

The hindlimb consists of the femur, patella, tibiotarsus, fibula, tarsometatarsus and digits (Figure 6.5). The femur has a double connection with the pelvic girdle since above the hip joint there is a joint between the femoral trochanter and the ilium. The tibia after a few months fuses with the proximal row of tarsal bones to form a tibiotarsus. The tibia and fibula constitute the 'drumstick' part of the limb. The distal row of tarsal bones fuses with the metatarsal bones to form a tarsometatarsus. The hock joint between the tibiotarsus and the tarsometatarsus has a lateral cartilaginous meniscus. Behind the hock joint is a fibrocartilage block, the tibial cartilage, over and through which travel a number of tendons. The hock joint is examined routinely in the slaughterhouse. The tarsometatarsus has a bony process which forms the core of the spur. The four digits, I–IV, have two, three, four and five phalanges respectively. In chickens and turkeys the tendons of many of the hindlimb and wing muscles may ossify. This bone formation in chickens starts at about 90 days.

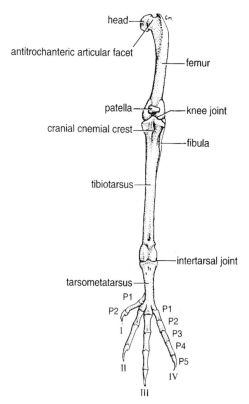

Figure 6.5 The left pelvic limb of a bird. With permission from King and McLelland (1).

General features

The typical avian long bone has an exceptionally thin cortex and a medullary cavity which contains a network of trabeculae to increase the strength of the bone. In hens just before the laying season a cancellous type of bone is laid down in the medullary cavity. This acts as a source of calcium for the manufacture of eggshells and increases the weight of the chicken skeleton by about 20%. Many of the bones in the post-cranial skeleton are aerated by extensions of the lungs.

Birds have two types of muscles, red and white, depending on the relative proportion of the red and white muscle fibres they possess. Red muscles, like the breast muscles of pigeons and the leg muscles of chickens, are characterized by large numbers of red fibres. Red fibres are rich in myoglobin and use fat rather than glycogen as a source of energy. These muscles are adapted for sustained activity. White muscles, like the breast muscles of chickens, contain more white fibres which use glycogen as a source of energy. These muscles, therefore, are characterized as being powerful but only acting over a short period.

Neck

Running down the right side of the neck is the oesophagus which compared with that of mammals has a much larger diameter. At the thoracic inlet the oesophagus is enlarged to form the crop (Figure 6.6). In chickens, pheasants and turkeys the crop is a ventral spherical chamber closely attached by skeletal muscle to the overlying skin. Consequently in the live bird it can easily be palpated. When the stomach is full, food may be stored in the crop where prior to chemical digestion in the stomach it undergoes softening and swelling. If the stomach is empty, however, the food bypasses the crop and enters the stomach directly. In the slaughterhouse the oesophagus in the evisceration process is cut below the crop, and to prevent contamination of the carcase by food the birds are not fed for 2–8 hours before death. The crop in pigeons is also a large ventral diverticulum of the oesophagus but is divided into two large lateral sacs. As well as storing food in this species it produces in both males and females 'crop milk', a desquamation of the epithelium which is fed to the chick at hatching. The crop of ducks and geese, in contrast, is a relatively indistinct fusiform widening of the oesophagus which is sometimes difficult to identify.

To the left of the oesophagus lies the trachea, which has a relatively large calibre and is surrounded by complete cartilage rings. It is enclosed except dorsally by skeletal muscle.

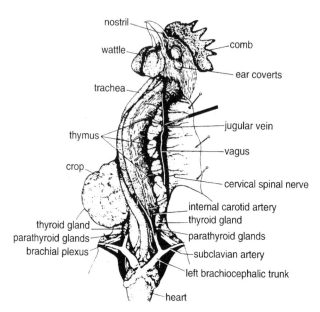

nostril
wattle
comb
ear coverts
trachea
thymus
crop
jugular vein
vagus
cervical spinal nerve
internal carotid artery
thyroid gland
thyroid gland
parathyroid glands
parathyroid glands
brachial plexus
subclavian artery
left brachiocephalic trunk
heart

Figure 6.6 The neck of a young male chicken. With permission from Nonidez and Goodale (3), and John Wiley & Sons, Inc.

In young birds the neck also contains the thymus, which, in the chicken, consists on each side of between four and seven pale lobes. The thymus has a similar microscopic structure to that of mammals and reaches its maximum size between 4 weeks and 17 weeks. It starts to regress at sexual maturity. The thymus contains primary lymphoid tissue which differentiates into T lymphocytes.

Running the length of the neck are the right and left jugular veins. In the chicken the right jugular vein is larger than the left because of the oblique anastomosis just below the head, diverting blood away from the left side. The jugular vein may be used for injections or collecting blood. The other veins that can be used for this purpose include the ulnar vein which is visible through the skin on the underside of the wing and the caudal tibial vein where it crosses the medial surface of the hock. The jugular veins are severed in throat cutting. Closely attached to the jugular vein are two cranial nerves, the vagus and the glossopharyngeal, so that inserting a needle into the vein may result in nerve damage.

A number of structures are situated at the thoracic inlet. The paired oval, reddish-brown thyroid gland lies medial to the jugular vein. Just behind the thyroid are the two parathyroid glands and the ultimobranchial gland; these organs are usually covered with fat and difficult to see. Lateral to the thyroid gland is the brachial nerve plexus. Caudal and medial to the thyroid gland in the midline is the syrinx at the junction of the trachea and the right and left primary bronchi. The syrinx is the site of sound production and consists of a series of variably ossified cartilages, vibrating membranes and muscles. Its narrow lumen may result in blockage in respiratory infections. In the male duck the syrinx has an enormous bony dilatation on the left side, the syringeal bulla, which appears almost to fill the thoracic inlet.

The axial skeleton of the neck and its associated musculature are sometimes removed from the bird to form part of the giblets. Embedded in this musculature are the paired internal carotid arteries which should be severed in slaughter by throat cutting.

Thoracoabdominal cavity

Liver and post-hepatic septum

On evisceration some of the contents of the thoracoabdominal cavity are removed. Two structures are then visible – the liver in the cranial part of the cavity surrounding the apex of the heart, and the post-hepatic septum caudally (Figure 6.7). The thoracic position of the liver is made possible by the

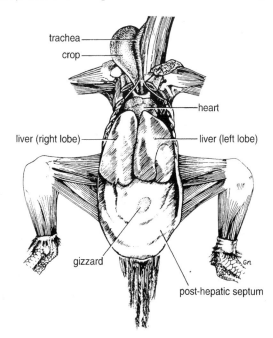

Figure 6.7   The first stage in the dissection of the thoracoabdominal cavity of a 3-week-old female chicken. The sternum and abdominal wall have been removed. With permission from King and McLelland (1).

absence of a diaphragm. The liver in the chicken has left and right lobes, the left lobe being partly subdivided into lateral and medial parts. In the chicken the lobes are equal in size but in the duck, goose and pigeon the right lobe is much larger than the left and the left lobe is not subdivided. The edges of the lobes are sharp. In all domestic birds except the pigeon a gallbladder is present on the visceral surface of the right lobe. Damaging the gallbladder in the slaughterhouse is a common cause of carcase contamination. The right lobe of the liver is penetrated by the caudal vena cava. The colour of the liver depends very much on diet and can vary from mahogany-brown to yellow. A yellow liver is also seen in chicks in the first 2 weeks after hatching and is due to pigments it absorbs along with the lipids of the contents of the yolk sac. The hepatoenteric duct draining the liver and the cysticoenteric duct draining the gallbladder empty into the terminal part of the duodenum. In the pigeon which has no gallbladder the liver is drained by two ducts. The liver, without the gallbladder, forms part of the giblets.

The post-hepatic septum is a double-layered peritoneal membrane which covers the viscera in the caudal half of the thoracoabdominal cavity. It arises from the roof of the cavity and ends caudally on the body wall below the cloaca. The left part of the septum encloses the gizzard. The post-hepatic septum divides the peritoneal cavity into a superficial hepatic peritoneal cavity containing the liver and a deep intestinal peritoneal cavity containing the intestines and urogenital organs. The hepatic peritoneal cavity is further subdivided but this is difficult to see other than by careful dissection. Entry to the intestinal peritoneal cavity can only conveniently be made by incising the post-hepatic septum. In young chicks the septum is a clear, glistening membrane through which the viscera are visible. With age, however, the septum usually becomes extensively filled with fat. A lack of fat here could indicate inanition. The division of the peritoneal cavity into two parts by the post-hepatic septum is important in restricting the spread of some diseases.

Stomach, duodenum and pancreas

Removal of the post-hepatic septum exposes the stomach on the left and duodenal loop on the right (Figure 6.8).

The stomach consists of two chambers, the cranial proventriculus and the caudal gizzard. Between the two chambers is the intermediate zone which is marked on the outside in the domestic birds by a constriction. The proventriculus (Figures 6.9 and 6.10) is a spindle-shaped organ in the walls of which are the glands which secrete gastric juice. The glands open at the tips of papillae which project into the lumen and are visible to the naked eye (Figure 6.10).

The gizzard (Figures 6.9 and 6.10) in the domestic birds is a large, muscular organ and is concerned with the physical breakdown of the food prior to

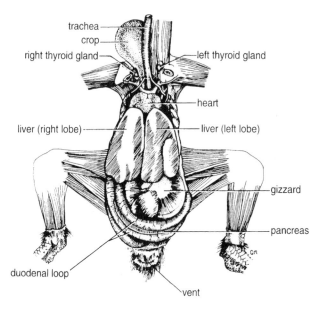

Figure 6.8 The second stage in the dissection of the thoracoabdominal cavity of a 3-week-old female chicken. The post-hepatic septum has been removed. With permission from King and McLelland (1).

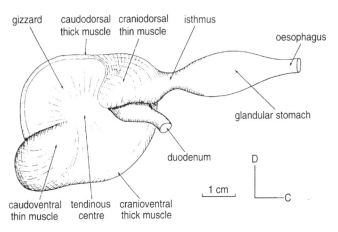

Figure 6.9 The stomach of the chicken, right lateral view. C, cranial; D, dorsal. With permission from McLelland (4) and WB Saunders (Philadelphia).

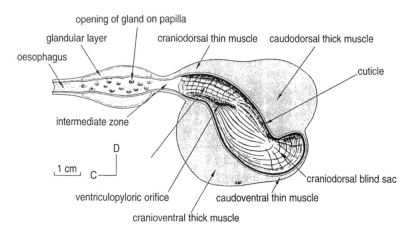

opening of gland on papilla

glandular layer   craniodorsal thin muscle   caudodorsal thick muscle

oesophagus

cuticle

intermediate zone

D

1 cm   C

ventriculopyloric orifice   caudoventral thin muscle

craniodorsal blind sac

cranioventral thick muscle

Figure 6.10   A longitudinal section of the stomach of the chicken, left lateral view. C, cranial; D, dorsal. With permission from McLelland (4) and WB Saunders (Philadelphia).

chemical digestion. The musculature is arranged into four groups of thick and thin muscles (Figure 6.9). The muscles attach to tendinous centres in the lateral walls. The asymmetrical arrangement of the muscles leads to rotatory and crushing movements when the gizzard contracts. When the gizzard is opened up a body, and cranial and caudal blind sacs can be identified (Figure 6.10). The entrance to the duodenum is in the cranial part of the body. The inner surface of the gizzard is lined by a hard membrane, the cuticle, which is secreted by the gizzard glands. Like the muscle, the cuticle is asymmetrically developed. It is a green or yellow colour due to bile regurgitated from the duodenum, and is removed by machine before the gizzard is added to the giblets. The lumen of the gizzard contains large amounts of grit which along with the well-developed muscle and the hard inner cuticle is responsible for breaking up the food. On the right side of the junction between the proventriculus and gizzard is the small, dark-red spleen. In the chicken the spleen is spherical, while in the duck it is triangular and in the pigeon elongated. It does not appear to vary in size.

The U-shaped duodenal loop has descending and ascending parts held together by mesentery (Figures 6.8 and 6.11). Between the two parts lies the pale-red or yellow pancreas. The pancreas in the chicken has four lobes. The three pancreatic ducts open, along with the bile ducts, on a papilla at the distal end of the duodenum.

Intestines

When the stomach and the duodenum are removed the remainder of the intestinal tract is exposed. The arrangement of the jejunum and ileum

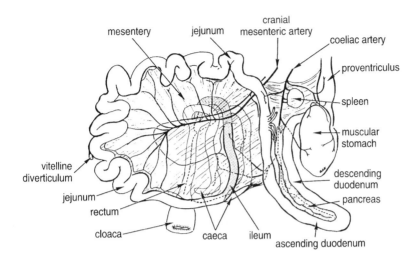

Figure 6.11 Ventral view of the gastrointestinal tract of the chicken. With permission from McLelland (4) and WB Saunders (Philadelphia).

depends on the species. In the chicken, turkey and pheasant they are arranged in garland-like coils at the edge of the mesentery (Figure 6.11). Where the jejunum ends and the ileum begins is arbitrarily taken as the point where the yolk sac and the yolk duct open into the antimesenteric side of the gut. The yolk of the yolk sac is absorbed into the blood stream by about 10 days after hatching and the sac is converted to scar tissue. The yolk is responsible for the yellow colour of the liver at this time. The yolk duct remains in the adult as a small papilla, the vitelline diverticulum (Figure 6.11), which is thought to have a lymphoepithelial function. In the duck, goose and pigeon the jejunum and ileum are arranged in fixed, U-shaped loops held together by mesentery (Figure 6.12). The jejunal and ileal loops are separated by the axial loop which carries near its tip the vitelline diverticulum. In the pigeon the largest of the three loops forms outer centripetal and inner centrifugal coils which are held together by mesentery. Protruding from the inner surface of the jejunum and ileum are nodules of aggregated lymphoid tissue which are visible to the naked eye. In the chicken one of these nodules is reported to occur regularly in the ileum about 10 cm from the junction with the rectum. In ducks and geese the aggregated lymphoid nodules are present as annular bands, four bands occurring in the duck and seven bands in the goose.

The large intestine consists of paired caeca and the rectum (Figures 6.11 and 6.12). The rectum is a straight tube extending from the ileum to the cloaca. At the ileorectal junction the terminal part of the ileum protrudes into the rectum. The rectum is supported by a mesorectum in which is situated the

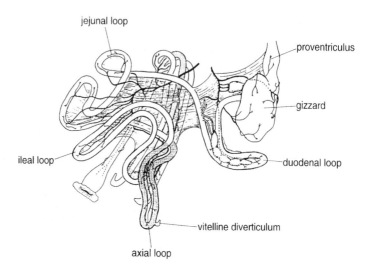

Figure 6.12   Ventral view of the gastrointestinal tract of the domestic goose. With permission from McLelland (4) and WB Saunders (Philadelphia).

intestinal nerve. Arising from the lateral walls of the rectum near the ileorectal junction are the right and left caeca. The caeca in all the domestic species except the pigeon are very large and have a characteristic green colour. The largest caeca occur in grouse. In chickens each caecum extends at first cranially before bending caudally to end near the cloaca. The orifices of the ileum and the two caeca are surrounded by sphincters. Well-developed caeca like these are important in the bacterial fermentation of cellulose and along with the rectum are involved in the reabsorption of ureteral urine. In the wall of each caecum close to the junction with the rectum is a large aggregated lymphoid nodule, the caecal tonsil, which is visible to the naked eye. The caecal contents are the source of the viscous semi-liquid droppings which are interposed with the well-formed cylindrical droppings of rectal origin. The caeca in the pigeon are vestigial and contain lymphoid tissue.

Between the various coils and loops of the intestine lie the paired abdominal air sacs which are recognized by their transparent and fragile walls.

Genital tract

Removal of the intestines exposes the genital tracts. The male reproductive system consists on each side of a testis, epididymis and ductus deferens. The right and left testes are situated on the roof of the thoracoabdominal cavity overlying the cranial ends of the kidneys. In the young bird they are small, bean-shaped and yellow in colour owing to fat in the interstitial cells but in mature, sexually active birds they are large and white. The surface of the sexually active testis is extremely vascular. In birds like the pigeon which are seasonal breeders the testes disintegrate during the non-breeding phase and are reconstructed for the next breeding season. The epididymis into which the seminiferous tubules open is not very obvious since it lies dorsal to the testis. Since the efferent ductules of the epididymis open into the whole length of the epididymal duct a head, body and tail cannot be recognized as in mammals. If the testes are reflected the small, yellow adrenal glands can be seen. They are attached to the cranial end of the epididymis. The ductus deferens is a zig-zag tube which extends caudally on the ventral surface of the kidney to end in the cloaca. The ductus deferens, epididymal duct and efferent ductules are the sites of sperm storage and maturation. There are no accessory genital glands.

In the female only the ovary and oviduct on the left side develop fully and become functional although they are present in the right side in the embryo and remnants persist in the adult. In the sexually active bird the left ovary (Figure 6.13) resembles a bunch of grapes, with four or five large mature follicles hanging down by stalks from the ventral surface. The follicles have a yellow colour due to yolk which is made in the liver. The pale band on the surface of the follicle is the stigma and is the site where the wall of the follicle ruptures at ovulation. Covered by the mature follicles are thousands of smaller immature follicles. Immediately after ovulation the follicle becomes a thin-walled sac which in the chicken regresses in about 10 days. There is no corpus luteum. In the chick the ovary is small and individual follicles can only be made out with difficulty. The ovary has a similar appearance in the adult domestic birds during the moult and in the non-breeding state.

In the in-lay chicken the left oviduct (Figure 6.13) may be about 65 cm in length. There are six parts including the infundibulum, magnum, isthmus, the tubular part of the uterus, the pouch of the uterus, and the vagina. The whole oviduct is suspended by a dorsal peritoneal ligament. The wall of the oviduct is packed with glands which secrete the egg white and the shell. The inner surface is greatly increased by mucosal folds which vary in appearance in the different regions. The tallest folds are in the magnum while in the uterus they are in the form of leaf-like lamellae. The muscle of the oviduct forms a sphincter in the cranial part of the vagina. In the chicken the egg stays in the infundibulum for 15 minutes, in the magnum for 3 hours, in the isthmus for 75 minutes, in the uterus for 20 hours and in the vagina for a few seconds. The glands of the infundibulum and magnum secrete the albumen of the egg, the glands of the isthmus secrete the shell membranes, and the glands of the uterus secrete the shell. The infundibulum is the site of fertilization. In the cranial vagina are a number of spaces, the spermatic

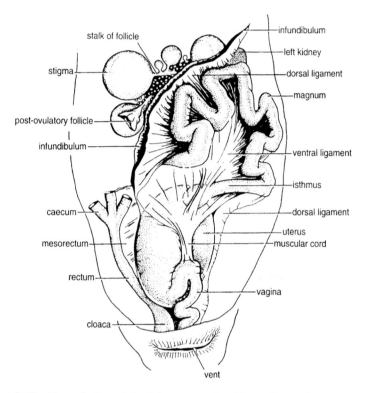

Figure 6.13 Ventral view of the left ovary and oviduct of an in-lay chicken. With permission from King and McLelland (1).

fossulae, which are the site of sperm storage. When the bird goes out of lay the length of the oviduct is drastically reduced to about 15 cm.

Remnants of the right female genital tract persist in the adult. The remnant of the right gonad is usually not obvious. However, if the left ovary is destroyed by disease the right gonad enlarges and in the chicken in 90% of cases is testis-like. Sperm production would only occur, however, if the left gonad was damaged during the first 3 weeks after hatching since then the primordial germ cells are still present. Remnants of the right oviduct are much more obvious and occur as a fluid-filled, bladder-like structure of variable size attached to the cloaca.

Cloaca

The cloaca is the common chamber into which the digestive and urogenital systems open (Figure 6.14). It is subdivided by folds into three compart-

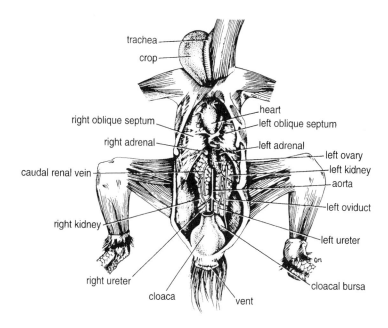

trachea
crop
heart
right oblique septum
left oblique septum
right adrenal
left adrenal
left ovary
caudal renal vein
left kidney
aorta
left oviduct
right kidney
left ureter
right ureter
cloacal bursa
cloaca
vent

Figure 6.14 The third stage in the dissection of the thoracoabdominal cavity of a 3-week-old female chicken. The liver, stomach and intestines have been removed. The lungs lie below the oblique septa. With permission from King and McLelland (1).

ments arranged one behind the other. From cranial to caudal are the coprodeum, urodeum and proctodeum. Into the urodeum open the urogenital ducts. In the male the ductus deferens opens laterally at the end of a small papilla. Above it is the opening of the ureter. On the left side in the female is the opening of the left oviduct, although in young chickens, ducks and geese the opening is closed by a membrane until sexual maturity. The opening of the proctodeum to the outside is bounded by the dorsal and ventral lips of the vent which are inverted into the cloaca. In the roof of the proctodeum is the cloacal bursa, a median diverticulum which contains much lymphoid tissue in its wall. The cloacal bursa is the site of differentiation of B lymphocytes. It begins to regress at about 8–12 weeks although a nodular remnant is still to be seen in the adult.

On the ventral lip of the vent is the phallus. The phallus in the chicken consists of a series of small interconnecting lymphatic bodies. Since the ventral lip of the vent is directed into the cloaca the phallus is pointing towards the interior of the bird. At tumescence enlargement of the phallus with lymph everts the lip of the vent so that the phallus is extruded. The phallus of the duck is very different from that of the chicken. It is a large, tubular structure which is invaginated into a sac in the ventrolateral wall of the proctodeum. On tumescence it is partly everted so that it protrudes cranially. Its spiral appearance is because the two lymphatic bodies are entwined around each other. Unlike in the chicken the duck phallus is inserted into the female's vagina.

Kidneys

Removing the reproductive organs exposes the kidneys. The kidneys (Figure 6.14) are brownish-red structures embedded in the concavity formed by the ventral surfaces on the synsacrum and the pelvis. They extend from the lungs cranially to the end of the synsacrum caudally. Passing through the cranial part of each kidney is the sacral nerve plexus, a branch of which is the ischiadic nerve. These nerves can easily be examined post-mortem. Because of the relationship of the kidney to the skeleton and the structures passing through it, it is difficult to remove the kidney intact. In the slaughterhouse the kidney may be taken out by suction. The avian kidney is supplied with blood from two sources, the aorta and the renal portal veins. The renal portal blood comes from the rectum, pelvis and hindlimbs and enters a venous ring on the ventral surface of the kidneys. Blood in the venous portal ring can either enter the kidney or be diverted away from the kidney into the caudal vena cava via the common iliac vein or into the hepatic portal circulation via the caudal mesenteric vein, a large vessel in the mesorectum. The flow in the common iliac vein is controlled by the renal portal valve. Note that blood in the caudal mesenteric vein usually flows towards the kidneys but the flow may be reversed towards the liver. The venous return from the hindlimb into the renal portal system means that substances injected into a hindlimb may enter the kidney before the systemic circulation. The kidneys are drained by the ureters directly into the cloaca. A bladder and urethra are absent. The kidney excretion consists of white semi-solid urates which combine with the faeces in the cloaca.

Heart and lungs

Removal of the liver exposes the heart and lungs in the cranial part of the thoracoabdominal cavity.

The avian heart (Figure 6.14) is relatively large compared with that of mammals because of the high energy requirements of flight. Structurally, however, it is similar. Differences include the presence of right and left cranial venae cavae entering the right atrium and a muscular flap between the right atrium and right ventricle instead of a cuspid valve. The coronary groove between the atria and ventricles contains much fat and can be examined for signs of inanition.

The quadrilateral or triangular lungs lie in the craniodorsal part of the thoracoabdominal cavity. Each lung lies tight up against the ribs, a number of which are embedded in grooves in the lung. To remove the lung in the slaughterhouse, therefore, a suction lung gun may be employed. Unlike mammalian lungs, the avian lungs are not divided into lobes. An important point functionally is that they are virtually immobile. Each primary bronchus (Figure 6.15) enters the lung on the medial surface and extends all the way through the lung to the caudal border. Arising from the primary bronchus are four groups of secondary bronchi which are named according to the part of the lung they supply. They include in the chicken four large medioventrals, eight large mediodorsals, eight large lateroventrals, and 25 very small laterodorsals. Arising from the secondary bronchi are hundreds of parabronchi which anastomose with each other joining together secondary bronchi within the same group and secondary bronchi of different groups. The walls of the parabronchi contain the gaseous exchange tissue consisting of air and blood capillaries. Unlike the mammalian alveoli the air capillaries are not blind-ending.

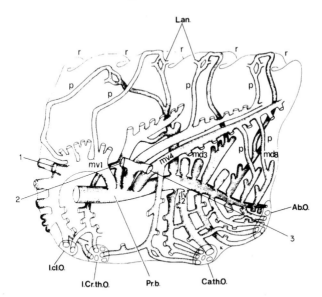

Figure 6.15 Medial view of the right lung of the chicken drawn as though transparent to show the bronchi. mv, md, lv, medioventral, mediodorsal and lateroventral secondary bronchi; p, parabronchi; L.an., anastomoses between parabronchi; Ab.O., Ca.th.O., l.cl. O., l.Cr.th.O., and 1, 2 and 3, sites of connections of air sacs to bronchi of lungs; Pr.b., primary bronchus; r, grooves of ribs. With permission from King (5) and Academic Press (New York).

Arising from the primary and secondary bronchi are the air sacs (Figure 6.16). The air sacs are delicate, thin-walled, transparent structures which when picked up post-mortem tend to disintegrate. Most of the sacs also connect to the lung by parabronchi. There are two unpaired air sacs and three paired sacs. The unpaired air sacs are common to both lungs and lie at the thoracic inlet. They include the cervical air sac above the trachea and oesophagus and the clavicular sac below the trachea and oesophagus. The cervical sac has tubular diverticula which extend up the bones and muscles of the neck. The clavicular sac also has large diverticula which extend between the bones and muscles of the thoracic girdles and shoulder joints. The paired air sacs include the cranial and caudal thoracic sacs below the lungs and the abdominal sacs between the viscera caudal to the lungs. The abdominal sac has a perirenal diverticulum which extends between the kidney and pelvis and a femoral diverticulum which surrounds the head of the femur and extends between the thigh muscles. Diverticula of the air sacs should be taken into account when trimming carcases in the condition of air sacculitis. In turkeys there is an unpaired cervicoclavicular sac and paired medial clavicular, cranial thoracic and abdominal sacs.

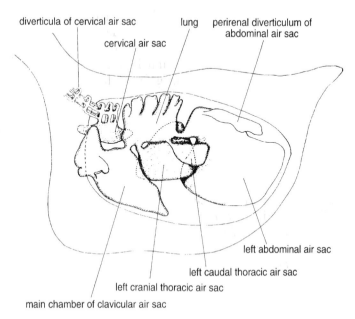

Figure 6.16 Diagrammatic view of the left lung and air sacs of an adult chicken. With permission from King (5) and Academic Press (New York).

Movement of air through the lungs is brought about by the air sacs following movements of the body wall. When air enters the lung in inspiration most of it goes immediately via the primary and secondary bronchi to the caudal thoracic and abdominal air sacs. At expiration this air re-enters the lung via the parabronchi and passes forwards in a caudal to cranial direction undergoing gaseous exchange. At the next inspiration this air comes under the influence of the cervical, clavicular and cranial thoracic air sacs which pull the air into them. At expiration the air is expelled from the cranial sacs into the primary bronchus and trachea. Because the air sacs have diverticula which extend into many of the bones, fracture of the bones could result in infection of the sacs.

Lymphoid system

The primary lymphoid tissue in birds is contained in the thymus and cloacal bursa. The majority of birds have no lymph nodes. Exceptions include ducks and geese which have one pair at the thoracic inlet and one pair close to the kidneys. These nodes, however, are not always easy to find. Other lymphoid tissue in birds occurs as nodules in the walls of lymph vessels, in the spleen, in the bone marrow, and as solitary and aggregated nodules in most tissues and organs. In the chicken the best developed of the aggregated nodules occur in the roof of the oropharynx and in the small intestine and caeca. In the duck, in addition to the annular bands of lymphoid tissue in the small intestine, there is a large aggregated nodule in the terminal part of the oesophagus.

Nervous system

Most of the nerves which can easily be examined post-mortem have already been described. They include the vagus and glossopharyngeal nerves close to the jugular vein, the cervical spinal nerves, the brachial nerve plexuses at the thoracic inlet, the intercostal nerves, the sacral nerve plexuses in the kidneys, the intestinal nerve running alongside the rectum, and the ischiadic nerves behind the femurs. As in mammals the spinal cord has cervical and lumbosacral enlargements associated with the innervation of the wing and hindlimb. However, the lumbosacral enlargement is unusual in that it has a dorsal fossa in which lies a large gelatinous body, the function of which is unknown.

References

1. King AS, McLelland J. *Birds, their structure and function*. London: Baillière Tindall, 1984.
2. Raikow RJ, Locomotor systems. In: King AS, McLelland J (eds) *Form and function in birds*. Vol. 3. London: Academic Press, 1984.
3. Nonidez JF and Goodale HD. Histological studies on the endocrines of chickens deprived of ultraviolet light. *Am J Anat* 1927 38: 319–41.
4. McLelland J. Aves digestive system. In: Getty R (ed.) *Sisson and Grossman's the anatomy of the domestic animals*. Vol 2. Philadelphia: Saunders.
5. King AS. Structural and functional aspect of the avian lung and air sacs. In: Felts WSL, Harrison RJ (eds) *International review of general and experimental zoology*. Vol. 2. New York: Academic Press, 1966.

CHAPTER 7

Control of Microbial Hazards in Poultry Processing

Introduction

Microbial contamination of poultry meat and its control are important for two reasons. Firstly, poultry is a significant reservoir of bacterial food-borne pathogens, such as *Salmonella* and *Campylobacter*, and is often implicated in incidents of human food poisoning. Secondly, the raw meat is highly susceptible to microbial spoilage when held in the unfrozen state, and shelf-life is related to initial levels of contamination with spoilage micro-organisms. Because of the nature of poultry meat and the means by which it is produced, some microbial contamination is inevitable, but needs to be minimized by effective hygiene control in the processing plant. The extent to which this objective is possible and the means of achieving it are considered in this chapter.

Part of the problem for the processor is that birds arriving for slaughter are heavily contaminated with a wide variety of micro-organisms, which are carried in the alimentary tract, among the feathers and on the skin. The different stages of processing result in many of these organisms being removed, although further contamination is likely as birds pass through the process. Sources of such contamination include contact surfaces, process water and aerosols, while any handling of carcases will also contribute to the spread of micro-organisms. The net effect of processing is to change the skin microflora from one in which Gram-positive rods and cocci are dominant to a flora comprising mainly Gram-negative genera, including Enterobacteriaceae and the main spoilage bacteria, *Pseudomonas* spp., which, however, are normally present in only low numbers.

Poultry processing is highly intensive in the larger slaughterhouses, with production rates of 6000 carcases per hour or more on a single line and birds virtually touching each other on the processing line. This situation is particularly conducive to microbial cross-contamination, allowing little opportunity to sanitize implements or equipment between carcases. Also, the skin is kept intact, thus retaining many of the organisms present on the birds. In addition, the process has become increasingly automated and involves some equipment for which the design is less than ideal for hygiene control. Since carcases remain whole throughout the process, there is a particular challenge in removing the viscera rapidly and without breakage through a relatively small opening in the abdomen.

Bacteria of public health concern

Food poisoning associated with poultry meat is common in many countries and the organisms of greatest concern are host non-specific salmonellae, especially invasive serotypes such as *Salmonella enteritidis*, *S. typhimurium* and *S. virchow*, and *Campylobacter jejuni* and *C. coli*. Both salmonellae and campylobacters are frequently found on poultry meat in much of the developed world.

Other common food-poisoning organisms are *Clostridium perfringens* and *Staphylococcus aureus*, although, in each case, many of the strains present do not produce detectable enterotoxin. Generally, the organisms occur in low numbers and the rare enterotoxigenic strains only become hazardous when the meat is held under conditions permitting rapid microbial growth. In recent years there has been considerable interest in food-borne pathogens that can multiply at low temperatures and are capable of growth on chilled poultry. These include *Aeromonas* spp., *Listeria monocytogenes* and *Yersinia enterocolitica*. The organisms are frequently found on raw poultry, but their public health significance in this context is still unclear; the strains of *Y. enterocolitica* normally belong to serotypes other than those associated with human yersiniosis.

Poultry products are rarely involved in incidents of human botulism, and *Clostridium botulinum* appears to be uncommon on raw poultry. Although outbreaks of type C botulism have occurred in commercial poultry flocks, and the organism may become a contaminant of processed carcases, there is no firm evidence that type C strains can cause human botulism. It is possible that some poultry products may be contaminated with other types of *C. botulinum* because of ingredients such as spices, which often contain a variety of spore-forming bacteria.

Salmonella

Young poultry are particularly susceptible to *Salmonella* infection and, under the usual conditions of intensive rearing, the organisms spread readily to other birds in the house. The salmonellae may be acquired:

- By transmission from parent to progeny via the hatchery.
- From contaminated feed.
- From environmental sources such as rodents and other wild mammals and birds.

The infection can persist for long periods and is usually asymptomatic. The organisms colonize the caeca, where populations in young chicks may reach 10^8–10^9/g of caecal content. Thus, heavy shedding of salmonella organisms can result in considerable contamination of the rearing environment and the outsides of the birds. The infection tends to decline with age, but contamination of the skin and feathers is likely to persist, as indicated in Table 7.1, which compares two different rearing systems in experimental trials.

At the processing plant, the incidence of *Salmonella*-infected flocks varies widely from day, to day, as does the proportion of contaminated carcases at the end of the process; however, the numbers of salmonellae on individual birds are usually low (< 2–1000 per 100 g of skin). This suggests that the organisms do not normally multiply in the processing plant and, with a lower growth limit of about 7 °C, are effectively prevented from doing so by the chilling process. Even at 10 °C, only slow growth can occur, and carcase temperatures are rapidly reduced to this point by cooling in either cold air or water.

Table 7.1 Persistence of *Salmonella typhimurium* in artificially infected broilers reared under different conditions.

Rearing system	In caecal content		On feathers	
	Week 2	Week 6	Week 2	Week 6
Floor pens	34	5	26	53
Cages	65	15	64	56

Numbers are percentages of positive birds; 200 birds per group, inoculated at 1 day old with 10^5 salmonellae per chick. Data from reference 2, with permission.

Campylobacter

Both *Campylobacter jejuni* and *C. coli* can be isolated from poultry, but *C. jejuni* is more common and is the species most often associated with human campylobacteriosis. The organisms are carried asymptomatically in the alimentary tracts of chickens, turkeys and ducks and are excreted in large numbers, even up to the point of slaughter. In general, poultry flocks are more often infected with *Campylobacter* than *Salmonella* and numbers on contaminated skin are usually higher – up to 10^5/g of neck skin in some cases. Campylobacters require a reduced-oxygen atmosphere for growth and usually are unable to multiply below 30 °C, so that growth in the processing plant seems unlikely. Since the infective dose for humans appears to be less than 500 cells, however, the mere presence of large numbers on the skin is potentially hazardous, and the organisms can be readily transmitted in the handling of raw poultry, either directly or via another item of food.

Although cross-contamination undoubtedly occurs during processing, levels of *Campylobacter* contamination on the skin may be reduced tenfold to a thousandfold by the end of the process. This reduction parallels that observed with total viable counts. Even greater reductions might be expected because campylobacters are more sensitive to adverse conditions than many other organisms, especially to drying, freezing and cold storage. In practice, none of these factors has sufficient effect to ensure the elimination of campylobacters. Air chilling, for example, reduces levels of *Campylobacter* contamination on pig carcases, owing to the drying effect, but is less effective with poultry, because the carcase remains whole and the inner parts retain moisture, even after prolonged chilling. Campylobacters are more sensitive to chlorine and monochloramine than *Escherichia coli*, but are not eliminated from poultry carcases by chilling in chlorinated water. Once in contact with the skin, the organisms may be protected from the chlorine, although, when used properly, chlorine greatly reduces the risk of cross-contamination via the chill water. There is evidence that water-chilled frozen carcases carry fewer campylobacters than those that are air-chilled and sold fresh.

Listeria monocytogenes

Contamination of poultry with *Listeria* spp. is well documented, and surveys have shown that 15–66% of fresh or frozen samples contain *L. monocytogenes*. However, the level of skin contamination is usually below 10 colony-forming units per cm^2. Among the strains isolated from poultry, serotype 4b, which is most often responsible for human listeriosis, is relatively uncommon.

Live poultry can become intestinal carriers of *L. monocytogenes* during rearing, e.g. from contaminated feed, and carcase contamination may occur in the processing plant. Carcases acquire listerias mainly through contact with contaminated surfaces and processing equipment, and there is a possibility that some items of equipment, such as the automatic carcase opener, may support growth of the organisms. Only rarely have listerias been isolated from the skin and intestines of birds arriving for slaughter.

Listeria monocytogenes grows better on poultry than on other kinds of meat and grows best in the presence of air. Although able to multiply at chill temperatures, the organism has a lag phase of many days at temperatures close to 0 °C and a correspondingly long generation time. Therefore, numbers can be kept at a low level on the product by adequate refrigeration.

Clostridium perfringens

Like *Listeria*, *Clostridium perfringens* is ubiquitous and is found in soil, dust and the intestinal tracts of most warm-blooded animals, including poultry. Levels of intestinal carriage in poultry may reach 10^5/g of gut content, but are highly variable.

Human food poisoning due to *C. perfringens* is usually associated with type A strains, which tend to be haemolytic on blood agar, with relatively heat-sensitive spores, or non-haemolytic, with spores that are highly heat-resistant. Only the former organisms are found in the live bird, but the latter may contaminate the meat subsequently and are capable of surviving prolonged cooking. When meat contaminated with *C. perfringens* is held under favourable conditions, the organism, which has an optimum generation time of about 10–12 minutes, rapidly reaches hazardous levels. In the processing plant, however, growth is unlikely because *C. perfringens* is an obligate anaerobe, with a minimum growth temperature in raw poultry of above 15 °C. The main problem is one of faecal contamination and dissemination during processing. Although carcases are often contaminated initially with *C. perfringens*, numbers of organisms decline as birds pass through the process and it finally occurs mainly as spores. Where present, counts from the finished product are usually about 10^2/g of neck skin.

Staphylococcus aureus

As in other food animals, coagulase-positive staphylococci are frequently present on the skin and in the nasopharynx of poultry, with a tendency for populations to increase during rearing. Only very low numbers are present in the alimentary tracts of normal, healthy birds.

The proportion of processed carcases carrying *Staphylococcus aureus* varies widely, as do the numbers of staphylococci on individual birds. In some studies, more than 80% of birds were positive. Levels of contamination may be higher on end-of-lay hens than on broilers, sometimes exceeding 10^3/cm² of skin. Among the relatively few strains that form food-poisoning enterotoxins, those producing types C and D toxins are the most common. These are rarely involved in food-poisoning incidents, however, and illness usually arises from the contamination of cooked food by an infected individual and subsequent temperature abuse of the food.

Apart from the staphylococci introduced by birds entering the processing plant, some items of processing machinery can become colonized with *S. aureus* and are thus a focus for carcase contamination, often leading to increases of a hundredfold or more in the numbers present on the skin. The main culprit in this respect is the defeathering machinery, where the atmosphere is warm and moist, and residual blood and faecal material are available as sources of nutrients for microbial growth. Also, the rubber 'fingers' or flails become worn and cracked during use and are penetrated by micro-organisms. Experience has shown that routine cleaning and disinfection of the equipment fails to remove or destroy organisms that have penetrated the rubber. Such organisms may thus become endemic to the processing plant and, in the case of certain strains of *S. aureus*, may persist for months or even years. Endemic strains of *S. aureus* are highly adherent and tend to be more resistant to chlorine than other strains, which may help their persistence in the plant. Some endemic strains are enterotoxin producers and these organisms can contaminate all carcases passing through the machines in which they have become established. Meat with unusually high numbers of *S. aureus* is not normally used in manufactured products.

Verocytotoxin-producing *Escherichia coli* (VTEC)

Various serotypes of *E. coli* are capable of producing verocytotoxin, but 0157:H7 is the one most often involved in human illness. Enteric disease caused by the organism may lead to the development of haemolytic uraemic syndrome, and death can result. The organism is rare or absent from poultry meat in the UK, but has been isolated from this source in the USA. Although mainly associated with cattle, it is capable of colonizing the alimentary tract of the young chick. Since this is a faecal organism, its control in the processing plant would depend upon the control of faecal contamination in general.

Spoilage micro-organisms

Under the usual aerobic storage conditions, spoilage of poultry meat is invariably due to the growth and metabolic activities of certain kinds of bacteria. These are termed 'cold tolerant' or 'psychrotrophic' by virtue of their ability to grow under chill conditions, although they grow faster as the temperature is raised towards their optimum of about 25 °C. The principal spoilage bacteria of aerobically stored poultry are pigmented and non-pigmented strains of *Pseudomonas* spp., which are accompanied on spoiled meat by populations of *Acinetobacter* and *Psychrobacter* spp. (the spoilage association). Spoilage is evident when the pseudomonads reach populations of about $10^8/cm^2$ and 'off' odours are detectable. The main species involved are *Pseud. fluorescens*, *Pseud. fragi* and *Pseud. putida*. If shelf-life is extended under chill conditions by the use of modified atmospheres enriched with carbon dioxide, the aerobic spoilage organisms are inhibited and a slower-growing, Gram-positive flora develops. This includes various lactic acid bacteria and *Brochothrix thermosphacta*.

The origin of the spoilage organisms is mainly the rearing environment of the birds. Being psychrotrophic, the organisms are unable to grow at body temperature and are not carried in the intestines. They are sometimes present in plant water supplies, but can be eliminated at the processing plant by superchlorination of the process water.

Pseudomonads are brought into the plant on the outsides of the birds. They are relatively heat-sensitive and are virtually eliminated during scalding. Recontamination of carcases occurs at subsequent stages of processing (Table 7.2); thus, pseudomonads may be useful as indicators of hygiene control in the processing plant.

Table 7.2 Effect of processing on contamination of chicken carcases with *Pseudomonas* spp.

| | Plant no. | | | |
Stage	1	2	3	4
After:				
bleeding	2.3	2.5	< 2.0	< 2.0
scalding	< 2.0	< 2.4	< 2.0	< 2.0
defeathering	2.5	3.2	2.3	< 2.1
evisceration	3.0	3.4	< 2.1	< 2.1
washing	2.7	2.7	< 2.1	< 2.2
chilling	3.3	3.9	2.6	3.2
packaging	3.9	4.0	2.9	3.5

Numbers shown are the geometric mean (log_{10}) c.f.u./g of neck skin: 15 samples examined in each case. Data from reference 8, with permission.

Microbiological hazards in processing

There are two kinds of microbiological hazard in processing:

- Those concerned with measurable increases in carcase contamination, which may result from mishandling or poor temperature control.
- Cross-contamination, in which minority organisms such as *Salmonella* may spread from one bird to another, usually in very small numbers, but

with the effect of increasing the incidence of contaminated carcases at the end of the process.

A different situation may be observed with *Campylobacter*, which is often present in a greater proportion of the birds in positive flocks and is carried in larger numbers in the intestines. With this organism, cross-contamination undoubtedly occurs during processing, but is less significant when most of the birds are already contaminated. Nevertheless, measures to avoid transmission from *Campylobacter*-positive to negative flocks are clearly important. Despite the above problems, processing reduces levels of carcase contamination when carried out in a hygienic manner.

A major reason for minimizing contamination in the processing plant is that, once in contact with the skin, micro-organisms may become irreversibly attached to the carcase surface. Not surprisingly, the washing of carcases during processing normally removes only a small proportion of the organisms present, and even the most effective spray-washer is unlikely to reduce microbial numbers on the skin by more than tenfold. The assumption is that attached organisms are resistant to the washing process. In addition, surface attachment appears to protect bacteria from the effects of scalding and contact with chlorinated water.

Studies on bacterial attachment to poultry skin have revealed a complex situation. Early work on *E. coli* showed that the flagella were implicated in the attachment process, since little or no attachment could be demonstrated with non-motile bacteria. Attachment increased with contact time and was directly related to the number of cells present. The rate of attachment was influenced by conditions of pH and temperature. Unattached cells in the film of moisture over the surface of the skin could be washed away by rinsing. However, the 'film flora' appears to be the source of those organisms that become attached to the skin.

Later work showed that flagellated and non-flagellated organisms attach to poultry skin with equal facility. Also, examination of the microtopography of chicken skin has shown a multiplicity of crevices and capillary-sized channels and a propensity for the skin to swell when wetted, thus trapping bacteria located in the crevices and channels. Therefore, many of the bacteria present on the skin may be either attached or entrapped, depending on their location.

In view of the difficulty in removing attached or entrapped bacteria, it is clear that the period of contact between bacteria and the carcase surface should be kept to a minimum. This has led to more frequent washing of carcases during the evisceration process and hence removal of a large proportion of the recently acquired contaminants. With regard to water immersion chilling, contamination and subsequent attachment can be reduced by limiting the build-up of micro-organisms in the chill water.

Effects of processing on carcase contamination

PRE-SLAUGHTER HANDLING AND TRANSPORTATION TO THE PROCESSING
PLANT

It is normal practice to withhold feed for several hours at least to reduce the
natural distension of the intestines and therefore minimize gut breakage
during processing. Despite this precaution, however, there is still a spread of
faecal material during the period of transfer from farm to processing plant,
and a parallel increase in microbial contamination of skin and feathers.
There is little evidence that the stress of transportation increases the number
of birds shedding salmonellae.

Transport crates and vehicles can be a potent source of flock-to-flock
transmission for enteric food-borne pathogens, and need to be properly
cleaned and disinfected after delivering birds to the processing plant.
Effective cleaning methods and equipment are now available, especially for
loose crate and modular transport systems, but lorries of the fixed crate type
are more difficult to deal with effectively. Measures taken on the farm to
reduce *Salmonella* infection will be largely nullified if the transporters are
inadequately cleaned and sanitized before re-use.

Hanging birds on the processing line causes them to flap their wings,
thereby scattering dust and micro-organisms. The hanging-on bay is, therefore, a highly contaminated area and must be physically separated from all
other parts of the processing plant.

STUNNING, EXSANGUINATION AND SCALDING

Stunning of birds in a water-bath stunner should occur without the heads
being totally immersed in the water. When immersion does occur, there is a
risk of the birds inhaling contaminated water, which may penetrate the
lungs and subsequently leak into edible parts of the carcase. The slaughter
knife may introduce contaminants into the blood stream before circulation
finally ceases; however, this has not been studied in poultry.

On entering the scalding tank, each bird introduces many millions of bacteria into the water. Thus, the water becomes heavily contaminated and any
inhalation of scald water leads to contamination of both the blood and respiratory system of the bird. By this means, it has been shown that
Clostridium perfringens, for example, can reach the heart and liver. It is
important, therefore, that birds are bled for an adequate period prior to
scalding. Severing the trachea, as in the kosher method of slaughter, is also
effective.

The net effect of passing birds through the scalding tank is to reduce external contamination, while any destruction of organisms in the water is a reflection of the temperature used. Although fresh water is added continuously to replace that removed by the birds as they leave the tank, the amount used is not sufficient to prevent a build-up of organisms in the scald water, even when an overflow is maintained.

The temperature varies between 50 °C and 63 °C, depending on the type of bird being processed (e.g. turkeys require a higher temperature than chickens to loosen all the feathers) and the nature of the final product (fresh or frozen). Birds intended for air chilling are usually scalded at 50–52 °C to ensure that the cuticle remains intact during defeathering, thus avoiding any subsequent surface discolouration. Spoilage bacteria are readily destroyed in the scald water, even at 50 °C, but at this temperature Enterobacteriaceae (including salmonellae) tend to survive and are only eliminated at about 60 °C (Table 7.3). Bacterial spores, on the other hand, are likely to survive at all normal scald temperatures.

When minority organisms, such as salmonellae, are introduced into the processing plant and scalding is carried out at 50–52 °C, cross-contamination in the scalding tank is unavoidable, although the problem also occurs at other stages of processing. Scalding has been improved in relation to hygiene control by the introduction of a multistage counterflow system, which allows the water in each tank to be changed, as required, during processing. With this equipment, carcase contamination is reduced by about 60%. There are also alternatives to the conventional immersion process, including spray or steam scalding, and combined scalding and plucking, in which water sprays are used. None of these methods has been widely adopted by industry and, in some cases, they are unsuitable for birds that will be sold as chilled products.

Avoiding the need to immerse the birds in heavily contaminated water clearly reduces levels of internal contamination, and counts from air sacs may be up to a thousandfold lower in consequence. Another approach for

Table 7.3 Control of Enterobacteriaceae in scald water by temperature.

Scald water temp. (°C)	No. of tests	Count	
		Range (log_{10} c.f.u./ml)	Mean (log_{10} c.f.u./ml)
50	15	2.7–4.0	3.9
52	10	2.6–3.0	2.8
53	10	1.7–2.7	2.4
59	10	0–1.3	0.8
62	15	0–2.2	1.5
62.5	5	0	0

Data from reference 3, with permission.

conventional scalding tanks is to add an organic acid, e.g. acetic or propionic acid, or adjust the water pH to 9.0 by addition of sodium hydroxide or sodium carbonate. At pH 9.0, the heat resistance of salmonellae is significantly reduced. All these additives can reduce microbial levels in the scald water, but have less effect on carcase contamination. However, their use is not encouraged by current legislation within the European Union.

MECHANICAL DEFEATHERING

The plucking process has important microbiological implications. The scouring or flailing of carcases with a large number of flexible rubber 'fingers' causes widespread dissemination of micro-organisms. Experiments with a readily identifiable 'marker' organism have shown that at least 200 carcases can be cross-contaminated during the defeathering process from a single inoculated bird. The organisms are spread mainly from the surfaces of the birds rather than extruded faeces. The extensive aerial dispersion can only be contained at present by ensuring complete separation of the scalding and defeathering area from the remainder of the process.

Being warm and moist, conditions inside the machinery favour the growth of micro-organisms, especially staphylococci, as discussed previously. Defeathering increases levels of skin contamination with these organisms and spreads any salmonellae present.

The processing of ducks involves scalding at 60 °C, followed by immersion of carcases in hot, molten wax. When set, the wax is removed by hand, along with the feathers. The higher processing temperatures involved appear to have a beneficial effect in reducing carcase contamination and can lead to total viable counts from skin of 10^3 c.f.u./cm^2 or less and counts of coliform bacteria below 10^2/c.f.u./cm^2.

REMOVAL OF EDIBLE AND INEDIBLE VISCERA

Evisceration is carried out manually in the smaller processing plants, while larger ones use automatic equipment involving several different machines, each concerned with a specific operation. Either approach can result in clean removal of parts, or may lead to extensive gut breakage and the spread of faecal material. Some of the machinery in current use causes a significant degree of damage to the intestines, because the carcases vary in size and the equipment is not automatically adjustable. However, the newer machines operate according to a different principle. After carefully controlled opening of the abdomen, the viscera are removed and transferred to a separate processing line, which runs parallel to that carrying the carcases and at the same speed, so that carcases and organs can be correlated for inspection purposes. In this system, contact between carcases and exposed viscera is eliminated, while hearts, lungs and livers are removed automatically, without the need for manual handling. The newer equipment reduces faecal contamination of both carcases and organs and hence the spread of food-borne enteric pathogens at the evisceration stage.

Once removed from the carcase, the giblets should be washed and cooled promptly to prevent microbial growth.

Studies involving 'marker' organisms have shown that cross-contamination of carcases occurs widely during evisceration and certain items of equipment (such as the older type of head-puller) may become a source of *Salmonella*. This problem can be minimized by strategically placed spray jets, which are directed at the points of carcase contact and use water containing at least 40 mg/l of free available chlorine.

The use of carcase injection procedures for introducing salt or polyphosphate solution into freshly eviscerated birds is now relatively uncommon. When carcases are injected, there is a risk of transferring skin organisms to the deep muscle tissue. Care in preparing and handling the injection solution is essential, as is the spray-washing of carcases prior to injection.

CLEANING OF CARCASES

Carcases are spray-washed after evisceration to remove blood spots and other minor organic soiling. With a well-designed spray-washer, significant numbers of micro-organisms are also removed from both the inner and outer surfaces of the carcase. Where water immersion chilling is used, the cleaning process ensures that large numbers of organisms are not introduced into the chill water. In automated chicken processing plants, an inside-outside washer of the carousel type is normally used for the final wash, but carcases may also be washed at intermediate stages of evisceration to remove as many faecal organisms as possible before attachment or entrapment can occur, as discussed earlier (Figure 7.1). Water used in spray-washing may be superchlorinated at 50 mg/l or more of free available chlorine. The chlorine has little direct effect in reducing carcase contamination, but does help to reduce the build-up of micro-organisms on equipment and working surfaces and eliminates any spoilage bacteria in the water supply.

CARCASE CHILLING

In high-throughput processing plants, carcases reach the chilling stage with a body temperature of at least 30 °C and need to be chilled promptly and

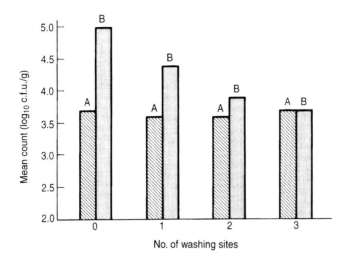

Figure 7.1 Removal of Enterobacteriaceae from carcases by spray-washing at up to three different stages of evisceration prior to chilling: A, counts after defeathering; B, counts after evisceration. Data from reference 10, with permission.

efficiently to prevent the growth of any food-borne pathogens present, while delaying that of psychrotrophic spoilage bacteria.

There are two main methods of chilling: one involves a continuous, in-line, water immersion system; the other is air chilling, which is either a continuous process or one that involves batch chilling. With water chillers, the birds are subjected to agitation during immersion and this removes many of the organisms contaminating the inner and outer surfaces of each carcase. Since large numbers of birds are present in the chilling system at any one time, opportunities exist for cross-contamination, and control measures are necessary to prevent any excessive accumulation of organisms in the chill water.

The key factors in controlling conditions in water chillers are temperature and the amount of water used. An adequate flow of fresh water not only aids the cooling of carcases, but prevents the chiller temperature from reaching a point at which microbial growth in the water would become a problem. In a well-controlled system, microbial levels in the water usually do not exceed 10^5/ml and may be lower. European Union regulations (Table 7.4) specify a number of controls, including the need for counterflow chilling, in which carcases move against the flow of water and therefore leave the chilling system in the cleanest water. Other requirements include temperature limits for water in different parts of the system, a maximum residence time for carcases in the first section, and specified levels of water usage that vary

Table 7.4　European Union requirements for water immersion chilling.

1. Water usage in pre-chill spray-washing (1.5 litres per carcase for the average size of chicken
2. Only counterflow water chilling
3. Limits for water temperature (16 °C at carcase entry point, 4 °C at exit)
4. Water usage in chilling system (2.5 litres per carcase for the average size of chicken)
5. Time limit for retention of carcases in first part of the system (30 min)

with carcase size. These are coupled with water usage requirements for spray-washing at the end of the evisceration line to ensure that carcases are as clean as possible before being chilled.

Under controlled conditions, water immersion chilling has a washing effect on the carcases and there is a net removal of residual contaminants. Total viable counts and counts of coliform bacteria may be reduced by 50–90%, with little change in the incidence of carcases contaminated with *Salmonella*. In some countries, further control is achieved by superchlorination of the chill water or the use of chlorine dioxide. By maintaining a total chlorine residual of 45–50 mg/l and a water usage of 2.5 litres per carcase, it is possible to keep the water used in chilling broilers virtually free from viable organisms, including clostridial spores. As with spray-washing, the chlorine has little direct effect on carcase contamination because of the rapid rate of inactivation, but it does help to limit cross-contamination by destroying organisms in the water.

When turkeys are processed, longer periods of chilling are needed because the carcases are larger, and static slush ice tanks may be used as a secondary process. This strategy also ensures that the product is suitably 'aged' before being frozen. Unless the water is chlorinated, psychrotrophic spoilage bacteria will multiply slowly in the tanks, increasing fivefold at 0 °C within 24 hours.

A possible alternative to immersion chilling is spray chilling, which utilizes chilled water and has a very high water requirement. The spraying process may reduce opportunities for cross-contamination of carcases, but is only suitable for the smaller kind of chicken.

Air-chilling requires the use of low scald temperatures to safeguard product appearance and keeping quality, and is essentially a dry process, so that there is no washing effect to remove micro-organisms. Although the outer surfaces of air-chilled birds are relatively dry, there is no advantage of extending shelf-life, if the product is packaged prior to storage. Under these conditions, the skin surface rapidly rehydrates inside the pack.

Air chilling is less likely than water immersion chilling to cause cross-contamination, but micro-organisms may still circulate in the currents of cold air and the carcases are often packed closely together in the chiller.

Other methods of 'dry' chilling include the use of liquid nitrogen or carbon dioxide. From the microbiological viewpoint, the effects of cryogenic chilling are similar to those of air chilling. The use of carbon dioxide snow for secondary chilling causes crust-freezing of the product and subsequent equilibration of the surface temperature to about minus 2 °C, thus extending shelf-life. This method is now used more rarely and appears to be unacceptable within the EU, because the product is temporarily frozen at the surface.

HANDLING OF CARCASES AFTER CHILLING

While chilled carcases would not support the growth of mesophilic bacteria such as *Salmonella*, any exceptional delays in freezing the product or transferring it to the second stage of chilling, before distribution, may lead to multiplication of spoilage organisms. There is also the possibility of contaminating the product during grading, trussing and packaging. Table 7.2 shows increases in product contamination with *Pseudomonas* spp. at the packaging stage.

Where the carcases are frozen, reductions in counts of vegetative bacteria up to tenfold may be expected, but Gram-positive organisms such as staphylococci and bacterial spores are generally more resistant to the freezing process. During frozen storage there is likely to be a decline in numbers of *Campylobacter* and *Salmonella*, although the organisms are not usually eliminated by this means.

STAFF HYGIENE

The level of contamination increases with handling during the packaging stage (as shown in Table 7.2) but also it occurs at other handling stages of the process. Therefore the staff should keep as clean as possible. They should wash their hands at regular intervals or when they become contaminated, using the sinks provided, and dry their hands on disposable towels. Clean protective clothing, covering their normal clothing and hair, and waterproof footwear should be worn to enter any workroom. Jewellery, except perhaps for wedding rings and ear sleepers, should not be worn in workrooms. Those employed in the workrooms should keep their nails short and clean and not wear nail varnish. In some premises staff wear colour-coded overalls with a different colour for those working in the cleaner parts, so that management can detect staff who are in the wrong area.

Training programmes should be arranged for the staff working in the premises. These should include every member of staff, whether they are working on the processing line, on storage of dry goods or on the final product, and should also include the management, the quality assurance staff, the cleaners and the cooks in the canteen. The training will vary, depending on the responsibility of the person being trained, but all should be given some training in basic microbiology and how food-poisoning organisms can be spread in a food factory. Staff working on particular tasks should be taught more details about that particular process, but they should also understand how their task fits into the whole. Sometimes staff want to wear gloves; if this is permitted, the gloves must be kept clean and replaced when they have any holes in them. Some people consider wearing gloves is more of a risk than keeping hands clean by frequent washing.

Few hand-held implements are now used in slaughtering premises, although knives are frequently used in cutting rooms. Where implements are used, sterilizers, operating by water at 82 °C, should be provided near to the work stations. Batch sterilization can also be used, where the knives are collected at regular intervals and replaced by ones that have been sterilized. The operators may find it easier to have two sterilized implements because they can continue to work even if they contaminate one implement. Facilities for holding implements so that they do not become contaminated will be required if more than one implement is provided. Some staff in cutting rooms wear chain-mail gloves to protect their hands. These should also be immersed in hot water at break times.

WATER

Water is used extensively in slaughterhouses and comes into contact with people, equipment, carcases and poultry meat. It is necessary to ensure that the water does not contaminate meat with bacteria which could cause food poisoning in humans. Water also contains spoilage bacteria which contaminate the premises and the meat. Most premises receive water from an official supply which normally complies with the bacteriological, physical and chemical standards laid down in legislation by the country concerned. The requirements for potable water within the EU are contained in Directive 80/778/EEC (see Chapter 12).

VERMIN AND FLIES

Vermin can spread bacteria within a premises, and these may cause disease in consumers of the meat. The design of the premises should ensure that the possibility of vermin entering is kept to a minimum, but poisoned bait or traps can be used to deal with any rats and mice that do enter the premises. Flies should be excluded from the workrooms, and this must be taken into account during the construction of the building. Doors should be self-closing and kept closed when not in use. Fly traps which attract flies with light and then electrocute them may be used, but they must not be placed over areas where meat is present.

CLEANING AND DISINFECTION

Waste products from processing should be removed on a continuous basis. Feathers are removed in a floor channel using recirculated water, or by a transfer belt. The waste products from evisceration are discarded, either onto a moving belt or into a water trough placed under the suspended carcases, and are removed from the room, either in a drainage channel in the floor or in pipes by suction or air pressure. Unfit carcases or meat should be held in lockable, waterproof containers and removed on a regular basis to the room for holding unfit meat to await collection.

There should be a cleaning programme which is known to all cleaning staff. It is normal to clean workrooms during the breaks in production when there is no product left in the room, to be followed at the end of the day's work by cleaning and disinfection of the changing rooms, empty storage rooms and workrooms. The programme should describe how the cleaning and disinfection is to be done and the frequency with which it is to be carried out. The ceiling, for instance, may not require cleaning daily but must be included on a regular basis. Storage rooms have to be cleaned and disinfected when they are empty and so drainage from these areas should either be in the rooms themselves or just outside so that wash water does not contaminate other areas.

There are five basic stages in a cleaning and disinfection programme although some of these stages may be combined. The first is the removal of the gross dirt using a squeegee or brush. This is followed by a wash-down with water using a hose pipe with a low pressure so that dirt is not splashed around the premises. Washing with warm water helps to remove some of the fat, but steam hides the work area and is not easy to work with. This stage is followed by washing the surfaces and equipment with a detergent solution to ensure that all the dirt and fat are removed. A solution of a sanitizer or disinfectant is then applied and finally is washed off with clean water. It is preferable for the room to be left to dry before it is used again.

Detergents and sanitizers have different components depending on the task for which they are designed. The pH of the detergent is one aspect. Acid detergents are used principally to dissolve rust and scale from hard water.

Alkalis are used to remove protein and grease, converting fats to soaps and splitting long protein molecules. Strong acids and alkalis are both likely to cause corrosion if used frequently, so the milder compounds are normally used.

Detergents hold the dirt in suspension, provided it is broken up by spraying with the detergent solution using hoses or (in small premises) scrubbing brushes. Detergents may contain substances known as emulsifiers or surfactants which coat small deposits of grease with a water-soluble skin, enabling them to be washed away. Dispersants may also be used in the formula; these give the particles an electric charge which repels other particles, so keeping them in solution. Foaming agents can be used to cover the surface in a foam which has the advantage of penetrating into crevices. The detergent should also be biodegradable.

Disinfectants and sanitizers usually contain quaternary ammonium compounds, amphoteric compounds or halogens, e.g. chlorine. Chlorine solution is not stable in hot water and is ineffective on a dirty surface; all disinfectants need clean surfaces on which to act.

It is important that the manufacturer's instructions are followed. Just by looking at or smelling a detergent it is not possible to tell how to use it, and certainly mixing two detergents may prove to be ineffective – particularly if one is acid and the other alkali.

WASTE DISPOSAL

Waste must not be allowed to accumulate within the premises, but must constantly be moved to the areas designated for waste storage. The waste is then normally removed by skip or other waterproof container to a waste processing premises which will sterilize the material by heat, producing a meat, bone and feather meal or meals. These are sometimes included in animal feed, although the public tends to disapprove of this, claiming it is a form of cannibalism. Alternatively the meal is used in fertilizers or disposed of at designated sites.

Systems of dealing with the organic matter which also provide gases which can be used to generate heat have been constructed. Anaerobic digestion can be used to produce a mixture of carbon dioxide and methane gas. The gas can be collected and used commercially to heat water or drive a generator. Aerobic digestion or incineration after the removal of water has also been used.

The waste should be removed from the poultry slaughterhouse in such a way that contamination is not spread around the yard or premises. The bay should be cleaned out when it is emptied, but again not in a way that contaminates the yard.

The waste water is frequently screened as it leaves the premises to remove pieces of meat, feathers or offal which have been washed into the drainage system. Fat traps can also be fitted, consisting of tanks where the fat rises to the surface and is then scraped off into a container. These two water treatment areas must be kept clean and the solids removed as frequently as possible, without contaminating the surroundings of the premises. As legislation reduces the permitted pollution of rivers, further treatment of water may be necessary, although if it can be treated at the local sewerage plant this is preferable. However, preliminary treatment to reduce the solids in the water is becoming more necessary. Sedimentation in tanks or pumping the water through a series of tanks helps to remove the solids, which settle to the bottom and must be removed at intervals.

Decontamination of the end-product

Over the years, processing plants have been improved structurally, and also operationally, by the introduction of hygiene control measures based on the Hazard Analysis Critical Control Point (HACCP) system, as discussed below. However, these steps are unlikely to eliminate all food-borne pathogens from carcases, and therefore an end-of-line decontamination process would be an attractive proposition. Such an approach should not be introduced to replace good hygiene practices, but rather to augment them.

Many different substances have been considered as potential decontaminants, but in most cases these have been ineffective or have led to tainting or unacceptable discolouration of the product. The more feasible options are considered below.

CHLORINE

Chlorine is normally used throughout the process, but could be considered as a decontamination treatment. However, its use is not permitted in all countries and in some there are restrictions on the chlorine concentrations that can be used. Although chlorine appears to have little direct effect on carcase contamination and is readily inactivated by organic material, it helps to control the build-up of micro-organisms on equipment. Addition of chlorine to chill water prevents carcases from being seeded with spoilage bacteria that would otherwise accumulate in the chilling system, and usefully extends the shelf-life of fresh poultry. Chlorine is most active against micro-organisms in the form of undissociated hypochlorous acid, which requires acid conditions. Other factors include the concentration of chlorine used, contact time and temperature. In chilling systems, much of the added chlorine will have combined with amino nitrogen to form chloramines. These are less active against micro-organisms than free chlorine, but are still effective at appropriate concentrations. Concentrations of free chlorine below 500 mg/l do not appear to taint poultry meat; however, there has been some concern about the possible formation of carcinogens, such as chloroform and chloramines, in the meat.

ORGANIC ACIDS

The substances of particular interest in this context are acetic and lactic acids, which are widely accepted for food use. In parts of Europe, lactic acid is favoured because it is a naturally occurring, non-toxic compound, used for various purposes in the meat industry. The antimicrobial activity of organic acids depends upon:

- The pH.
- The degree of dissociation of the acid.
- The acid molecule itself.

In practice, the efficacy of an acid in reducing microbial counts from meat will depend upon the concentration used, the method of application, time and temperature of treatment and the extent of microbial entrapment or attachment to the product surface. Treatment involves either dipping the carcase in a solution of appropriate strength, or the use of a spray system. Hot treatment (about 55 °C) may be more effective than the use of cold solutions, especially with acetic acid. The bacteriostatic effect of acid treatment may be prolonged on storage of the meat, thus extending shelf-life.

TRISODIUM PHOSPHATE

There is interest in using trisodium phosphate (TSP) to reduce *Salmonella* contamination of carcases. This substance is already an ingredient of certain food products. The carcases may be treated after chilling by immersion in 9.5% w/w TSP for 15 seconds. Treatment has been shown to reduce total viable counts by about 50% and the incidence of *Salmonella*-contaminated carcases from 9.5% to 0%. It is less effective against *Campylobacter*.

IONIZING RADIATION

Food irradiation in general is a contentious issue with consumers, in spite of widespread recognition among scientists that it is a safe and effective means of destroying micro-organisms in foods, with minimal effects on product quality. Irradiation kills bacteria by virtue of its effect on cellular DNA and other macromolecules, on which viability depends. Gamma-irradiation from a source such as cobalt-60 has high penetrative capability and will destroy organisms at the surface and in the depths of meat.

Both vegetative pathogens and spoilage bacteria are relatively sensitive to irradiation and low-dose treatment would be sufficient to reduce microbial hazards and extend shelf-life. Use of a low treatment dose is important to avoid significant organoleptic changes in the meat. In this context, the maximum dose for chilled poultry is 2.5–3.0 kGy, with higher doses being possible for frozen products. Although acceptable on scientific grounds, the intention to use irradiation would raise logistical questions. Would treatment be carried out by poultry processors or at regional centres? Is sufficient cobalt-60 available to meet the demand? Would the capital costs be prohibitive?

Application of the HACCP system

The HACCP system is a structured approach to the identification, assessment and control of microbial hazards associated with food production and handling. Application of the system involves seven basic steps or components:

1. Identification of hazards and assessment of their severity and risk of occurrence in any specific situation.
2. Determination of critical control points (CCPs) at which hazards can be controlled. A CCP may be a raw material, or a location, practice, procedure or stage in a production process.
3. Establishment of limits and tolerances that indicate when an operation is being controlled at a CCP.
4. Development and use of monitoring procedures to ensure that each CCP is being controlled.
5. Identification of any corrective action needed when a CCP is not under control.
6. Verification of controls to ensure that the HACCP system is working.
7. Keeping of records, including those of any corrective action.

In the context of the HACCP concept, a hazard is defined as the unacceptable contamination, growth and/or survival by micro-organisms of concern to safety or spoilage and/or the unacceptable production or persistence in foods of products of microbial metabolism such as toxins. In some cases, a hazard can be eliminated (CCP1), while in others the hazard can be minimized, but not eliminated (CCP2).

The HACCP approach to controlling food safety is fully endorsed in many countries, as well as by international organizations such as the International Commission on Microbiological Specifications for Foods, the *Codex Alimentarius* Commission and the European Community.

The HACCP principles are applicable to all sectors of the poultry meat industry – breeding, hatching, rearing, feed production and processing.

During operations at the processing plant, the birds pass through a number of different stages at which microbiological hazards can occur, as described above. In practice, control of hygiene is made difficult by the rapid rate of production at the larger slaughterhouses and the close proximity of the birds, which favours microbial transmission.

In controlling any gross increase in carcase contamination, chilling is the only CCP1, and, in this process, growth of most food-borne pathogens is prevented. Even *Listeria monocytogenes*, which can grow slowly under chill conditions and is a common contaminant of poultry meat, does not appear to multiply significantly in chillers during the working day. Water immersion chilling, which is now largely restricted in Europe to carcases intended for freezing, is a good example of a CCP1 because the requirements for hygienic chiller operation (see Table 7.4) are soundly based on scientific evidence. In contrast, the establishment of a CCP2 tends to be more a matter of personal judgement and experience. Washing of carcases, however, is clearly a CCP2 because carcase contamination is reduced by this means, especially when the birds are washed at different stages of the evisceration process and prior to chilling.

Reducing the incidence of cross-contamination is more difficult to achieve and quantify, and there are no *critical* control points in this respect. The problem of cross-contamination is largely due to the nature of the process and the high rate of processing, which allows little opportunity for intervention measures between individual birds. Only recently has equipment aimed at improving hygiene become available.

Extensive automation in modern processing includes the stages at which viscera are removed. Breakage of the viscera and contamination of carcases with intestinal organisms tend to occur because of natural variations in bird size and the inability of the machines to adjust to differences between individual birds. At present, only careful adjustment of the machines between flocks will reduce gut breakage to any degree (a possible CCP2 for gross contamination), but this type of equipment is not amenable to complete control. However, the recent developments in automatic evisceration machinery appear to improve the hygiene situation and will gradually be adopted by the industry.

Tests for monitoring CCPs need to be simple and provide a rapid response, so that any corrective action can be taken promptly. Examples are measurements of temperature (especially in scalding and chilling), water flow rate, chlorine concentrations in process water and visual checks on the standard of evisceration. It is important that checks are carried out periodically, with sufficient frequency, and that the results are properly recorded. The checks will aim to ensure that critical values are being met and control is maintained. Monitoring should always be carried out at the points most relevant to the control objectives.

The EU Directive on Health Problems Affecting Trade in Fresh Poultry Meat (92/116) makes no specific provision for the HACCP system, although the Food Hygiene Directive (93/43) does place such a requirement on operators, independently of enforcement authorities. Implementation of the HACCP approach is essentially a company responsibility as part of the normal quality assurance system, but in future it is likely that processing plant operators will apply HACCP principles in conjunction with the enforcement authority. Thus, a new role for the inspectorate could encompass the supervision and verification of a critical control point approach to product safety.

References

1. Bailey JS, Thomson JE, Cox NA, Shackelford AD. Chlorine spray-washing to reduce bacterial contamination of poultry processing equipment. *Poult Sci* 1986; **65**: 1120–3.
2. Bailey JS, Cox NA. Internal colonisation and external carriage of artifically inoculated *Salmonella typhimurium* from floor pen and cage reared chickens. *Poult Sci* 1999; **70** (supplement 1): 142.
3. Büchli K, van Schothorst M, Kampelmacher EM. Untersuchungen über die hygienische Beschaffenheit von mit Wasser resp. Luft gekühlten Schlachtgeflügel. *Archiv für Lebensmittelhygiene* 1966; **17**: 97–9.
4. James WO, Brewer RL, Prucha JC, Williams WO, Parham DR. Effects of chlorination of chill water on the bacteriologic profile of raw chicken carcasses and giblets. *J Am Vet Med Assoc* 1992; **200**: 60–3.
5. James WO, Prucha JC, Brewer RL *et al*. Effects of countercurrent scalding and postscald spray on the bacteriologic profile of raw chicken carcasses. *J Am Vet Med Assoc* 1992; **201**: 705–8.
6. James WO, Williams WO, Prucha JC, Johnston R, Christensen W. Profile of selected bacterial counts and *Salmonella* prevalence on raw poultry in a poultry slaughter establishment. *J Am Vet Med Assoc* 1992; **200**: 57–9.
7. Mead GC, Dodd CER. Incidence, origin and significance of staphylococci on processed poultry. *J Appl Bact Symp Supp* 1990; 81S–91S.
8. Mead GC, Hudson WR, Hinton MH. Microbiological survey of five poultry processing plants in the UK. *Br Poult Sci* 1993; **34**: 497–503.
9. Mulder RWAW, Dorresteijn LWJ, van der Broek J. Cross contamination during the scalding and plucking of broilers. *Br Poult Sci* 1978; **19**: 61–70.
10. Notermans S, Terbijhe RJ, van Schothorst M. Removing faecal contamination

of broilers by spray-cleaning during evisceration. *Br Poult Sci* 1980; **21:** 115–21.

11. Oosterom J, Notermans S, Karman H, Engels GB. Origin and prevalence of *Campylobacter jejuni* in poultry processing. *J Food Prot* 1983; **46:** 339–44.

12. Tompkin RB. The use of HACCP in the production of meat and poultry products. *J Food Prot* 1990; **53:** 795–803.

CHAPTER 8

Food Poisoning Associated with Poultry Meat

Introduction

Food poisoning is not defined in the legislation which makes it a notifiable disease in the UK, and it is more accurate to use the term 'food-borne disease'. This has been defined by the World Health Organization (WHO) as 'any disease of an infectious or toxic nature caused by or thought to be caused by the consumption of food or water'. This chapter deals with food-borne disease caused by the consumption of micro-organisms or their toxins associated with poultry meat, the source of which may be from poultry, humans or the environment.

Food-borne infections are a major public health problem in all parts of the developed world. In many countries there has been a significant increase in reports of food-borne infections in recent years. In England and Wales the Public Health (Control of Diseases) Act 1984 makes food poisoning a notifiable disease and in Scotland the Public Health (Notification of Infectious Diseases) (Scotland) Regulation 1988 carries out the same function. Notifications of food poisoning collected under this legislation more than quadrupled between 1980 and 1993, rising from 17 300 to over 74 000. Similarly, reports of laboratory isolates of gastrointestinal pathogens have shown dramatic increases both in the UK and elsewhere.

Poultry (both meat and products) have been identified as a major source of food-borne infection. In 1992 the Committee on the Microbiological Safety of Food stated, 'we see poultry and their products as the most important source of human gastrointestinal infections arising from food'. The Committee also went on to attribute the size of the problem to the transformation of the poultry industry by 'greatly increasing the size of production units and throughputs of slaughterhouses and of processing plants', which permitted cross-infection and cross-contamination to occur. As a result the Committee noted 'the high proportion of carcases contaminated with salmonella and campylobacter'.

Poultry meat is rightly regarded as a major vehicle in the epidemiology of food-borne infections and it is therefore appropriate to consider in detail the organisms involved and the clinical disease produced in those affected. It is equally relevant to attempt to quantify the size of the problem of food-borne disease and to understand the limitations of all the methods used to calculate the numbers of people involved.

Surveillance of food-borne infections

It is important to realize that during surveillance of any disease process many cases are lost to the reporting system. No one surveillance method is capable of providing an accurate estimate of the numbers involved, and a combination of methods such as statutory notifications, laboratory reporting and outbreak investigations is necessary to give the best information. The data collected are most useful in terms of identifying trends rather than giving accurate counts of the numbers involved.

In any population only a proportion of those infected will become clinically unwell (Figure 8.1). Not all of those who are ill will seek medical attention, and those who do are usually the most severely affected or the most vulnerable, such as the very young or very old. A variable proportion of those seen by a doctor will be tested for the presence of enteropathogens, and again this will often depend on the severity of the symptoms or the age of the patient. Microbiological laboratories will not always successfully isolate and identify the presence of a pathogen even if it is present. This is a

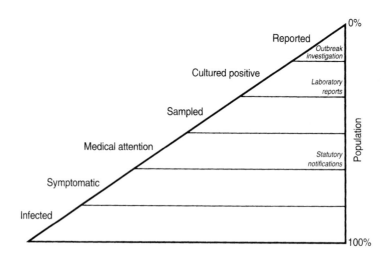

Figure 8.1 Disease surveillance.

particular problem with viral infections, and unless a virological cause is suspected and appropriate tests such as electron microscopy requested, these may not be carried out. Even when the laboratory isolates a pathogen it may not be reported under a recognized surveillance system. Not all confirmed cases, which are linked to a common source and part of an outbreak, will be identified as such by the investigating authorities, and the source of the outbreak may not be investigated or confirmed.

Unfortunately the proportion of under-reporting varies considerably, with different organisms and in different patient age groups. It is likely that children will receive more medical attention and therefore be represented in greater numbers in those patients seen by doctors. More laboratory samples are likely to be taken from the young. The severity of the disease can also affect the proportion detected, e.g. botulism is very rare but is so clinically severe that few cases will go undetected and unreported. On the other hand, *Salmonella* infections may be mild and no treatment sought or laboratory confirmation requested. The extent of investigation carried out may depend on the apparent number of persons affected, e.g. the source of *Campylobacter* infections, which commonly occur as single sporadic cases, is less likely to be investigated than are outbreaks of salmonellosis. The apparent rise in food-borne disease itself may be self-fuelling – media reports and scares may influence the number of people seeking medical attention, notifications made and samples submitted, so perpetuating the reported increase.

Each of the methods of data collection therefore has its limitations and these should be recognized.

Statutory notifications of food poisoning

In England and Wales notifications of food poisoning have dramatically increased since 1980 (Figure 8.2). This large increase was also recorded in Northern Ireland but was less evident in Scotland. It is difficult to believe that there were sufficient differences in food sources and eating practices between Scotland and other parts of the UK in the early 1980s, to explain the fact that the reported rate of food poisoning in Scotland was almost three times that in England and Wales. Nor is it easy to explain why the rate in England and Wales rose from 20 per 100 000 population to more than 80 per 100 000 between 1982 and 1993. It is likely that at least part of the reported increase was due to improvements in the methods of recording notifications in England and Wales and in Northern Ireland, together with the unquantifiable effects on notifications, as a consequence of media controversy.

Although food poisoning is still a major and increasing concern, it is

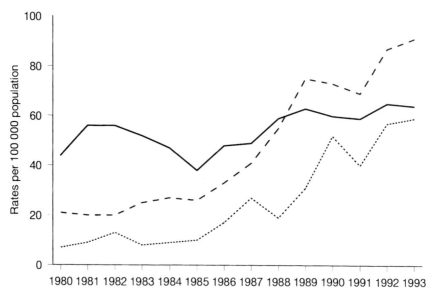

Figure 8.2 Food poisoning in the UK, 1980–93. Solid line, Scotland; dashed line, England and Wales; dotted line, Northern Ireland.

probably incorrect to assume that the incidence of clinical disease has increased by as much as the figures suggest.

Laboratory reports of enteric infections

In the UK, laboratory isolations of enteropathogens from clinically affected persons form a major part of surveillance for food-borne disease.

Reported isolation rates for *Salmonella* spp. have increased in recent years, although this has varied geographically within the UK (Figure 8.3). This trend has also been reported in most industrialized countries. While average reported rates have not changed markedly in Scotland, in England and Wales rates have increased significantly from 20 per 100 000 population to about 60 per 100 000. Again this apparent increase is at least partly due to an improved reporting system and does not necessarily mean that there has been a threefold increase in clinical cases of salmonellosis in England and Wales.

What has been apparent from the laboratory reports is the change in the specific salmonellae reported. Prior to the middle 1980s *Salmonella typhimurium* was the single most important serotype in humans, while *S. enteritidis* accounted for less than 10% of all human infections in the UK.

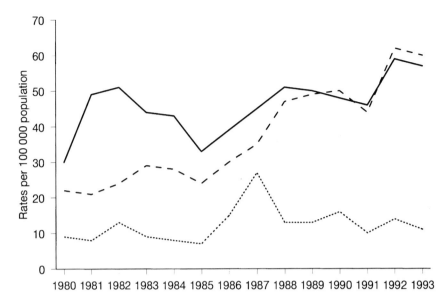

Figure 8.3 Laboratory reports of isolates of *Salmonella* spp. in the UK, 1980–93, given as isolation rates per 100 000 population. Solid line, Scotland; dashed line, England and Wales; dotted line, Northern Ireland.

By 1993 the proportion due to *S. enteritidis* had risen to over 50% (Figure 8.4). In particular *S. enteritidis* phage type 4 has dominated the reports in recent years in the UK, but other phage types are involved in other countries, e.g. phage types 8 and 13a in the USA. In the UK other serotypes have at different times risen in importance, only to subsequently fall in numbers reported. Many of these have been associated with poultry, e.g. *S. agona*, *S. hadar*, *S. virchow* and *S. wangata*.

Since 1980 there has been a steady increase in the reported rates of laboratory isolations of *Campylobacter* spp. (Figure 8.5) and in the UK it is now the most frequently reported bacterial cause of human gastroenteritis. At least part of this increase has been due to an improvement in the methodologies available to laboratories to isolate *Campylobacter* spp. and as a consequence more laboratories are routinely examining faeces for this organism. In the UK a total of over 43 000 isolates were reported in both 1992 and 1993, and the trends have been very similar in all geographical areas.

Unlike *Salmonella* spp. there is a poorly developed typing scheme for *Campylobacter* spp., most of which are reported as species and not further typed. This makes epidemiological investigation very difficult and it is not possible to say if any of the increase is due to changes in eating practices or

foods consumed. It has been suggested that a shift, within poultry consumption patterns, from frozen to fresh poultry meat may be a contribut-
ing factor due to the better survival of campylobacters on fresh poultry
meat.

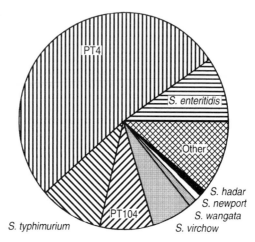

Figure 8.4   Human *Salmonella* serotypes isolated in Scotland in 1993.

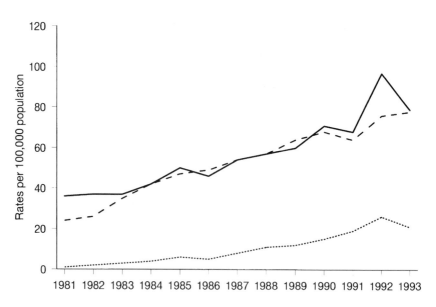

Figure 8.5   Laboratory reports of isolates of *Campylobacter* spp. in the UK,
1981–93, given as isolation rates per 100 000 population. Solid line, Scotland;
dashed line, England and Wales; dotted line, Northern Ireland.

Outbreak investigations

Outbreaks of food-borne infection are extensively investigated in most countries, although this is often carried out in different ways and by different authorities. In 1980 the WHO European Zone Regional Office, Copenhagen, introduced a surveillance programme for Europe. It is difficult to directly compare data from different countries because of the different systems of collecting information, but there are considerable similarities in the foods and organisms involved and the trends observed.

In Europe, *Salmonella* predominates as the reported cause of the majority of outbreaks, while *Campylobacter* is uncommonly reported under the programme despite being the most frequently isolated cause of gastroenteritis. Other organisms are also frequently reported, such as *Bacillus cereus* in the Netherlands, *Clostridium perfringens* in Denmark and Germany yet in the UK these are of lesser importance (Figure 8.6).

The major vehicles of transmission may vary from country to country. In the UK poultry meat is the most frequently identified food, while in Spain it is eggs, in Sweden salads, and in Denmark meat products predominate. However, in many outbreaks the responsible food vehicle is not identified. For example, in Scotland in 1993 a suspected food vehicle was only identified in 27% of outbreaks of food-borne infection. Where a food vehicle was implicated, poultry meat was the food most commonly identified (Figure 8.7).

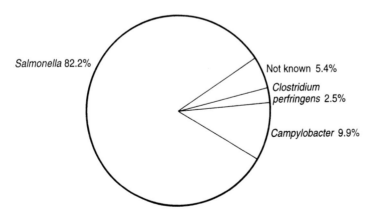

Figure 8.6 Food-borne disease in Scotland, 1993; proportion of outbreaks by agent.

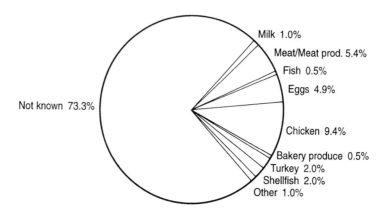

Figure 8.7 Food-borne disease in Scotland, 1993; proportion of outbreaks by food.

One serious limitation on the investigation of food-borne infection is the lack of information available on people affected by sporadic cases of disease, although the total number of persons affected is much greater than the total involved in outbreaks. Little or no information is available on sources of infection for sporadic cases and it may be incorrect to extrapolate from the information available on outbreaks.

Food-borne pathogens

The majority of cases of food-borne infection are attributed to bacteria, which may originate from animal, human or environmental sources. In part, this distribution may be due to the difficulty in identifying other causes such as chemical contaminants. In a significant number of outbreaks no agent is identified and it is likely that many of these are due to viral infections. Where a virological source is suspected, or more rarely confirmed, the most likely origin of the virus is human, either as direct food contamination (e.g. hepatitis A), or following indirect contamination via sewage (e.g. small round structured virus, SRSV). Poultry meat *per se* is unlikely to be an important source of viral gastroenteritis but it is possible for an infected person to contaminate poultry meat. This is particularly likely with 'ready-to-eat' products, not requiring further cooking.

The incubation periods and human symptoms of the major food-transmitted pathogens are summarized in Table 8.1.

Table 8.1　Food-borne agents: summary of incubation and clinical features.

Agent	Incubation period	Main symptoms
Salmonella spp.	6–72 hours (usually 12–36 hours)	Diarrhoea, abdominal pain, nausea, maybe vomiting, fever
Campylobacter spp.	1–10 days (usually 3–5 days)	Abdominal pain, profuse diarrhoea, malaise, headache, fever
Staphylococcus aureus	1–6 hours	Vomiting, prostration of short duration
Clostridium perfringens	6–24 hours (usually 10–12 hours)	Colic, diarrhoea of short duration
Listeria monocytogenes	3–21 days (may be longer)	Flu-like illness, meningitis, abortion, premature labour
Yersinia enterocolitica	3–7 days	Diarrhoea, severe pain, low-grade fever
Bacillus cereus	1–5 hours (preformed toxin)	Severe vomiting, abdominal pain, diarrhoea
Viruses Norwalk group, e.g. small round structured virus (SRSV)	18–16 hours 24–72 hours	Vomiting, abdominal pain, diarrhoea, fever, headache

Salmonella

Of all the organisms causing food-borne infection, *Salmonella* is most frequently associated with the poultry industry.

Salmonella spp. are members of the Enterobacteriaceae; they are Gram-negative and able to grow on a wide variety of simple media between 7 °C and 45 °C. They can therefore grow and multiply on many foods, although they are subsequently destroyed by cooking or pasteurization. There are more than 2200 different serotypes of *Salmonella*, differentiated by the Kauffmann–White typing scheme, which identifies the presence of different somatic (O) and flagellar (H) antigens.

Although some *Salmonella* serotypes are almost species-specific – e.g. *S. typhi* in humans and *S. pullorum* in poultry – the majority are able to infect (but not necessarily cause illness in) a wide range of hosts – e.g. *S. enteritidis*. At any one time a relatively small number of different salmonellae are present in animal and human populations. These are constantly changing as different salmonellae increase in importance as enteropathogens and then disappear, for reasons not entirely understood. Other outbreaks can be attributed to specific causes; for example, in 1990 importation of Danish poultry resulted in outbreaks of *S. berta* in England and Wales. Poultry can harbour many different serotypes, the majority of which cause little clinical sign of infection in the birds but which may subsequently cause human illness, e.g. *S. enteritidis*, *S. hadar* and *S. virchow*.

Salmonella serotypes can be further subdivided by a variety of methods. Phage typing is an extremely important method of differentiation and is based on the susceptibility of a given salmonella to a range of different viruses (bacteriophages). *Salmonella enteritidis* phage type 4 has emerged in recent years as a particular problem in the broiler industry in the UK, and while the same phage type has become common in much of Europe, other phage types such as 8 and 13a are more prevalent in the USA. Other typing methods include antibiotic resistance patterns and plasmid profiling, which further differentiate strains and allow human cases to be identified as part of an outbreak and suspected origins confirmed.

PATHOGENESIS

After ingestion and passage through the stomach, salmonellae multiply in the small intestine and colon. They attach to surface receptors of the epithelial cells and penetrate the cell, migrating into the lamina propria. The subsequent inflammatory response results in clinical symptoms, predominantly diarrhoea.

The number of organisms required to result in infection and illness (the 'infectious dose') is still a matter of debate. Traditionally it has been claimed that 10^6–10^9 organisms must be consumed for illness to occur. However, there are well-documented cases where much smaller numbers of bacteria (less than 1000) have caused infection. This may partly depend on the nature of the food; fatty foods may protect the salmonellae from gastric acid, or liquids may pass through the stomach quickly and again allow bacterial survival. If the consumer is especially susceptible, e.g. following intestinal surgery, or is taking antacids (which suppress the effects of gastric acid), infection may be more easily established.

CLINICAL FEATURES

The incubation period is usually 12–36 hours, but can vary between 6 hours and 72 hours. The most common symptom is diarrhoea, which may be accompanied by fever, headache, nausea and abdominal pain. Vomiting is less common. Infection is usually self-limiting, resolving within 7 days. A number of those infected may carry, and excrete, the organism for long periods even when clinically normal, and this may cause some difficulty in deciding how soon they should return to work, especially if they are employed in the food industry. Workers will not normally be excluded from work by the health authorities once they have been 'symptom free' for 48 hours. It is not now the norm to rely on the demonstration of serial negative stool samples before allowing return to work (Table 8.2). Illness may be more severe in the young or elderly, or in the immunocompromised. Fortunately (apart from *S. typhi* and *S. paratyphi*) bacteraemia is uncommon, although some poultry-associated *Salmonella* spp., e.g. *S. virchow*, are

Table 8.2 Criteria required for return to work for food handlers. Food handlers other than those whose work involves touching unwrapped food to be consumed raw or without further cooking present a minimal risk of spreading gastrointestinal illness if they are well and have normal stools. The circumstances of each case, excreter, carrier or contact should be considered individually and factors such as their type of employment and standards of personal hygiene should be taken into account. Where the work involves touching unwrapped foods to be consumed raw or without further cooking the criteria listed here are recommended before allowing return to work.

Organism	Return to work after
Bacillus cereus	No exclusion from work
Campylobacter spp.	Forty eight hours after the first normal stool
Clostridium botulinum	No exclusion from work
Clostridium perfringens	Forty eight hours after the first normal stool
Cryptosporidium spp.	Forty eight hours after the first normal stool
Giardia spp.	Forty eight hours after the first normal stool
Hepatitis A	Seven days after onset of jaundice and/or symptoms
Salmonella spp. (excluding typhoid and paratyphoid infections)	Forty eight hours after the first normal stool. No microbiological clearance is required where adequate hygiene is practised
Salmonella typhi and *S. paratyphi*	Six consecutive negative stool specimens taken at two week intervals starting two weeks after completion of antibiotic treatment
Shigella spp.	Forty eight hours after the first normal stool
Staphylococcus aureus	Successful treatment of septic lesions
Verocytotoxin producing *Escherichia coli* (usually O157)	Two negative faecal specimens at least 48 hours apart
Vibrio cholera	Forty eight hours after the first normal stool
Vibrio parahaemolyticus	Forty eight hours after the first normal stool
Viral gastroenteritis	Forty eight hours after the first normal stool
Yersinia spp.	Forty eight hours after the first normal stool

Adapted from the Public Health Laboratory Service *Communicable Disease Report*, Review Number 11, 1995, ISSN 1350–9349.

more invasive and can cause systemic disease. Infections are not commonly fatal and deaths are usually associated with some other underlying pathology, although rarely an otherwise healthy individual may die from the effects of salmonellosis.

SOURCE

Poultry meat is a major source of human *Salmonella* infection. In one survey as many as 25% of flocks were shown to be infected, with up to 4% of individual birds carrying the organism in the intestine or on feet or feathers. The source of organisms in infected flocks can include vertical transmission from breeding flocks, hatchery cross-contamination, feed, and rearing site contamination, including vermin and visitors to the site. During scalding, plucking and defeathering, contamination from relatively few birds can spread to many carcases. A number of surveys in the UK have shown retail carcase contamination rates varying between 45% and 80%. Although the number of carcases carrying salmonellae appears to be declining, the proportion of contamination with *S. enteritidis* has been increasing. Each contaminated carcase may carry relatively few organisms, but during subsequent mishandling these can multiply and cause a health risk. The industry can improve this contamination rate by paying attention to hygiene at slaughter.

While many poultry carcases may carry *Salmonella* organisms, very few actually cause illness, and this is often due to subsequent mishandling or contamination of other foods. In 1992 over 350 cases of *S. wangata* infection were reported in the north of England and in Scotland, and were identified as part of an extended outbreak, which was only recognized as a result of the uncommon serotype involved. Investigation by environmental health officers and medical authorities identified that the problem was largely confined to consumers of halal poultry, either directly or through commercial food outlets using halal poultry. Although it was subsequently discovered that several breeding flocks, hatcheries and broiler flocks were infected, human illness only occurred in the halal food chain where lack of hygiene and absence of temperature control had allowed initially low numbers of organisms to multiply, resulting in human infection.

The importance of cross-contamination was demonstrated in one study which compared the salmonellae present in poultry carcases delivered to a hospital kitchen with the salmonellae subsequently isolated from the drains from the patients' accommodation. Despite apparently satisfactory hygiene in the kitchen and proper cooking of the poultry, the salmonellae from the drains were statistically linked to those in the poultry, demonstrating transfer from the kitchen to the patients.

Although the poultry may itself be properly cooked, other foods may act as the vehicle following cross-contamination. This was the likely cause of a major outbreak in a long-stay hospital which resulted in more than 450 cases in patients and staff and 19 deaths. Results of the epidemiological investigation and laboratory typing suggested that, although the food vehicle causing the outbreak was a beef meal, the organism was probably introduced into the kitchen by poultry meat.

Campylobacter

Campylobacter organisms were first isolated in 1913 although they were classified as *Vibrio* spp. at that time. They were originally thought to be primarily animal pathogens, associated with infertility (e.g. *Vibrio fetus*) and it was not until the mid-1970s that their association with human enteritis was recognized. Since then, as laboratory methods have been refined and become more widely available, they have been recognized in the UK and many other countries as the most common cause of bacterial enteric infection in humans.

Campylobacters are small, slender, spirally curved, highly motile bacilli. They are Gram-negative and microaerophilic, requiring less oxygen than that normally present in air (5%). This lower oxygen requirement explains the difficulty of their culture and recognition as human pathogens. They grow best at 42–43 °C and not at all at temperatures below 30 °C. Unlike other bacteria they are unlikely to grow on food kept at room temperature. Campylobacters are heat-sensitive and easily destroyed by cooking.

Although 13 species of *Campylobacter* are recognized, only *C. jejuni* and *C. coli* are of major importance as human pathogens. However, most medical laboratories do not identify the species involved, restricting identification as far as *Campylobacter* spp. Serotyping is not as well developed for *Campylobacter* as it is for *Salmonella*, and although schemes such as Penner (65 serogroups) and Lior (100 serogroups) have been developed, they are not generally available. A combination of the two schemes can be used for better strain differentiation but does not greatly assist epidemiological investigation. More modern typing methods such as DNA analysis may offer better prospects for strain identification, but are not routinely carried out. This inability to link isolates from people, animals, food and other sources has limited the understanding of the epidemiology of *Campylobacter* infections.

PATHOGENESIS

An oral dose as low as 500 organisms may be sufficient to cause symptoms in people, although the number of organisms ingested does not appear to affect either the incubation period or the severity of the symptoms. The jejunum and ileum are infected initially but subsequently this extends distally as far as the rectum. While the organisms are invasive, the exact pathogenic mechanism is not clearly understood, although there is evidence that campylobacters produce one or more cytotoxins similar to that of *Vibrio cholera*.

CLINICAL FEATURES

The normal incubation period is 3–5 days; however, this can be extended to up to 10 days. Clinically there is often severe abdominal pain and bloody diarrhoea. The pain is such that a diagnosis of acute appendicitis may be mistakenly made. The abdominal pain may be accompanied by fever and nausea, although vomiting is uncommon.

Infection is usually self-limiting, resolving within a week, although excretion may continue for several weeks. Complications are rare and though bacteraemia has been recorded, death is unlikely to occur. Occasionally reactive arthritis or peripheral polyneuropathy (Guillain–Barré syndrome) may occur several weeks after the acute diarrhoeic phase.

SOURCE

The absence of typing detail hinders identification of sources of infection. Campylobacters are often present in the intestinal flora of animals and birds and potentially any food which is faecally contaminated during processing may be a source of human infection. Subsequent spread from person to person may occur, but most human infections appear as sporadic cases. Poultry have been recognized as a major reservoir of campylobacters and up to 50% of broiler flocks may be infected. Contamination rates in broilers have been shown to vary from 30% to 100% at the point of sale. Unlike *Salmonella* contamination, it would appear that broilers usually become infected at the rearing site, and the organism has rarely been isolated from hatcheries or newly hatched chicks. Drinking water may be an important source of infection for the chicks, with survival of the campylobacters – even after disinfection – in biofilm within pipes. Once infection is present *Campylobacter* can spread quickly within the flock, although there is little evidence of clinical disease in infected flocks.

During processing the organism can be distributed over the surface of the birds (skin and abdominal cavity) with 10^6–10^7 organisms present per bird. Campylobacters can be trapped in feather follicles and may not be subsequently removed by washing and disinfection. Contamination is higher in fresh than in frozen birds, since freezing reduces the number of organisms, although once frozen they can remain viable for many months. This may partly explain the reported increase in *Campylobacter* infections as the poultry trade moves from frozen to fresh birds.

Other sources of human infection include milk, cooked meats and water. Contact with animals, including pets, and farm animals can also result in human infection.

EPIDEMIOLOGY

Campylobacter does not multiply in foods at room temperature, and numbers of organisms on food may remain low and are destroyed by cooking. Outbreaks are uncommon except for water and milk-associated outbreaks.

The infection has a marked seasonal distribution, peaking early in the summer months – several weeks before the peak of *Salmonella* isolates. This may be due to change in eating habits in early summer with an increase in pre-cooked cold meat consumption and barbecues – both of which are particularly susceptible to cross-contamination between raw and cooked foods. Cross-contamination has been well demonstrated, passing from raw chicken to hands, cloths, etc. *Campylobacter* can survive for considerable periods on hands if not properly washed.

The role of poultry in the epidemiology of *Campylobacter* was demonstrated in one investigation which described the similarity between campylobacters isolated from poultry from a single poultry producer and those in the local human population consuming broilers from that company. Following active intervention to remove *Campylobacter* from the broiler flock the specific serotypes of *Campylobacter* involved disappeared from the local population.

Listeria monocytogenes

Listeria species are widespread in the environment where they survive for long periods of time. Although there are several species, only *Listeria monocytogenes* is thought to cause human infection. This species has long been recognized as an animal and human pathogen, but it was only in the 1980s that the food-borne route of transmission was identified as being important. Infection with *Listeria* is much less common than other food-borne infections such as salmonellosis and campylobacteriosis, but may clinically be much more severe.

Listeria monocytogenes is a short, Gram-positive rod which grows well on a wide variety of media (including foods). The organism can grow over a wide temperature range (0–42 °C) and can multiply slowly at refrigeration temperatures which inhibit other food-borne pathogens. This ability to survive and grow at low temperatures means that foods which are prepared and subsequently refrigerated (e.g. pre-cooked foods, cheeses, etc.) may be a particular risk. Although *Listeria* is more heat-tolerant than other food-borne pathogens, it is destroyed by cooking and pasteurization.

Strains of *L. monocytogenes* can be grouped by serotyping, but most strains isolated from humans and foods in the UK belong to only two types, 4 and 1/2. Further refinement of identification of *L. monocytogenes* strains has still to confirm the suspected the link between types isolated from the environment, animals, food and humans.

PATHOGENESIS AND CLINICAL FEATURES

Although ingestion is the usual route of entry of *L. monocytogenes*, the main symptoms in humans are systemic rather than intestinal. Most healthy people carrying *L. monocytogenes* in the gastrointestinal tract are symptomless, and up to 5% of the healthy population may be excreters at any one time. Illness is most likely to occur in individuals with impaired resistance such as pregnant women and their unborn children, neonates and the elderly. Only rarely do apparently healthy individuals become ill.

The number of organisms required to cause infection is unknown, but has been shown to be as low as 100 for susceptible individuals. The incubation period is thought to range from a few days to several weeks. Symptoms can vary considerably from a flu-like illness, fever, septicaemia, meningitis and abortion. The overall case mortality rate is about 30%.

SOURCE

Listeria is ubiquitous, being widely found in the environment and on foods. One survey demonstrated the presence of *Listeria* in 24% of broiler flocks. As many as 60% of raw chicken samples have been shown to be contaminated, and 12% of precooked chicken samples. *Listeria* contamination in a wide variety of other raw and cooked foods has also been shown to be high. Soft cheese and pâtés have been particularly implicated: levels in cheese have been as high as 10^4/g.

Only in very few instances has a suspected foodstuff been confirmed as having the same strain of *L. monocytogenes* as in patients.

EPIDEMIOLOGY

Fortunately listeriosis is a relatively uncommon disease in the UK, with approximately 100 cases per year reported most years. During the late 1980s there was a significant increase to over 300 cases per year. This resulted in advice from the Chief Medical Officer to susceptible groups (e.g. pregnant women) to avoid higher-risk foods such as pâté and soft cheeses. Subsequently the incidence returned to about 100 cases per year.

Most human cases are sporadic and because of the sometimes very long incubation period it is particularly difficult to identify the foods involved. Where case–control studies have been carried out these have identified undercooked chicken and cook-chill food as potential sources.

When outbreaks occur, they can be extensive. During 1992 over 270 cases were reported in France, and were traced to pork tongue.

Clostridium perfringens

Clostridium perfringens has long been recognized as a human pathogen, causing (for example) gas gangrene. It was first identified as a cause of food-borne illness in the 1940s and is now seen as a common cause of food poisoning throughout the world. The incidence has been falling in recent years in the UK, possibly as a result of better understanding of the importance of thorough cooking and subsequent chilling. Although most clostridia are widespread in the environment (e.g. soil), *C. perfringens* is also a commensal in the gut of humans, animals and birds.

The clostridia are large, spore-forming, Gram-negative anaerobic bacilli. They can grow rapidly over a wide temperature range (15–50 °C) and optimally at 43–47 °C. The spores are heat-resistant and may survive cooking. *Clostridium perfringens* can be classified into five types (A–E) depending on the extracellular toxins that are produced, but only type A is important in food poisoning.

PATHOGENESIS AND CLINICAL FEATURES

When a contaminated food – usually meat contaminated with animal faeces – is cooked, the heat drives off dissolved oxygen creating anaerobic conditions and induces sporulation. During cooling the spores germinate and can multiply rapidly (generation time 12 minutes). When food containing large numbers of bacteria is eaten the bacteria reach the small intestine where they sporulate, releasing enterotoxin which damages the villi and inhibits absorption. This usually results in abdominal pain and diarrhoea but rarely vomiting. Symptoms usually appear 10–12 hours after ingestion of the contaminated food and last 24–48 hours. The infection is rarely fatal.

SOURCE

Clostridium perfringens is part of the normal gut flora of all food-producing animals and birds. During the slaughter process contamination of the carcase with faeces can occur. This contamination can survive until cooking, when heating and subsequent cooling produce the anaerobic conditions for bacterial multiplication. Foods particularly implicated include meats and poultry, particularly as stews and casseroles. The ideal conditions are most likely to be found when larger volumes of food are being prepared, since rapid cooling is more difficult to achieve. Large outbreaks may therefore occur if food is not thoroughly reheated (to above 75 °C) and where large volumes of food are prepared, e.g. in hospitals and commercial catering.

EPIDEMIOLOGY

In England and Wales between 1986 and 1989 there were 204 reported outbreaks of *Clostridium perfringens* infection, of which 35 were attributed to poultry products and 50 to mixed meats, pies, sausages, gravies and sauces. *Clostridium perfringens* was the most common cause of outbreaks in large-scale catering such as institutions and canteens, and accounted for 39 of 96 hospital outbreaks of food poisoning. A further 97 outbreaks were reported between 1992 and 1993, one of which affected 24 of 31 people who had eaten stewed chicken.

Staphylococcus aureus

Food poisoning caused by *Staphylococcus aureus* is unlike the majority of other bacterial causes since it follows the consumption of food containing preformed bacterial toxin. In addition the source of the bacteria is more likely to be human than animal.

Staphylococcus aureus organisms are Gram-positive, facultative anaerobic cocci. They produce a range of eight enterotoxins (A, B, C_1, C_2, C_3, D, E, F) in food, of which type A is the most common. These are thermostable and can survive boiling for 30 minutes. The toxins are produced during active growth of the bacteria and even if the food is subsequently cooked or reheated, killing the bacteria, toxin activity may remain. The toxins are produced over a wide range of temperatures (10–45 °C) with the optimum at

35–40 °C. Different strains of *S. aureus* can be identified by phage typing, which aids epidemiological investigation.

PATHOGENESIS AND CLINICAL FEATURES

The toxins do not act directly on the intestinal wall but rather on receptors in the intestine. This stimulates the vomiting centre in the brain via the vagus nerve. The main symptoms are nausea, vomiting, abdominal pain and prostration. This may be accompanied by diarrhoea but rarely fever. The incubation period is short because of the preformed toxin, occurring usually within 1–6 hours of ingestion. The majority of patients recover within 24 hours.

SOURCE

Stapylococcus aureus can be recovered from 40% of healthy people – from nostrils in particular. It is often present in infected skin lesions and can be shed in large numbers. Consequently food handlers are an important source of contamination with this organism, and personal hygiene is particularly important. In animals it may be present in skin and joint lesions, and in cows, goats and sheep it can cause mastitis.

EPIDEMIOLOGY

The foods most commonly implicated in staphylococcal food-borne disease include cooked meats, dairy produce and poultry. Prior cooking removes other bacteria and if the food is subsequently contaminated it provides an ideal medium for the growth of staphylococci. Poor handling of the food is an important factor and it is likely that most contamination occurs not at initial processing but during subsequent mishandling by food workers. Once a food is contaminated it can act as a source of contamination for other foods by cross-contamination.

Proper temperature control (e.g. refrigeration) is a major factor in reducing the risk of *S. aureus* outbreaks.

Viruses

In many outbreaks of food poisoning no causative organism is identified. It is likely that many of these are due to a viral agent. The difficulty in routinely identifying viruses in foods and faeces undoubtedly contributes to this under-diagnosis.

In outbreaks where a virus is identified the majority belong to the Norwalk group. In particular, one of the small round structured viruses (SRSV), along with others such as rotavirus and astrovirus, have been impli-cated. In theory any virus which can spread by the faecal–oral route can contaminate food and cause illness following consumption. Hepatitis A can be spread by this route. Usually these viruses are highly infectious at low doses.

Poultry are unlikely to be the primary source of these human viruses, but poultry meat can act as a vehicle following contamination either at the time of processing or more probably at a subsequent stage in food preparation by an infected food handler.

Most illnesses due to gastroenteritis viruses such as SRSV are self-limit-ing, with a duration of 24–48 hours.

Prevention

The major aim of poultry meat hygiene and inspection is to produce poultry meat which in the normal course of events will pose no risk to consumers. In microbiological terms this means freedom from pathogens and their products.

It is the responsibility of the industry to ensure that the whole of this food chain, which extends from the breeding and rearing farms, through slaugh-ter and further processing to cooking and subsequent consumption, is oper-ated in such a manner as to minimize the risk. The latter stages of this chain are normally beyond the control of the poultry producers.

If poultry meat is properly handled and cooked there should be no risk of food-borne disease even if *Salmonella, Campylobacter* or other pathogens were initially present on the carcase. This is, however, no justification for allowing potentially contaminated products to enter the kitchen. Just as great, if not greater, risks exist from the potential of cross-contamination from poultry meat to other foods.

The industry is continuing to strive to reduce the presence of potential food-poisoning organisms in the rearing flocks by improving attention to disease status and farm hygiene. Similarly, in the processing plant improve-ments such as multistage scalding, equipment design, multiple washing points, the use of organic acids and the application of the principles of HACCP all have a part to play in reducing cross-contamination. Nevertheless the reported incidence of food-borne infection continues to rise, although the figures have to be carefully interpreted. A large part of this can still be attributed to poultry meat consumption. A similar situation previously existed with milk. In this instance the solution in some countries was the introduction of compulsory heat treatment of milk, which had considerable effects on the incidence of milk-borne disease. One solution for the poultry industry might be the introduction of a similar 'safety net' by allowing irradiation of poultry meat. Discussion of this topic is outwith the scope of this book. However, irradiation is a process unfairly feared by consumers in many countries – yet accepted in others. This technology holds promise for the future, given consumer acceptance. In the meantime the poultry meat industry must continue to strive to reduce the level of pathogen contamination on the final product.

CHAPTER 9

Poultry Meat Inspection

Introduction

Poultry for slaughter for human consumption must undergo inspection for fitness for human consumption. This consists of a pre-slaughter health inspection and a post-mortem inspection. The official veterinary surgeon (OVS) and the poultry meat inspector (PMI) form the inspection team, with current legislation in the European Union permitting the use of suitably trained plant inspection assistants (PIAs), provided by the manager of the slaughterhouse workers, and properly supervised by the OVS and PMI.

The occupier of any licensed premises is required to ensure that the OVS, PMIs or PIAs are provided with adequate facilities to enable their duties to be carried out effectively.

The identity of poultry for slaughter must be proved on arrival in the slaughterhouse, and the occupier of any licensed premises must keep – and retain for at least 1 year – an adequate record of the number of birds (identified by species) received for slaughter, the number dead on arrival and the reason for any carcases considered unfit for human consumption by the inspection team, who must also keep records.

The inspection service has to determine whether or not to permit the slaughter of a consignment of birds. This is done on the basis of a veterinary certificate accompanying the consignment or on the basis of information provided by the producer. In the latter case, flocks must be under veterinary supervision and the OVS must be in possession of the producer's report on the flock for slaughter.

Pre-slaughter health inspection

Within the countries of the EU, a pre-slaughter health inspection is permitted at the slaughterhouse if the OVS has not received a production report and there is no veterinary attestation accompanying the consignment.

- The OVS may decide to permit slaughter on welfare grounds, with subsequent inspection of the premises of origin.

- Slaughter is also permitted if the producer has declared that no more than 20 000 domestic fowl, 15 000 ducks, or 10 000 turkeys or geese are reared each year, when the OVS may arrange for ante-mortem inspection to be carried out in the slaughterhouse.

A room or covered space, which is sufficiently large and easy to clean and disinfect, must be provided for this pre-slaughter inspection, which requires adequate lighting of at least 220 lux.

There is a requirement for welfare checks to be carried out on all poultry at the slaughterhouse to check for injuries that may have been sustained during transport.

Ante-mortem inspection permits the recognition of acute infectious diseases, acute diarrhoea, cachectic birds, dead birds, general contamination or abnormal smell. The inspector should determine:

- Whether the birds are showing signs of disease which can be transmitted to humans, i.e. zoonoses.
- Whether the birds are showing signs of disease or any condition that would make the meat unfit for human consumption.

An OVS, or an inspector acting under supervision, may require the occupier of a licensed premises or the producer of any group or bird not to slaughter any bird for human consumption where there is evidence that it would be unfit for human consumption. They may also forbid the slaughter for human consumption of birds in which clinical symptoms of ornithosis or salmonellosis have been established, or of any bird from the same group as the bird with symptoms.

An OVS may require the slaughter of a specified group of poultry subject to a control programme of infectious disease under the Zoonoses Order 1989 to comply with certain conditions. These include precautions to avoid contamination of other birds, and, at the end of the slaughter period, thorough cleaning and disinfection of any equipment, fittings and facilities immediately after use.

Post-mortem inspection

Inspection of individual parts of the birds is carried out by PMIs or PIAs. The parts requiring inspection are the surface of the bird (excluding head and feet if not for human consumption), the viscera and the internal body cavity.

Delayed evisceration is permitted provided uneviscerated birds are held at no more than 4 °C for a maximum of 15 days.

The OVS is also required to examine a random sample of the carcases and viscera of birds passed at post-mortem inspection and a random sample of rejected birds, to monitor the standards of the meat inspectors.

Slaughtered birds are opened so that the cavities and the viscera can be inspected. The viscera may be detached or left attached to the carcase by their natural connections. If they are detached they must remain identifiable as belonging to a given carcase.

Post-mortem inspection is carried out on the whole bird after defeathering and on the evisceration line; both places require adequate lighting of 540 lux. The inspector must have sufficient room to inspect the carcase and viscera. When it is not possible to examine the whole bird easily, a mirror is provided. All surfaces in this area must be easily cleaned and disinfected, with ready access to facilities for cleaning hands and for cleaning and sterilizing tools. A hang-back rack to hold detained birds is also required, and trimming may take place on this rack.

Arrangements must be made to ensure the removal of rejected meat so that it does not come into contact with meat declared fit for human consumption. The unfit meat must be placed, as soon as possible, in special rooms or containers. Arrangements must also be made to ensure that carcases and offal awaiting inspection or which are detained do not come into contact with carcases and offal already inspected.

This inspection should take place immediately after slaughter and should include:

- Visual examination.
- Palpation and incision if considered necessary.
- Investigation of abnormalities in consistency, colour or smell.
- Laboratory investigations where deemed necessary.

Conditions which are relatively common and should be recognized at inspection are previously dead birds, putrefaction, imperfect bleeding, cachexia, bruising and fractures, septicaemia and toxaemia, air sacculitis, peritonitis, sinusitis, synovitis and arthritis, Marek's disease and leucosis complex, erysipelas (turkeys), and tuberculosis and neoplasms (hens). TUMOURS

With septicaemia and toxaemia it is not easy, and usually impossible, to identify the causal organism from macroscopic examination alone. This is also true of chronic infections when there is a large amount of thick pus.

In the EU Poultry Meat Hygiene Directive (92/116/EEC), indications of unfitness for human consumption are given, as follows:

1. Birds shall be declared totally unfit for human consumption where the post-mortem health inspection reveals any of the following diseases or conditions:

   - Generalized infectious disease and chronic localization in organs of pathogenic micro-organisms transmissible to humans.

- Systematic mycosis and local lesions in organs suspected of having been caused by pathogenic agents transmissible to humans, or their toxins.
- Extensive subcutaneous or muscular parasitism and systemic parasitism.
- Poisoning.
- Cachexia.
- Abnormal smell, colour or taste.
- Malignant or multiple tumours.
- General soiling or contamination.
- Major lesions and ecchymosis.
- Extensive mechanical lesions, including those due to extensive scalding.
- Insufficient bleeding.
- Ascites.
- Residues of substances exceeding the authorized standards or residues of prohibited substances.

Parts of a slaughtered bird which show localized lesions or contaminations not affecting the rest of the meat shall be declared unfit for human consumption.

2. In the case of birds, the head separated from the carcase with the exception of the tongue, and the comb, wattles and caruncles and the following viscera shall be declared unfit for human consumption: trachea, lungs and crop, oesophagus, intestine, gallbladder, and other parts unfit for human consumption.

Birds dead before slaughter

The prevalence of birds arriving dead on arrival at processing plants varies. The causes of death are not well understood but mortality can be influenced by time of day, duration of transport and waiting time, the catching team and the number of birds per crate in hot weather (1). In a survey of six processing plants the overall prevalence of birds arriving dead was 0.19% (2). Half the birds had died of heart failure, with congestive heart failure without ascites in most cases.

The dead birds should not be presented for processing but detained at ante-mortem inspection. If, inadvertently, they are not detained at the ante-mortem point, they may be identified by the muscle which is a darker red than normal as seen through the skin, along with engorged vessels supplying the viscera, a more pronounced picture than with badly bled carcases (see below).

Judgement
Carcases and offal are unfit for human consumption.

Badly bled carcases

In carcases that are insufficiently bled the skin is a cherry-red colour, which may extend over part or all of the carcase and be most obvious in the neck region.

Judgement
Carcases and offal are unfit for human consumption.

Putrefaction

As staleness develops in the carcase, the eyes become dark and sunken. The feet are hard and stiff, the flesh loose, flabby and darker colour. An unpleasant odour develops and a green colour appears, especially in the region of the vent and crop.

Judgement
The bird should be detained. Carcases and offal are unfit for human consumption.

Ascites (dropsy) and oedema

Ascites is an accumulation of excess fluid in the abdominal cavity. It is obvious in the region of the vent if the carcase is suspended by the head. The fluid may be present in great quantity and is often associated with diseases of the abdominal cavity, e.g. egg peritonitis and tumours. It may be present with other chronic diseases. Putrefaction rapidly ensues, with the green colour first seen around the vent.

Muscle tissues can also be affected – this is generalized oedema.

Judgement
Affected birds should be identified and removed at the whole bird, pre-evisceration inspection point and rejected for human consumption.

Cachexia, emaciation

It is difficult to differentiate between poorness and emaciation but the latter is associated with disease. Where there is a reduced food intake and loss of body weight in an acute illness the cause of emaciation may not be obvious. In the worst cases recognition is easy, but many adult birds look emaciated at the end of the laying period.

Judgement
Look at the viscera and state of the fat surrounding the organs for evidence of degenerative change. If there is degenerative change the whole carcase and offal should be considered unfit for human consumption.

Skin conditions

Skin lesions follow disease or injury. This can occur on the farm, at loading or unloading, or from machine damage during processing.

Skin damage on the farm can arise from birds scratching each other's backs when there is panic, lack of food or overcrowding. Abrasions may become infected and possibly lead to emaciation.

Judgement
If damage is localized with the carcase in good condition, then trim to remove all affected tissues. If the carcase is in poor condition it should be rejected.

MAREK'S DISEASE

The skin form of Marek's disease has swollen, whitish, nodular feather follicles which may coalesce. It is particularly noticeable along the large feather tracts of the neck and breast areas. (See 'Tumour' section for judgement.)

ABSCESSES

Abscesses are less common in poultry than in other animals. They occur in bumblefoot and breast blisters, or follow feather pecking or cannibalism. The pus tends to be dry and odourless, with the abscess poorly encapsulated or circumscribed.

Judgement
Trim the affected parts if localized. If bone and/or muscle are widely affected, reject the carcase.

BREAST BLISTERS

Breast blisters are common and caused by injury (probably repeated injury) to the breast bone. They vary in size and can become large and may become infected, with abscess formation. They are common in birds affected with infectious synovitis.

Judgement

Infected, haemorrhagic or enlarged breast blisters should be trimmed. The affected tissue may be adherent to the keel bone and when this happens part of the bone will have to be removed with the affected tissues. Trimming of small, non-infected, non-haemorrhagic blisters may be deferred until after chilling, when a proportion of them will have disappeared.

BRUISING

Bruising can occur during crating, transport, uncrating and shackling of the legs. The skin of poultry is loosely attached to the underlying muscle and is easily under-run. Bruises may be highly coloured with red, blue and green colours predominating, depending on the age of the lesion. If there are also skin lacerations these may become septic.

Judgement

Judgement should be based on the extent and nature of the bruising and the practicability of carrying out trimming:

- Extensive bruising or ecchymosis renders the whole carcase unfit.
- When the bruising is localized, the carcase may be passed following removal by trimming of all affected parts. When trimming, the extension of blood between muscles, bones, etc. should be considered and care must be taken to ensure that all affected tissues are removed.
- Provided that the carcase is otherwise fit, superficial, discreet, uncomplicated bruises not exceeding 2 cm in diameter may be left untrimmed.
- If secondary infection is present with under-running, reject the carcase.

RED-SKINNED CARCASES

Broiler chicken carcases may be seen with the entire carcase bright red instead of the normal bleached colour. This is thought to be the result of a physiological response to heat when inadequate time has been allowed for bleeding out before the bird enters the scalding tank (3).

Action
Ensure that the stun is effective and that the bleed-out time is adequate.

Judgement
Reject carcase and offal.

RED WING-TIPS

Reddened wing-tips may be found in broilers, associated with excessive flapping while hanging from the shackles.

Judgement
Trimming is required only in worst cases.

MELANOSIS

The deposition of black melanin pigment in abnormal sites may be seen in all species.

Judgement
Carcases with small deposits of melanin in the skin may be passed. Otherwise it is rare for such infiltrations to be localized, and deposits of melanin in any other area justify classification of the carcase and offal as unfit.

DERMATITIS

Dermatitis is associated with reduced immune competence in affected flocks. It has been found with a greater incidence in the presence of Gumboro disease.
    Gangrenous dermatitis is primarily on the legs but can be found on the flanks and involves both staphylococci and clostridia.

Judgement
Reject affected birds.

OVERSCALD

Overscald can occur either in the scalding tank or during singeing, when carcases are left in the equipment for too long. The skin is slimy to touch and strips easily from the underlying meat, which is whiter than usual.

Where overscalding of the carcase is in doubt, a cut should be made into the pectoral muscle. If the flesh has a cooked appearance to a depth of more than 2 mm, then the carcase should be considered to have been overscalded.

Judgement
Except in the case of large turkeys, where salvage of unscalded meat may be possible after trimming, overscalded carcases and offal should be considered unfit.

Muscle conditions

GREEN MUSCLE DISEASE (OREGON DISEASE)

Green muscle disease, an ischaemic necrosis of the deep pectoral (supra-coracoid) muscle, is classically described in turkey breeding flocks, but may be seen less frequently in fattening turkeys, broiler breeders and young poultry. In turkeys it appears to occur more often in females than in males.

The affected breast may appear slightly concave and the lesion may be unilateral or bilateral. Deep within the affected muscle will be found a characteristic green, necrotic or fibrous lesion.

The condition in the whole carcase may be most readily detected by a light-probe. When the probe is inserted into the cavity of the bird in a darkened room, the affected muscle will cast a shadow.

Judgement
The affected muscle must be removed by trimming; it is unfit and must be rejected.

Broken bones

Fractures may be sustained ante-mortem, when they are normally associated with haemorrhage, or post-mortem by machine damage, when haemorrhage is absent.

BROKEN BONES ASSOCIATED WITH HAEMORRHAGE

Judgement
The affected tissues should be trimmed from the carcase. Where a limb is affected, the cut should normally be made at a joint which ensures that all

the affected tissue is removed. Where one side of the pelvis only is affected, the backbone should be split from the tail forward until the affected tissues can be removed by making a second cut laterally from the backbone. If the whole pelvis is affected the posterior of the carcase should be removed by cutting through the vertebral column anterior to the pelvis.

BROKEN BONES WITHOUT HAEMORRHAGE

Judgement

- *Broken bone with ruptured skin:* this lesion is usually sustained in the plucking machines and as the skin is broken, the affected bone and associated muscle should be removed. This usually means making the same cuts as described above.
- *Broken bone with no ruptured skin:* the assessment of this lesion usually depends on the seriousness of the fracture. If there are several pieces of broken bone then trimming should be carried out as described above. If there is a straight break of one bone, this can usually be left as fit for human consumption.

Joint lesions

MYCOPLASMA SYNOVIAE INFECTION

Mycoplasma synoviae infection may affect the synovial membranes associated with joints, tendon sheaths and bursae. At first, thickening and oedema are seen, but later the exudate is creamy and in older birds may be caseous and orange. In chickens, lesions also occur commonly in the respiratory tract, but this is rare in turkeys.

Judgement
If infection is generalized, carcase and offal should be considered unfit. Localized lesions require trimming.

GREEN LEG DISEASE

Ruptured gastrocnemius (green leg disease) may be associated with viral arthritis or staphylococcal infection.

Judgement
Remove affected tissue.

STAPHYLOCOCCAL INFECTION

Localized staphylococcal infection of the foot (bumble foot), with a bulbous lesion of the ball of the foot, is thought to be due to foreign body penetration or bruising. It may become generalized and affect joints and synovial bursae, including the sternal bursa.

Judgement
Remove affected tissues if localized. If the condition is generalized, the carcase and offal should be rejected.

PEROSIS, TWISTED LEGS, TIBIAL DYSCHONDROPLASIA AND RICKETS

Judgement
In cases of severe deformity the affected parts must be removed, and the carcase judged on its merits.

Liver conditions

Bird livers contain varying amounts of fat, leading to variation in colour from dark red to reddish yellow. Livers of very fat birds may rupture (cf. *pâté de foie gras*).

Chronic lesions where there is extensive fibrosis of the livers in turkeys and ducks, with discolouration in all species, can be found.

Judgement
If the carcase is satisfactory it can be passed as fit with the liver rejected.

FATTY LIVER – HAEMORRHAGIC SYNDROME

Fatty liver is considered to be of dietary origin. The liver is enlarged, fatty, friable and often associated with subcapsular haemorrhages which may be long-standing or massive with rupture of the liver.

Judgement
If carcase and offal are otherwise fit, rejection of the liver is usually sufficient.

LIVER GRANULOMAS OF TURKEYS

Liver granulomas are fairly common in turkeys. They are usually firmly embedded in the liver and consist of light-coloured, spheroid masses having a hard, caseous core. They may be numerous (up to 20 or more), and are either unencapsulated or surrounded by a dense, fibrous capsule.

Judgement
If the carcase and offal are otherwise fit, reject the liver.

Reproductive system disorders in laying poultry

IMPACTION OF THE OVIDUCT

Impaction of the oviduct only may occur, with no associated systemic effects. There may be an associated peritonitis which feels slimy to the touch.

Judgement
Reject the oviduct and pass the carcase and offal. Condemn the whole carcase and offal if peritonitis is present.

SALPINGITIS

Salpingitis may be associated with large quantities of inspissated yolk material in the oviduct. The condition may also be associated with *Escherichia coli* infection in immature chickens and ducks. There may be a hard, white, 'cheesy' cast in immature oviducts.

Judgement
It is possible to strip out and condemn the diseased organ if the carcase is acceptable. Where the condition is associated with an abnormal smell or systemic effects, the carcase and offal should be considered unfit.

EGG PERITONITIS

Egg peritonitis occurs in lay hens, ducks and turkeys, when free egg yolk in the peritoneal cavity becomes infected with *E. coli* or other organisms. This condition should not be confused with the presence of free egg yolk in the peritoneal cavity, which may occur in normal, healthy birds and is not a cause for rejection.

Judgement
This condition should be detected at the whole bird inspection station to prevent opening of the abdominal cavity. Egg peritonitis usually merits total

rejection of the carcase but in chronic cases where there is no systemic reaction or abnormal smell, the breast muscle, legs and wings can be salvaged providing the knife making the salvage cuts does not enter the abdominal cavity.

Bacterial infections and septicaemia

The most common organism in bacterial infections is *Escherichia coli*. Other common organisms include *Staphylococcus* spp., *Pasteurella* spp. and *Salmonella* spp. Bacterial infections may be triggered by *Mycoplasma* or viral infections.

In the acute stage of infections the birds may be septicaemic with poor bleeding, petechial haemorrhages, and swollen, congested organs. In the later stages chronic lesions are present.

At post-mortem inspection it is very difficult to determine the causal organism from macroscopic examination, as the findings are very similar and more than one organism may be present.

Judgement
All cases of acute infection and septicaemia are rejected. Multiple chronic lesions also merit total condemnation, but the odd chronic lesion may be trimmed.

AIR SACCULITIS

Air sacculitis is a term used to embrace several diseases which cannot be distinguished accurately at post-mortem inspection in the slaughterhouse. These diseases include chronic respiratory disease (CRD) in chickens and turkeys, *E. coli* and *Salmonella* septicaemia in all species, and *Pasteurella* septicaemia in ducks. Lesions may be seen in the air sacs, pericardium, peritoneum, liver, oviduct and infraorbital sinuses.

- *Air sacs* may be affected by a scarcely perceptible cloudiness or contain catarrhal exudate. In the later stages of disease, they may be much thickened and contain caseous exudate.
- *Heart and liver*: one or both organs may be congested and affected with a fibrinous or fibrinopurulent pericarditis or perihepatitis. A grossly distended pericardial sac containing a mucopurulent exudate is typical of *Salmonella enteritidis* septicaemia.
- *Oviduct*: there may be salpingitis, characterized by an inactive oviduct filled with caseous exudate. This condition is particularly common in

ducks, but may also be seen in broilers. It should not be confused with the salpingitis of egg-laying birds (see above).

Judgement
A guide to the assessment of carcases is given in Table 9.1.

Table 9.1 Assessment of carcases with infectious lesions.

Lesion	Judgement
Septicaemic carcase	Carcase and offal unfit
Pericarditis	Carcase and offal unfit
Perihepatitis	Carcase and offal unfit
Salpingitis	Oviduct unfit. Pass carcase
Mild air sacculitis (no accumulation of exudate)	Remove air sacs. Pass carcase
Air sacculitis with catarrhal exudate (small amounts) OR Air sacculitis with caseous exudate	Remove affected air sacs, and: (a) If clavicular sac affected – humerus, deep pectoral muscles and neck unfit (b) If abdominal air sac affected, remove the kidneys also NB: if pericarditis or perihepatitis also present – total rejection
Air sacculitis with catarrhal exudate (large amounts)	If clavicular air sac affected the legs can be salvaged If clavicular air sac not affected the legs, breast muscle and wings can be salvaged NB: if pericarditis and/or perihepatitis also present – total rejection

CHLAMYDIAL INFECTION

Ornithosis is the term given to the condition of birds caused by *Chlamydia psittaci*, which in humans and psittacine birds is called psittacosis. All types of poultry and wild birds are affected, which has a risk to human health from inhalation of infected dust. A particular risk has been established in the slaughterhouse with ducks.

Clinical disease is not normally recognized but ducks can show a conjunctivitis. When present it may be either acute or chronic, with non-specific post-mortem findings. Lesions include thickened, inflamed air sacs with yellowish-white exudate, pneumonia, perihepatitis and enlargement of the liver and spleen.

Judgement
Affected carcases are rejected. Birds suspected at the pre-slaughter inspection of being affected must not be slaughtered, as discussed at the beginning of this chapter.

CLOSTRIDIAL INFECTION

- *Botulism*: most poultry outbreaks of botulism are caused by *Clostridium botulinum* type C, but A and B can occur. Clinical signs are weakness, incoordination of the legs first, then the wings and neck, followed by flaccid paralysis. In young birds similar signs have been seen with an acute form of Marek's disease.
- *Gangrenous dermatitis* is a disease of broilers, due to *Clostridium septicum* or *C. oedematiens*, in which the skin and muscle are gangrenous.

Judgement
Birds affected with these diseases should be culled on the farm and not taken to the slaughterhouse. All birds with clostridial infections must be rejected.

ESCHERICHIA COLI INFECTION

Infection with *E. coli* commonly affects birds of 4–12 weeks of age. Such infections are predisposed to or exacerbated by *Mycoplasma*, viral infections such as Newcastle disease or infectious bronchitis, or by coccidiosis.

In the acute form the carcase is septicaemic with swollen and congested liver, spleen, kidneys and red-brown muscles. Petechial haemorrhages are widely distributed but most obvious in the heart and the mesenteric fat.

Chronic lesions are an extensive serofibrinous pericarditis, perihepatitis and peritonitis. The fibrinous adherent material can most easily be seen on the surface of the liver. *Escherichia coli* may be involved in air sacculitis and egg peritonitis; it may also be implicated in arthritis, when it most often affects the hocks, where there is pus formation.

Judgement
Remove at the whole-bird stage if possible. If the lesion is localized, then local seizure is possible, otherwise total rejection is necessary (cf. air sacculitis).

COLI GRANULOMA

Coli granuloma is thought to be the result of previous *E. coli* infection. Small cauliflower-like lesions and small yellow/white granulomas are found on intestines and caeca. It is not very common.

Judgement
As it is a chronic condition, if the carcase is satisfactory then only condemn the intestinal tract.

ERYSIPELAS

Erysipelas is primarily a disease of turkeys and the affected birds are listless with, rarely, a swelling of the snood. Mature domestic fowl may also be affected. Where possible, affected birds should be detained on ante-mortem inspection but if they inadvertently reach the post-mortem inspection station they will show typical signs of septicaemia. The liver is often enlarged, congested, friable and sometimes light-brown in colour. The intestines are commonly congested and there may be catarrhal enteritis. A valvular endocarditis may be present in more chronic cases.

Judgement
Carcases and offal should be considered unfit for human consumption.

PASTEURELLOSIS, FOWL CHOLERA

Birds suffering from acute pasteurellosis will exhibit post-mortem signs typical of septicaemic carcases. Petechial and ecchymotic haemorrhages are frequently found and are widely distributed. The liver may be swollen and contain multiple small focal areas of necrosis. The lungs of turkeys are affected more severely than those of chickens and pneumonia is common. A naso-ocular discharge may be seen.

The chronic infection is characterized by localized exudative, purulent or necrotic lesions which may affect respiratory tract, lungs, hock joints, sternal bursa, footpads, peritoneal cavity and oviduct. The liver may be yellow or black in colour with necrotic areas. There can be swollen heads, combs and wattles; occasionally the only lesion seen is an abscess in the wattle.

Judgement
Localized chronic lesions may be trimmed. In cases of acute or generalized infection, carcases and offal must be considered unfit for human consumption.

SALMONELLOSIS

A number of poultry diseases are caused by bacteria of the *Salmonella* group. The major concern is that poultry are asymptomatic carriers of food-poisoning organisms, e.g. *Salmonella enteritidis* and *S. typhimurium*. Specific poultry disease is caused by *S. pullorum* and *S. gallinarum*, currently not a problem in the UK.

- *Salmonella pullorum* causes pullorum disease or bacillary white diarrhoea (BWD). In the acute form in adults the liver is enlarged with multiple necrotic foci and a fibrinous exudate. The heart is enlarged and may be misshapen, the spleen friable with necrotic foci, and the kidneys are enlarged. In the chronic form, which is more commonly seen, there is an acute or chronic pericarditis and the ova are discoloured, shrunken and sometimes cystic.
- *Salmonella gallinarum* causes a serious septicaemic disease, fowl typhoid, affecting mainly adult birds. The liver has a typical bronzed appearance.
- *Salmonella enteritidis* and *S. typhimurium* infections generally show no significant lesions. In some cases of *S. enteritidis* infection there may be a pericarditis, perihepatitis and air sacculitis. The thickened pericardial sac is distended with a considerable quantity of turbid fluid.

Judgement

Suspect birds should be removed at the whole bird, pre-evisceration inspection point, and are unfit for human consumption. If this condition is detected at the evisceration inspection point, the carcase and offal are unfit for human consumption.

HYDROPERICARDIUM

Hydropericardium must not be confused with *Salmonella enteritidis* or *E. coli* infection. Excessive fluid is present but no adhesions. The pericardial sac is white and thickened.

Judgement
Offal is considered unfit for human consumption.

STAPHYLOCOCCUS AUREUS INFECTION

Infection with *Staphylococcus aureus* is quite common, especially in the post-septicaemic chronic form as arthritis, synovitis, etc. with swollen joints and twisted backs. Staphylococcal septicaemia occurs in older birds and is characterized by pneumonia, focal lesions in the liver and sometimes arthritis. May be associated with other pathogenic organisms. Specific conditions include 'bumble foot', infected breast blisters and gangrenous dermatitis.

Judgement
See above.

Tuberculosis usually affects older birds, with lesions seen most commonly in the liver, kidneys, intestinal tract and bone marrow. The lesions are irregularly shaped, greyish-white nodules varying in size from that of a pin's head to large masses. The tubercles can be shelled out from the surrounding tissue. When cut through, the nodules are firm with a dry, cheesy appearance. If the long bones are split lengthwise, small, spherical nodules may be found in the bone marrow.

Confirmation can be made by microscopic examination for the causal organism.

Judgement
Carcases and offal should be considered unfit for human consumption.

YERSINIA PSEUDOTUBERCULOSIS INFECTION

Infection with *Yersinia pseudotuberculosis* causes signs similar to fowl cholera. The chronic form may be seen in the slaughterhouse; there are multiple caseous, tubercle-like lesions in the liver and spleen, and sometimes in the lungs. A severe enteritis may also be present.

Judgement
Affected birds should be rejected.

Viral infections

Viral diseases, as such, are not likely to be seen at post-mortem inspection. They are likely to be involved with bacteria and mycoplasmas in some of the multifactorial diseases seen in poultry.

Judgement
All cases of acute infection and viraemia are rejected. Otherwise the carcase is judged for fitness before a decision is taken to seize localized lesions. Where secondary bacterial infection is also present, refer to action listed under bacterial infection.

ADENOVIRUS INFECTIONS

Adenovirus infections are widely distributed, with domestic avian species of all ages susceptible. These infections are specifically associated with conditions such as egg drop syndrome 1976, turkey haemorrhagic enteritis and marble spleen disease; the virus may also be a secondary pathogen with other viruses in infectious bursal disease and respiratory disease. In live birds signs of disease include diarrhoea, respiratory disease, tenosynovitis, poor growth and poor food conversion; in laying poultry, there is a fall in egg production.

AVIAN INFLUENZA

Avian influenza is unlikely to be seen at the slaughterhouse. In the acute form – fowl plague – there is a high mortality rate, with haemorrhagic lesions, most prominent in the gastrointestinal tract and trachea, and necrotic foci in the spleen and liver. Other forms include depression, respiratory and ocular involvement and decreased egg production.

Action
In some countries there is a requirement to notify the State Veterinary Service.

FOWL POX

Fowl pox is seen in any age of chickens or turkeys. The skin form affects the featherless parts of the head. Diphtheritic lesions are possible in the mouth, and may extend down the trachea to the lungs and even involve the rest of the bird.

INFECTIOUS BRONCHITIS

Infectious bronchitis is a severe respiratory disease with lesions in the trachea and air sacs. Nephritis occurs with some strains. The disease can be mild, with birds just off their feed for a few days, and a drop in egg production with impaired shell and egg quality. The disease may contribute to *E. coli* infection.

INFECTIOUS LARYNGOTRACHEITIS

Infectious laryngotracheitis is a mild disease; often much of the flock will be coughing. The tracheal epithelium is inflamed and there may be 'plugs' which obstruct the upper trachea and cause asphyxiation.

Clinical infectious bursal disease or Gumboro disease has a speedy onset with significant mortality in broiler flocks. The bursa of Fabricius is enlarged and inflamed, possibly with haemorrhages in the lower gastro-intestinal tract and caeca. The kidneys are pale and there may be pale edges to the liver.

There is impaired immunity to other diseases and secondary bacterial infection is possible.

AVIAN LEUCOSIS AND MAREK'S DISEASE

See 'Tumour' section.

Mycoplasmosis

Mycoplasma is implicated in several diseases in poultry; it is frequently associated with bacteria and possibly viruses.

Mycoplasma gallisepticum gives rise to air sacculitis and sinusitis. In turkeys there is a catarrhal inflammation of the infraorbital sinuses in which, in advanced cases, there is a yellowish inspissated pus which distends the sinus. In chronic respiratory disease in domestic fowls it is often associated with bacteria, such as *E. coli*, or viruses.

Infectious synovitis of poultry is caused by *M. synoviae* which also causes air sacculitis.

Osteodystrophy and bowing of legs of turkey stags can be seen.

Judgement
Based on body condition, localized lesions and bleeding (see also the section on air sacculitis), judgements range from local condemnation, to the carcase and offal being unfit for human consumption.

Fungal infections

ASPERGILLOSIS

Infections by *Aspergillus* species may be seen in all poultry and severe outbreaks are often associated with faulty management.

The respiratory system is most commonly affected, with yellow or white nodular plaques which may coalesce. Green, fructating bodies will be present in more generalized forms of the infection, occasionally resulting in septicaemia or emaciation.

Mixed infections are common and associated peritonitis may be seen.

Judgement

In cases of generalized air sacculitis, associated septicaemia or emaciation, the carcase and offal should be considered unfit.

Where the carcase is affected by a few plaques or caseous casts in the air sacs, the viscera including the lungs should be considered unfit and salvage of the carcase or carcase meat carried out along the lines indicated for air sacculitis in Table 9.1.

Parasitic infestations

PROTOZOA

Coccidiosis Coccidiosis in poultry is caused mainly by the *Eimeria* species, of which only three are of importance: *E. tenella, E. necatrix* and *E. acervulina.*

Caecal coccidiosis occurs mainly in young birds, caused by *E. tenella*; acute cases have the caeca filled with blood. In the chronic form the caeca are distended by dark-red, 'cheesy' masses. There is a marked drop in food consumption, with bloody diarrhoea, lassitude, emaciation and a high mortality rate.

Intestinal coccidiosis occurs in older birds and is caused by *E. necatrix* and *E. acervulina*. Birds lose weight with a drop in food consumption, and become droopy with reduced egg production.

Judgement

In all cases there is usually emaciation, with total seizure required.

Blackhead, histomoniasis or infectious enterohepatitis Blackhead is a specific disease chiefly of turkeys but may also affect chickens. Only turkeys have severe symptoms caused by *Histomonas meleagridis*. Affected birds go off their food, and show dullness, weakness and drooping wings and tail. In turkeys there are characteristic sulphur-yellow droppings. In the acute form death rapidly ensues, but a chronic wasting is seen in older birds.

Cyanosis or blackening of the wattles and skin of the head may take place – hence the name 'blackhead' – but is not a constant feature. Characteristic circular areas of focal necrosis are found in the liver. These lesions are depressed, yellow to yellowish-green with greyish peripheral regions which may extend deeply into the liver, which is enlarged. One or both caeca may be greatly enlarged with thickened walls and containing dark, cheesy masses.

Judgement
Depends on the condition of the carcase.

ROUNDWORMS

The roundworms of poultry are *Ascaridia galli (lineata)*, *Syngamus trachea* and *Heterakis gallinarum*.

Ascaridia galli *infection Ascaridia galli (lineata)* is a yellowish-white worm found in the small intestine of the fowl and turkey. Heavy infections cause haemorrhagic enteritis, anaemia, diarrhoea and emaciation, and may even cause complete obstruction of the intestine.

Judgement
Emaciated birds are rejected.

Syngamus trachea *infection Syngamus trachea* (gapeworm) inhabits the trachea of the fowl or turkey. The young worms migrate to the larger bronchi and then on to the trachea where they attach to the mucous membrane and suck blood, hence the red colour. Heavy infestations may cause pneumonia and catarrhal tracheitis.
  Young birds are most often affected with the characteristic signs of the disease known as 'gapes', from the gaping, extended beak and spasmodic gasping for breath.

Judgement
Emaciated birds are rejected, otherwise localized condemnation of affected parts.

Heterakis gallinarum *infection Heterakis gallinarum* occurs in the caeca of fowls and turkeys. It is important as the carrier of the protozoan parasite *Histamonas meleagridis*, which causes blackhead in turkeys and fowls.

Judgement
Emaciated birds are rejected (but see 'Blackhead' above).

TAPEWORMS

The three tapeworms of importance in poultry are *Davainea proglottina*, *Raillietina tetragona* and *Raillietina echinobothrida*. *Davainea proglottina* inhabits the duodenum of the fowl, *Raillietina tetragona* the small intestine of fowl, pigeon and turkeys, and *R. echinobothrida* the small intestine of fowl and turkeys. *Davainea proglottina* is the most pathogenic and causes a haemorrhagic enteritis, as may *Raillietina tetragona* and *R. echinobothrida* in heavy infestations. *Raillietina echinobothrida* also causes 'nodular' tapeworm disease' by burrowing into the duodenal mucosa and causing nodules very similar to tuberculosis nodules. The lesions are confined to the intestines, which is unusual in tuberculosis, with the small tapeworms usually found hanging from the inside of the lesions when the intestines are opened.

Judgement
Only birds that are emaciated are rejected.

Tumours

All common types of tumours are found; lymphoid tumours are the most common especially those associated with Marek's disease. The reproductive system is the most common site of tumour formation, especially the ovary. Other organs often affected are the liver, spleen, kidneys and alimentary tract.

It is difficult to distinguish between benign and malignant tumours in the slaughterhouse; however, tumours in poultry are *commonly malignant* and may affect any part of the body. Ascites is often associated with tumours of the viscera.

MAREK'S DISEASE

Marek's disease is seen in chickens and occasionally turkeys, and is caused by a herpesvirus. The disease may be seen in one or more of the the ocular, skin, visceral or nervous forms. Visceral lesions can affect any organ but are most commonly seen in the ovary, testes, heart, liver, proventriculus and kidneys.

In the acute form there is infiltration of lymphoid tumours in gonads, lungs, heart, muscle and skin. The acute form may cause death with few or no symptoms other than small lymphoid tumours in the viscera.

In the chronic form the lymphoid tumours are larger, pale, circumscribed and widely dispersed. In some cases nerves are visibly enlarged, with a change in colour from white to grey or yellow. The nerves most obviously affected are the brachial, sciatic and coeliac plexus, with paralysis seen in the 'classical form' with sciatic nerve involvement.

Judgement
Carcase and offal should be considered unfit for human consumption.

AVIAN LEUCOSIS COMPLEX

Avian leucosis complex embraces a number of diseases of poultry which are characterized by proliferation of the leucocytes. Lesions of leucosis and Marek's disease can be very similar. Four forms of the disease are recognized:

- *Lymphoid leucosis*: tumours almost invariably involve liver, spleen and cloacal bursa. The tumours are soft, smooth and glistening, and the cut surface appears slightly greyish to creamy white. The growths may be nodular or diffuse and in the latter case the liver can be extremely large.
- *Myeloid leucosis*: the lesions can again be diffuse or nodular. The diffuse form usually affects the liver, spleen and kidneys with a greyish infiltration. The organ can have a mottled or granular appearance.
- *Erythroleucosis*: the most characteristic lesion seen is a diffuse enlargement of the liver and spleen and, to a lesser extent, the kidneys. The organs are usually cherry-red to dark mahogany in colour and are soft and friable. The bone marrow is very soft or watery, dark blood-red or cherry-red, and haemorrhages may be present.
- *Osteopetrosis*: this disease is manifest in a thickening of the long bones occurring first in the diaphyses. On palpation and inspection the tibiotarsal bone is thicker and smoother than normal.

Judgement
Carcase and offal should be considered unfit for human consumption.

Contamination

FAECAL CONTAMINATION AND CONTAMINATION FROM THE CONTENTS OF THE ALIMENTARY TRACT

Contamination of carcases and equipment may result from the rupture of pendulous crops, containing sour-smelling material, during processing.

This may be avoided by the rejection of affected birds at the whole bird inspection point or, alternatively, affected turkeys and other birds in good condition may be detained and the crop trimmed out prior to evisceration.

Judgement
1. Contamination occurring where the skin is cut or the muscle exposed, e.g. the vent cut or the neck area, should be removed by trimming the affected surface.
2. Contamination of the skin can usually be washed off using a water spray *provided this is done immediately after the contamination took place* and the spray is of low pressure with a plentiful supply of water.
3. Slight to moderate contamination of the carcase cavity may be washed out using a spray, over which the carcase can be positioned vertically.
4. Gross contamination of the carcase cavity renders the whole carcase and offal totally unfit. However, it may be possible to salvage wings, fillets and neck, providing the necessary trimming is carried out hygienically.
5. Contaminated livers and hearts should always be considered unfit for human consumption.
6. Poultry meat, carcases and/or offal affected with general contamination by faecal material, bile, grease, disinfectants, etc. should be considered unfit for human consumption.

BILE STAINING

Any part of the carcase or offal affected with bile staining should be trimmed.

POULTRY MEAT FALLING FROM THE LINE OR CONVEYOR

Judgement
1. Offal falling onto the floor or any other potentially contaminated surface should be considered unfit.
2. Carcases or offal falling into a feather flume or evisceration trough should be considered unfit.
3. Carcases falling onto the floor or any other potentially contaminated surface should be judged as such.
4. Portions or deboned poultry meat falling onto the floor or any other potentially contaminated surface should be considered unfit.

CONTAMINATION FROM PLUCKING MACHINES

Judgement
Where plucking machines break the skin, the underlying musculature should be considered to be contaminated and trimmed from the carcase.

Birds falling into feather flumes or evisceration troughs are grossly contaminated and are rejected as unfit.

Missing viscera

Carcases presented with no viscera should not be passed as fit for human consumption.

Guidelines on trimming

Trimming must be carried out under the supervision of the inspectorate. The selection of lesions or parts that require trimming must not be delegated to the management of the slaughterhouse.

Minor blemishes such as bruising may be trimmed at one of the post-mortem inspection points – preferably that following evisceration, to reduce contamination of the exposed flesh. Trimming of these carcases may be delayed until after chilling, providing that:

- The carcases are segregated and remain identifiable.
- There is no risk of contamination to other carcases.
- Trimming is done under the constant supervision of an inspector.

Trimming of more serious conditions involving infection, e.g. septic back wounds in turkeys, air sacculitis with mucopurulent exudate, or moderate contamination by intestinal contents, is usually impracticable with high line speeds, and in these cases an adjacent trimming area should be provided.

Most trimming should be carried out by staff supplied by management. The mode of trimming may be adapted to suit the requirements of management, providing that all affected parts are removed. Care should be taken to ensure that there is no unnecessary wastage.

The weight of trimmed parts removed under the supervision of the inspectorate should be noted daily, or more often if necessary.

References

1. Bayliss PA, Hinton MH. *Appl Animal Behav Sci* 1990; **28**: 93.
2. Gregory NG, Austin SD. *Vet Record* 1992; **131**: 501–3.
3. Griffiths GL. *Br Vet J* 1985; **141**: 312–14.

CHAPTER 10

Small Producers

Introduction

Throughout the world there are people who produce for sale, small numbers of poultry carcases or small amounts of poultry meat or poultry meat products. They present a particular problem to the food hygienist or legislator as they carry out their activities in small premises which frequently do not have the same standards or facilities as those provided in the larger premises. It would, however, be unrealistic to expect small producers to build a processing plant to the same standards of structure and equipment that are necessary for the large producer, but to a person who suffers an attack of food poisoning, it is irrelevant whether the food was prepared in small or large premises. However, if the customer has a complaint it is easier, in most cases, to find out who manufactured the product or who produced the carcase if they were purchased from a local producer, than if they were purchased in a supermarket. So a small producer who sells directly to the customer does have a strong incentive to ensure that standards are adequate.

The role of the small producer

Niche markets

For economic survival, small producers of poultry meat have to find a niche in the market which does not bring them into direct competition with the large producers. They can do this by supplying small numbers of carcases or cuts either directly to the final consumer at a market or to a local butcher who wants a small amount of poultry. Another possibility is to market a product which is considered superior to the mass-produced one and hence can be sold at a higher price, but which would be uneconomic for the large producer because the market is relatively small, e.g. some farmers slaughter quail, guinea fowl or geese, and a few slaughter the very young broiler as poussin which weighs around 0.5 kilograms. The customer who buys from a farm shop is aware that the product has been produced on that farm which they can see, by the farmer who they can meet, rather than in a large factory, and this is another opening used by small producers. Other producers slaughter poultry for religious communities who require the birds to be slaughtered in a certain way. The birds are normally reared on the slaughterhouse owner's own premises although birds can be reared by other farmers on contract or birds can be purchased on the market.

The small poultry meat product manufacturer has a large choice about what can be sold on the market. Again, a niche can be created by using different recipes, perhaps with herbs, spices or marinades, regional dishes, or even family recipes. These specialities can be sold locally and the shopkeeper will hope to develop a clientele who will return for more; the recipes may even be modified to suit local tastes. The large producer has to sell country-wide through supermarkets, and therefore has to aim for a blander taste which should suit most palates. The small producer frequently manufactures meat products at the back of a retail shop or farm shop, and this permits the sharing of facilities between the two premises so that investment and overheads are kept to a minimum, compared with the larger producer who has, however, the economies of size.

Inevitably many small businesses are looking for ways of expanding and becoming more profitable. To do this they can extend the area in which they sell or extend their product range. However, with this expansion comes the dangers of poor control of hygiene. The production rooms can become too busy or the chillers may be unable to deal with the increased load. Transport over longer distances may become necessary, and the vans may be unable to maintain the correct temperature of the product over these longer journeys. It is not easy for small producers to get bigger, and many ambitious projects fail because management do not think out the repercussions of the growth, either in hygiene standards or in the ability to sell the increased production.

Definition of 'small'

Legislators find difficulty in defining 'small' in relation to the small producer, which they have to do in order to ensure some uniformity of enforcement. Some legislation may restrict the area in which the product can be sold to the local authority area in which the premises are situated. Alternatively the sales may be restricted to the local market. However, it is not easy to define an area in a way that does not penalize some producers, such as those who live on the boundary of one area and want to sell in the nearest town which may be in the neighbouring area. Other legislators like to control the size of the throughput by limiting the number of carcases produced or the weight of the products which can be sold. It is easier to monitor if the numbers apply to a daily production, although this does not suit poultry farmers who, for instance, may want to have a yearly production quota which allows them to concentrate their production at certain times, such as Christmas for turkey producers. If the criterion is the weight of the final product which is sold, the producer has to maintain records and these will be used by the enforcing authority to check that the producer keeps within the legal limits. This can lead to problems as it is difficult to check whether the records are correct and they may not be acceptable in court if a prosecution is brought.

Another definition of 'small' may be that it has to be a family business associated with a farm where the poultry is reared, the 'producer exemption'. The poultry from these premises are generally slaughtered on the farm and sold from the farm shop or at a local market. Other suggestions for a definition include a limit on the number and type of outlets from which the products may be sold, or a limit on the variety of poultry products that can be made on small premises. There is some merit in these suggestions, particularly the restriction on the variety of products, as some processes are potentially more dangerous than others, e.g. vacuum packaging. However, it is more satisfactory to ensure that management and staff are properly trained, than to try to legislate against certain products, as all products are potentially dangerous.

The European Union, in Directive 92/116/EEC, has decided to use the number of birds slaughtered as one of their criteria for defining 'small'. Slaughterhouses with a throughput of less than 10 000 birds per year and where the sales are only on the local market, are defined as 'small' and are exempt from the directive. This means that the national rules of the individual countries apply. Slaughterhouses with a throughput of less than 150 000 birds per year or cutting premises handling 3 tonnes of cut-up meat or less per week, are classed as small but have to comply with the directive, which has some different requirements for small premises. However, sales from these premises cannot go across borders to other European Union countries but are restricted to the local market. The USA has a similar procedure, whereby only poultry meat produced in federally approved and inspected premises may cross state borders.

The European Union has also introduced a directive (92/5/EEC as amended by Directive 92/45/EEC and read with Commission Decision 94/383/EEC) that applies to meat products. The documents define non-industrial or small meat product premises, as premises where production does not exceed 7.5 tonnes of finished meat products or 1 tonne of *foie gras* per week. They have to comply with the conditions which apply to non-industrial premises and can only have a national health mark. The difficulties in legally defining 'small' are demonstrated in these directives.

Traditional poultry production

Some farmers produce poultry carcases in a traditional way and claim that these are better-tasting and produced under higher standards of welfare than the mass-produced, fast-growing bird which goes to the supermarkets. These traditional carcases, however, cost more. The French '*Label Rouge*' traditional free range poultry is one of these types. In this scheme, supported by the Ministry of Agriculture, criteria are laid down for the production of these carcases. The breeds are selected for slower growth than the mass-produced birds, and there are strict conditions for the diet, e.g. no animal matter is allowed in the food. The birds are reared under traditional free range conditions and there is a minimum slaughter age of 81 days. Most of the carcases from birds reared under these conditions are sold '*effilé*', which means that the intestine has been removed through the vent, leaving the remainder of the offal in the cavity of the carcase. To monitor disease in these carcases, all the partially eviscerated carcases are inspected by meat inspectors, and at least 5% of carcases have to be completely eviscerated so that they can be fully inspected. There are problems with this partial inspection, as disease conditions in the viscera may be missed. However, all of the partially uneviscerated carcases are inspected, so that only normal-looking carcases are passed fit for human consumption. If disease is found in a number of birds the whole batch has to be fully eviscerated and inspected.

In other countries the 'New York dressed' carcases, also known as long-legged or uneviscerated poultry carcases, used to be common. There were advantages to this type of carcase. Traditionally the birds were killed by dislocation of the neck which also broke the blood vessels in the neck, allowing the blood to collect under the skin. They were then plucked by hand without the use of water. The skin was not cut or broken during these processes and it remained dry. During storage a dry, cool atmosphere was maintained. The bacteria do not appear to migrate through the intestinal wall of these carcases and bacterial growth on the skin is limited by the dryness, the cool temperature and an intact surface. This is, therefore, a satisfactory way of storing poultry carcases and ensuring that bacterial growth is limited. The meat from the hung carcases has a slightly gamy flavour, and becomes tender with hanging. After several days a green colouration can appear around the vent area and spread up the back of the carcase, and the meat becomes very gamy tasting and even inedible. However, in winter, turkey carcases can be hung for 20 or more days in a well-ventilated room and still be fit to eat. Before the bird can be eaten it has to be eviscerated and the head removed. Cuts have to be made during these processes and spoilage can then occur fairly rapidly, particularly on the cut surfaces.

There were two main hygienic problems with the New York dressed poultry which the legislators had to consider. Firstly, the carcase could not be properly inspected. If inspectors suspected disease in a carcase they used to cut between the ribs to inspect the liver, but this did not detect all the diseased birds. Secondly, the evisceration was delayed as long as possible to maintain the dry intact skin, and frequently the evisceration was done in a butcher's shop where there was a risk of contaminating other foods in the shop.

New York dressed poultry are still produced in some countries within the European Union, where their production is now controlled by Council Directive 92/116/EEC, to ensure that the carcases are properly inspected and produced hygienically. The 'Traditional Farm Fresh' turkeys in the UK are an example, being produced by a group of turkey farmers who are independently inspected to ensure that the turkeys are produced to the standards of welfare and production laid down by their Association. The turkeys may be bred to produce a slower-growing, heavier bird than the mass-produced ones. They can be black, bronze or white types. They are reared under good welfare conditions, sometimes on free range, to grow to the size required by the customers, by which time the heavier birds can be at least 20 weeks old. The slaughter of these birds is either by breaking the neck, or by stunning and cutting the blood vessels as performed in the large premises. The Humane Slaughter Association in England has produced a leaflet on the manual slaughter of turkeys (1). This recommends that for small birds, breaking the neck can be done by jerking the bird's head back while holding the legs with the other hand. For bigger birds, weighing more than 3 kg, they recommend that the neck be trapped under a heavy bar or preferably by using a cone which holds the bird while stretching the neck by means of a lever attached to the stand holding the cone.

Defeathering is normally carried out by dry plucking using manual labour, although some producers use scalding and wet plucking. The carcases are then hung in refrigerated stores held at a temperature of 4 °C or less. This ensures that most of the bacteria that can cause food poisoning, e.g. *Salmonella*, are not able to multiply. After a maximum of 15 days storage, the carcases are either eviscerated in the slaughterhouse or in a separate room in a licensed cutting premises, and the meat inspection of carcase and viscera is carried out in the same way as for other poultry. The legislation from the European Community, therefore, overcame the main public health risks associated with the old-style New York dressed poultry. Other species of birds are also produced to these standards; geese and ducks can also undergo a wax stripping to remove the smaller feathers which are difficult to remove by the other methods.

Another distinctive type of small poultry production is that associated with the production of *foie gras* from geese. The geese are force-fed to ensure that they produce a heavy, fatty liver. The European Union permits the stunning, bleeding and plucking of birds specially reared for this production, to be carried out on the farm in a special slaughter room. The uneviscerated carcase then has to be moved to an approved cutting premises equipped with a special room where the carcase is eviscerated and inspected in accordance with the normal requirements. During this evisceration the liver is removed and can be subsequently used in the manufacture of the special pâté.

Design and construction of small premises

The premises used by small producers must comply with the general requirements (see Chapter 3). However, because of the low throughput there are not the long hours of continuous production that are normal in large premises. Therefore, although hygiene of operation must always be of a high standard (see Chapter 7), some concessions for batch processing in the design of the premises are permitted.

On some slaughter premises the birds walk from their rearing houses to the slaughterhouse, and the route they take must be clean so that their feet do not get dirty. If the birds are brought into the slaughterhouse in crates, or crates are used to transport the products, there should be facilities for cleaning these crates. This may be done outside the buildings on a suitable area of drained concrete, with a supply of running water and disinfectant. Animals, other than the birds for slaughter, should be kept off the site, and anything that is likely to taint or contaminate the poultry meat or products, such as manure or slurry from the farm, must be keep well away from the food-producing areas.

Storage rooms for wrapping and packaging materials may be required, and refrigerated storage should be provided for the products, carcases or cut meat produced on the premises. If the premises is situated at the back of a shop which already has refrigerated storage, this may be used for the meat or products provided there is no risk of cross-contamination between the stored foods. If the carcases go immediately to a retail shop or to premises for further treatment and these premises are only a short distance away in terms of travelling time, then provided the transport is satisfactory and can maintain a low temperature, refrigerated storage for carcases may again be unnecessary in the slaughterhouse. There may be a need for separate storage, some refrigerated, for the raw materials held on premises which manufacture meat preparations or meat products. Boxed carcases, meat or products must not be stored in the same rooms as carcases, meat or products that are not in a box. Containers that are easy to clean and can be stored off the ground should be provided for meat and edible food, as well as lockable containers for unfit meat. There must be facilities for cleansing and disinfecting containers, and these may be cleaned in workrooms at the end of a shift. There should be adequate lighting, which should be equivalent to 220 lux in workrooms and 540 lux at inspection points. Lights should be shatterproof or protected by a shatterproof shade.

Changing rooms with lockers, toilets and wash-hand basins, and facilities for washing boots and aprons, should be provided, although in the smallest premises lockers need not be in a room but may be located in a corridor. Staff entering the buildings must have facilities for washing their boots and putting on protective clothing. Some facilities for the official inspectors to change into protective clothing should also be provided. Sometimes the small premises are associated with other premises, for instance a shop where the same staff may serve customers and work in the slaughterhouse or processing room. If toilet facilities are available on the site they may be used for both premises provided there are hand-washing facilities available of the standard required by legislation, and dirt is not taken into the food premises by dirty protective clothing. Toilets must not open directly into any room where food is present, and a ventilated lobby should be provided.

Equipment for cleansing and disinfecting the whole of the premises must be available and have its own storage area. Depending on what is delivered to and removed from the premises, there may be a requirement for reception bays and dispatch bays. If delivered materials and dispatched products are boxed, then a canopy over the bays may be adequate, rather than a sealed bay which is normally required. Refrigerated or insulated lorries or vans should be used for dispatch, the type of vehicle depending on the distance that the materials have to travel and how many drop-off points there are. Where there are many drop-off points to retail shops on one delivery route, an insulated van will be inadequate to maintain a low temperature, particularly in summer, so a refrigerated van should normally be provided. The box of the refrigerated vehicle should be brought down to the transit temperature of the product before loading is allowed to begin.

Poultry meat products

In poultry meat product manufacturing premises, the number of rooms required depends entirely on the processes being carried out. In most premises batch processing is carried out, i.e. the raw meat is prepared at one time, stored under refrigeration, and then it is all processed together. Where this happens the preparation of the raw meat should take place in one room and the processing and handling of the processed food should take place in another. It can be argued that only one room is required, providing the raw materials are all removed after preparation and the room is cleansed and disinfected before being used for processed food. However, the main cause of food poisoning with poultry products is recontamination after processing, and there will always be a risk of this if the raw preparation room is also used for handling the processed product. It is safer, therefore, to have two separate rooms.

The most frequent processing will be by heat, and the room used for cooking should be well ventilated to control condensation and the ambient temperature. The meat should be heated to at least 75 °C throughout, and this temperature should be maintained for at least 2 minutes; it is normal, however, to ensure that a higher temperature is reached. After heating the product must be cooled, either by spraying the fully wrapped product with cold water, or in a chiller which has to be capable of quickly bringing the temperature of the product down to 10 °C or less. When the product has been cooked and chilled it may be brought back into the processing room for any further processing and for wrapping, providing the room and all the equipment has been thoroughly cleansed and disinfected since the heating was carried out. The wrapped product is then normally put into a cleaned, dry, plastic crate, and this may also take place in the same room. If the food is smoked, a special room is required which must be properly ventilated, unless smoking is carried out at a separate time from the handling or processing of other foods.

If the process is continuous, as distinct from batch processing, a ventilated extra room must be provided for any further processing like cutting, deboning, wrapping and packing the meat product. During these processes the products must be kept cool.

The subsequent cooling and storage of the product must take place in a refrigerated store. The temperature depends on the type of product and how long it is to be stored, but should normally be no more than 5 °C.

Poultry slaughterhouses

Where there is a small throughput, the number of rooms needed in the slaughterhouse can vary, depending on the final product. There has to be a bay for the reception of live birds. If the birds are reared on the same premises as the slaughterhouse, the poultry may be brought by hand or in crates, sometimes on a trailer, or sometimes the birds walk to slaughter. In the reception bay the birds may be placed in shackles to convey them to the next room or they may be moved from one room to another by hand. The next room is for slaughtering and defeathering. The birds are stunned prior to bleeding, unless the slaughter is for certain religious communities when stunning is not permitted. Stunning can be carried out using an electrified water bath when the birds are suspended from shackles or they can be stunned by using an electrified knife or an electrified V-shaped stunner into which the head is placed (Figure 10.1). If the killing is done by incising the blood vessels in the neck, then a trough will be required to collect the blood. Sometimes the birds are placed into cones after cutting the blood vessels, and suspended over a trough (Figure 10.2).

Plucking may be done manually or by using plucking machines. Some of these machines batch-pluck the scalded birds by spinning several birds inside a rotating drum which drags the feathers from the birds as they rotate (Figure 10.3). Other machines are smaller versions of the ones used in large-scale premises. In yet another method the birds are presented manually to a revolving cylinder which drags the feathers from the skin (Figure 10.4); these cylinders may be fitted with rubber flails or the feathers may be caught

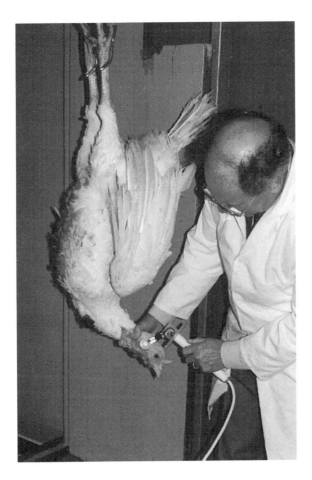

Figure 10.1 Hand-held electric stunner. (With kind permission of Poultryman (UK) Ltd.)

Figure 10.2   Bleeding cones. (With kind permission of Poultryman (UK) Ltd.)

Figure 10.3   Batch drum plucker. (With kind permission of Poultryman (UK) Ltd.)

Figure 10.4 Removal of wing feathers. (With kind permission of Poultryman (UK) Ltd.)

within channels in the cylinders, and the birds can be plucked either wet or dry by this type of machine.

The carcases are then moved into a second room for evisceration and further preparation – the room must be large enough to keep these two operations some distance apart. Evisceration is normally performed manually in these small premises, with the carcases either suspended from shackles or placed on tables. A lockable container should be provided to hold unfit or inedible meat or carcases. The carcases may be spray-washed after completion of evisceration to remove any contamination, but if the evisceration has been completed satisfactorily this washing can be omitted, leaving the skin relatively dry. The carcases may then be suspended on A frames or 'Christmas tree' shackles for chilling. These A-frames are constructed so that carcases will not drip onto the carcases below, and are on wheels so that they can be pushed into the chillers. The edible offal may be chilled on trays placed in trolleys which keep the containers off the floor. Refrigerated storage for cooling and storing the carcases should also have lockable facilities for holding carcases that need further examination. This can be an area that can be partitioned off, with the partitions placed against the wall when not in use. If the carcases are to go to an adjacent butcher's shop, a chiller or freezer in the shop may be used for cooling providing it has been cleaned, disinfected and dried prior to filling.

Where evisceration is delayed, there has to be a holding period in refrigerated storage after the completion of defeathering. These birds are then brought out at a later date for evisceration which may take place in these small premises, possibly in the defeathering room, provided the room has been thoroughly cleansed and disinfected before the uneviscerated carcases are returned to the room. Evisceration can either take place on a table or with the carcases suspended from shackles. Containers for the removal of waste should be provided.

Cutting premises

Poultry cutting or deboning premises must comply with the general requirements listed above and in Chapter 3, and consist of a cutting room with a refrigerated reception storage room which may also be used as the dispatch chiller. However, boxed carcases or meat must not be held in the same store as carcases or meat that are not in a box. The temperature of the meat during storage and cutting must not be allowed to rise above 4 °C and so, unless the meat is handled quickly, an air-conditioned cutting room may be required.

Evisceration of carcases that have been hung uneviscerated for a maximum of 15 days or carcases used for the preparation of *foie gras* may take place in a cutting premises, but a separate room properly constructed and equipped for evisceration must be provided.

Hygiene of operation in small premises

Hygiene is important in small premises, where there may be greater risk of cross-contamination than in large manufacturing premises. The staff should wear clean waterproof footwear, overalls and aprons, and the hair should be covered. People working in small premises are more likely to be engaged in more than one task, and so stringent precautions should be taken if a person goes from one task to another. There is a risk of staff moving from one room to another without taking the proper precautions of cleaning hands and protective clothing. This is particularly dangerous if the person goes from a dirtier to a cleaner area. Where rooms are used at different times for different processes, they must be properly cleansed, disinfected and dried before the second process can start. The staff should also change their protective clothing and wash their hands between handling raw and processed food. Supervision of staff is probably not as strict as in larger premises, so all staff members should receive training in the hygiene of production. With fewer people working in the premises there is a risk that people who are ill may feel obliged to come to work. If one of the staff is suffering from food poisoning or an infected skin lesion, that person should not work with food until cleared by a medical practitioner.

Hygiene of production

The hygiene of production is also important (see Chapters 7 and 12). Temperature control is essential for carcases and raw meat, and it is also essential that heated products reach the correct temperature (over 75 °C), and that subsequent cooling to a temperature of 10 °C or lower is as rapid as possible.

There is always a possibility that familiarity will lead to slackness in ensuring that the process is properly monitored and hygiene is maintained at a high standard. Details of the process should be recorded, including the temperatures of the meat at various stages in the processing. Meat products which are to be eaten without any further heating are a high-risk product, and detailed monitoring and recording of the processes should be ensured. Thermometers should be calibrated at least at 6-monthly intervals. Recalling the details of the process is not easy after a day or two unless they are recorded at the proper time. There is also a risk that short cuts may be taken without awareness of the significance of the change.

Changes to the process must always be carefully considered from the hygiene aspect, as should any changes, however small, in the ingredients of a product. There are codes of practice for some types of products which should be followed. Hazard Analysis Critical Control Point (HACCP) procedures are expensive to arrange (see Chapter 7), and if the premises has been operating for some time it may not be necessary to carry out a full investigation. However, if a new process is introduced or there are alterations to an existing process, then a confirmatory visit from a consultant to ensure the process is safe is necessary. Unless an HACCP investigation is done properly it can give a false sense of security to management and therefore it should only be done in consultation with an expert.

Record keeping

It is necessary for the small producer to keep records of the source of the birds and any other raw materials used in the product, and also the processes used in each batch, in case of future problems with the product. The product or wrapping should be marked with a batch number so that if any problems arise the processing can be investigated and if necessary the whole batch withdrawn from sale.

Evisceration

Evisceration procedures can cause cross-contamination. In small premises the evisceration can take place on the suspended carcase or the carcase can be placed on a table. The incision around the vent should be made without any cutting into rectum or cloaca and the rectum must be pulled gently so that it does not retract into the abdominal cavity. Evisceration can be carried out using only the hands or an evisceration implement can be used. Care must be taken to ensure that the intestinal tract is not broken and that the proventriculus is removed with the abdominal organs. In the past the lungs would be removed at the same time, but it is probably more hygienic to take the lungs out separately as there is less chance of the intestines being broken. The neck should be removed after the carcase has been inspected if the meat is intended for human consumption. Delayed evisceration is usually carried out on a table, when the cooled fat makes it easier to remove the viscera without rupturing the intestinal tract. If contamination does take place during evisceration it should either be trimmed or washed away, ensuring that the contamination is not washed into the cavity of the carcase. Implements and the hands of the staff must be kept clean during the process by frequent washing, preferably between carcases. After evisceration the carcase and offal must be cooled as quickly as possible to 4 °C and stored at this temperature or below.

Cutting and deboning

During cutting or deboning of the carcase the implements must be kept clean and sterilized, the cutting should be performed quickly and the meat put back into refrigerated storage immediately the cutting is completed. The cutting room should be well ventilated to ensure it remains cool. The temperature of the meat should not rise above 4 °C during cutting or deboning so the carcases and meat must not be held in the cutting room for any longer than is necessary.

Cleaning

The cleansing and disinfection of small premises may be neglected, especially at busy times. Cleansing and disinfection must be carried out effectively at least once a day and more often if there is a build-up of dirt in the premises. Waste materials must not be allowed to pile up in the workroom but should be removed to the waste bay or collection point at regular intervals. The gross dirt should be removed with squeegees or brushes and then the equipment, walls and floors should be cleaned with water and a suitable detergent, which is subsequently washed away. The ceiling should also be kept clean. The walls, floors and equipment should then be sprayed with a food-quality disinfectant. Care must be taken that all the products are removed from the workrooms when the rooms are being cleansed and disinfected. Containers must be washed and disinfected after emptying and before being brought back into workrooms. There is also a risk that vermin may be attracted by badly stored waste and this must be prevented.

Sometimes premises are not used for long periods. An example of this is where 'Traditional Farm Fresh' poultry is only produced at Christmas and Easter. Prior to a long break it is important that the premises are properly cleansed and disinfected after completion of the final day's activities, otherwise the dirt can become caked onto the floor and equipment, making it difficult to clean at a later date. Equipment may need to be dismantled and stored elsewhere so that it can be kept clean and dry. Sometimes the rooms are used for other activities; this can lead to the entry of vermin, and also dust can spread throughout the premises. In all cases rooms (including floors, walls, ceiling or roofs) and equipment (including any refrigeration equipment) must be cleansed and disinfected and the disinfectant washed away before production starts again. It may be worth taking some swabs of the cleansed surfaces before starting work, and sending them to a laboratory for a bacteriological examination, to check that the cleaning is satisfactory. The results will not be immediately available, but if they are not satisfactory, a higher standard of cleaning must be carried out in the future. Cracks in any of the surfaces should be repaired to ensure that dirt is not able to accumulate.

In poultry meat product premises the rooms should be dry before production starts again after cleaning. Advice should be sought on the correct detergent and disinfectant to use, and certainly ordinary farm disinfectants should not be used.

Water samples should be collected when work starts again after a long period (or at least annually) and sent to a laboratory for bacteriological examination to ensure that it is still potable. Water pipes should be inspected to see that the plumbing has not been changed during a break, and particularly that there are no dead ends where bacteria can grow and contaminate the water (see Chapter 12).

Reference

1. Manual of slaughter of turkeys (December 1994) South Mimms, Potters Bar, Hertfordshire EN6 3PA, UK.

CHAPTER 11

Residues in Poultry Products

Introduction

Poultry meat and eggs have received much less bad publicity related to chemical residues than other meats. Red meat in particular has attracted much attention. Examples have been the scandal of meat from calves injected with growth hormones being used for baby food with bizarre results, and the detection of residues of organochlorine and sulpha drugs in meat imported into the USA. However, poultry used to be injected with stilboestrol, normally in pellet form, to reduce the male characteristics in male birds kept for fattening, so these substances have been used and could have occurred as a residue in poultry meat. Indeed, there were rumours of early puberty in children as a result of eating poultry meat containing residues of stilboestrol. The poultry industry at present does not seem to use hormones to any extent, although there is little published evidence that these substances have been investigated in any extensive testing programme of poultry meat.

Most drugs given to poultry are included in food or water, and then absorbed from the gut wall. With some agents such as the coccidiostats little absorption takes place, and most of the drug remains in the gut. Injected drugs usually reach a high level in the blood relatively quickly; if the injection was intramuscular the drug can remain concentrated at the injection site for some time. Slow-release pellets can also be inserted under the skin, so the risks of drug residues occurring are greater when drugs are injected. Some residues build up over a long time – e.g. cadmium in the kidneys – which is a problem in older animals. The young age at which poultry is slaughtered means this problem is rare in modern poultry production.

Pesticide residues are more likely to arise from inadvertent introduction in food rather than deliberate usage. Animal feed is a compounded material derived from a wide range of sources both in terms of ingredients and their country of origin. Pesticides have been controlled for many years and international levels have been laid down for trade; this ensures that only in exceptional circumstances do feed constituents carry high levels of pesticides. Nevertheless there is always a possibility that some poultry meat could be contaminated. Potential environmental pollutants may also cause residues in poultry meat. There are accepted maximum residue limits (MRLs) for a wide range of pesticides, and accepted limits for other environmental pollutants such as polychlorinated biphenyl, dioxin, lead, cadmium, arsenic and mercury.

There is increasing interest, both nationally and within groups of countries, to include poultry meat within official plans. The European Union (EU) has been working on a directive for several years. An EU working party is looking at MRLs for more substances, and there is also an international group set up by the Food and Agriculture Organization (FAO) of the United Nations and the World Health Organization (WHO) which is also investigating the same subject. When standards have been agreed it should allow trade between countries to pass more freely.

Testing for residues is carried out at specially equipped laboratories. It is important that the methods are clearly defined and that the laboratories have a means of confirming that they are testing to the correct standard. The EU has designated certain laboratories to be Community Reference Laboratories whose task is to assist the national laboratories and ensure that the results from all the national laboratories are consistent. Some of the testing is capable of finding extremely minute traces of a substance, so until MRLs are set for these substances the results may not be of much use from an enforcement aspect. However, the finding of the residue is significant and suggests an MRL is necessary.

Reasons for concern about residues

Various reasons for concern about drug residues have been put forward. The principal concerns are drug resistance, toxicity, allergy and barrier to trade.

Drug resistance

A wide variety of species and strains of micro-organisms cause disease. To counteract them, antibiotics are used to kill the targeted organism. However, organisms that are resistant to the antibiotic may survive and because of the lack of competition from the other organisms may establish themselves, giving rise to a drug-resistant organism which causes disease. Such resistant strains could infect both the initial host animal or other animals including humans. This problem has long been recognized, and wherever possible drugs used in animal husbandry should be different from those used in human medicine. This is observed to a degree, but not entirely, with respect to some of the more effective antibiotics such as the penicillins, tetracyclines and aminoglycosides such as neomycin.

Toxicity

Drugs are substances toxic to various forms of life whether they be bacteria, worms or other life forms such as protozoa, and there have been concerns that exposure over a lifetime to residue levels of such substances could induce undesirable effects in humans. This could take the form of adjusting the nature and levels of microflora in the gut, through to causing mutagenic, teratogenic or carcinogenic effects. A discussion document was published by the Fédération Européenne de la Santé Animale, addressing the effects of antimicrobial residues in gut flora (1).

Allergy

People can become allergic to drugs and among the better known of such effects is sensitivity to penicillins. Other drugs have been recognized to cause allergic reactions, although less commonly. Some people can react badly to penicillins and it is feared that exposure to drugs in meat could cause such a reaction. These allergic reactions could be extremely difficult to diagnose as they would appear only occasionally after the consumption of meat containing sufficient residue of the allergenic drug.

Barriers to trade

The presence of residues can be regarded as unacceptable in imported meat, and this can cause problems with trade. Thus countries wishing to protect their consumers and stop meat being imported could use the excuse that unacceptable levels of residues were present in some imported meat. If a substance is banned, any level is regarded as unacceptable.

It is to counter such international problems that MRLs for drug residues are being set at national and international levels so that trade can proceed, free from disputes of this nature.

Sources of residues in poultry meat

Drug residues can occur in poultry meat through improper use of these substances. The demand for drugs is high in the intensive production poultry industry because of the need to maximize growth rate and the financial consequences of disease outbreaks.

Drugs are most readily supplied to the birds via feed or water, less commonly by injections. Properly used, drugs should not give rise to residues of significance as they will have been licensed for use with due consideration to this possibility, and the level of supply and the length of withdrawal of the drug prior to slaughter will have been designated. However, failure to observe the instructions, for whatever reason, may produce a residue problem. Failure to observe withdrawal periods is the most common occurrence; overdosing, causing need for longer withdrawal periods, and inadvertent administration of medicated feed are also possible sources. Another, less likely source is pick-up from contaminated faeces, which has been suggested as a route in pig production.

Pesticide residues could arise from direct treatment of birds, from their housing or the source of the litter. However, contamination of feed is the greatest potential source of this group of residues.

Poultry meat contamination with other residue types is rarer, and where it does occur is most likely to be attributable to the feed. For example, aflatoxin residues could result from mouldy feed, as could nitrosamine, although both compounds are more likely to harm the birds than leave residues. The problem of nitrosamine toxicity first showed itself in the UK as the result of the death of a flock of turkeys fed with a contaminated feed.

The other environmental contaminants are most likely to arise from feed grown on contaminated land. Again, this source seems reasonably remote.

These problems are not restricted to the birds themselves but may arise in the eggs produced.

Control of drugs

Drugs have to be licensed prior to use and they should only be used under the conditions of the licence. In the UK licences are issued to pharmaceutical companies jointly by the Department of Health and the Ministry of Agriculture, Fisheries and Food. These government departments are advised by an independent group of experts. Pharmaceutical companies have to submit extensive data for the group's consideration, showing that the drug:

- Is effective against the disease being treated.
- Does not adversely affect the animals at the proposed treatment level.
- Production is safe to the company's staff.
- Has no adverse reaction on people handling the drug thereafter, e.g. feed manufacturers or farmers.

- Has residue levels in all edible tissue of the treated animals at acceptably low levels after cessation of treatment, so that the consumer is protected from any inadvertent intake of the drug.

Once these matters have been satisfactorily addressed the expert group will recommend the licensing of that particular formulation of the drug for the treatment of specific animal species with a recommended withdrawal period.

Poultry farmers have to withdraw medicated food for at least the recommended period before sending the birds for slaughter. This can be difficult if birds are thinned out, when some go for slaughter and others remain, but it is still the farmer's responsibility to ensure that those going for slaughter have not eaten medicated food or drunk medicated water for at least the withdrawal period of the medicine being used.

At present pharmaceutical companies can submit data to individual countries or make multistate application for licensing, but it is intended that in future, for EU countries, a single application to the European Medicines Evaluation Agency will suffice for the licensing of a drug throughout the EU. The agency will license both human and veterinary medicines, and in the case of the latter will seek the advice of the Committee for Veterinary Medicinal Products (CVMP) based in Brussels.

The CVMP Residues Working Group also recommend MRLs for drugs which they consider should be licensed. In arriving at an MRL they consider toxicological data packages which include the following information:

- Single dose and repeated dose toxicity.
- Reproductive effects, including reproduction itself and embryo and fetus toxicity.
- Teratogenic, mutagenic and carcinogenic data.
- Pharmacodynamic and pharmacokinetic information in laboratory species.
- Microbiological effects and where possible observations in humans.

From all these data a 'no observed effect' level is determined, and depending on the nature of the observed effect a safety factor of 100, 1000 or more is used to reduce this amount to an acceptable daily intake (ADI) figure. The size of the factor is based on the severity of the effect observed; mild toxic effects such as nausea warrant the smaller factor, while mutagenic or carcinogenic effects require the larger factors. From the ADI an MRL is established for the various edible tissues such as muscle, liver, kidney, fat, milk and eggs, based on the likely maximum intake of that tissue by an individual.

This approach provides the average individual with an additional safety factor over the ADI, as the daily maximum intakes used are improbably high, e.g. 300 g lean muscle, 100 g liver, 100 g egg per day (2).

All new drug applications will involve the determination of an MRL and
the withdrawal period necessary to achieve this MRL. Older drugs may not
have had an MRL specified at the time of licensing and these will now have
to have such a value determined. It is the aim of the CVMP to achieve a total
review of all drugs without MRLs by 1997. Table 11.1 lists MRLs defined
for a selection of drugs by the UK, the EU and the international WHO/FAO
Codex Alimentarius. It will be seen that there is variable coverage by these
bodies, from no MRL for the ionophore coccidiostats, such as lasalocid,
monesin and narasin, to a single MRL for ronidazole and streptomycin, to
complete cover for others such as sulphadimidine and penicillin. While the
values given generally agree, there are occasionally differences between the
various bodies.

Table 11.1 Maximum residue limits recommended by the UK, EU and
WHO/FAO, in µg per kg of tissue or fluid, for drugs used in poultry production.

Drug	UK (µg/kg)	EU (µg/kg)	WHO/FAO (µg/kg)
DES	0	0	0
Trenbolone	0	0	2 (all)
Amipicillin	50 (tissues)	4 (milk) 50 (tissues)	
Benzylpenicillin	50 (tissues)	4 (milk) 50 (tissues)	4 (all)
Chloramphenicol	10 (all)	10 (all)	—
Chlortetracycline	100 (tissues) 600 (kidney) 300 (liver)	100 (muscle, milk) 600 (kidney) 300 (liver)	
Nitrofurans	5 (all)	5 (tissues)	
Sulphadimidine	100 (all)	100 (all)	100 (tissues) 25 (milk)
Sulphaquinoxaline	100 (all)	100 (all)	100 (tissues)
Dimetridazole	10 (all)	10 (all)	—
Fenbendazole	1000 (liver) 10 (other tissues)	1000 (liver) 10 (muscle, kidney, fat, milk)	100 (meat, fat, kidney, milk) 500 (liver)
Lasalocid	—	—	—
Monensin	—	—	—
Narasin	—	—	—
Ronidazole	—	2 (all)	—
Streptomycin	1000 (all)	—	—
Tylosin	—	—	—

A more extensive and authoritative summary of the control of drugs may be found in KN Woodward's chapter on this topic in *'Food Contaminants: Sources and Surveillance'*(3).

Drug supply

Drugs may be supplied to the animal production industry as 'prescription only' medicines or be placed in the Pharmaceutical Merchants' List. As the terms suggest the former drugs require a veterinary prescription, whereas the latter may be supplied by merchants without direct veterinary supervision. Drugs by either route should only be used in line with the licence. Veterinarians may also choose to prescribe a drug outwith the licence; this requires a Veterinary Written Direction when the medicine is to be incorporated in feed.

It has been suggested that in the past the farming community had well-stocked pharmacies on farm and accusations were made of misuse of drugs. These pharmacies, it was suggested, had been built up through lack of control by the veterinarians, by easy access to merchants and through the desire of farmers to have stocks of drugs available against disease so that they could self-treat rather than bear the cost of a veterinarian's visit. It was further suggested that farmers misused these drugs and did not administer them as required by the licence. For example, it was suggested that animals were treated with double doses to speed recovery and once reasonably recovered were sold off before any further symptoms appeared, without observance of the withdrawal period. A number of procedures have been introduced to prevent such practices.

Drugs may be delivered to the animals by injections or orally, through feed or water. The oral routes are more common in the poultry industry.

The supply of drugs in feed may be from feed mills who introduce the drugs at approved levels into feed, or they may be added at the farm. Medicated feed producers must have the equipment to produce suitable uniform products in a safe and consistent manner. They must account for all the drugs entering and leaving their premises, and must consider their production procedures. Codes of practice for the UK have been issued by the Ministry of Agriculture, Fisheries and Food (4, 5). Thus, production of a feed to which a drug is added must be followed by a clean feed to ensure effective clear-out of the drug from the mill. This clean feed should then be used as the base of the next feed being treated with the same drug whenever it is next produced. This clean-down of the plant is essential before production of further feeds, whether they be fortified with other drugs or not.

Records of all feedstuffs put though the mill and the order in which they were produced have to be kept, as well as samples of the various feeds. Records of drugs in and out of the mill premises are also necessary, as well as records of who was supplied with the feeds. Mills in the UK are periodically inspected or audited by Pharmaceutical Society Inspectors who will be interested in all such records, as well as sight of the prescriptions supplied where appropriate.

Farm control

On farms, fortified feeds should be kept separate from normal feedstuffs. This is to ensure no cross-contamination of feed occurs. If feeds are kept in bins or silos, careful cleaning out of the fortified feed bins should be undertaken to exclude mistakes being made. This is just as true for fortified feeds with different drugs present as for normal feed. The reason for these precautions is that pockets of feed can remain in the storage bin and contaminate subsequent feeds. This could be disastrous for a finishing or non-fortified feed, or where the withdrawal time of the earlier feed is considerably longer than that of the new fortified feed.

The farm is now probably the least controlled part of the chain, as farmers may not have sufficient storage bins or sufficient labour to allow thorough control of fortified feeds. Another area of difficulty may be where automatic feed facilities are available. While the majority of the poultry houses may use this, a separate feed for finishing birds will be necessary.

Importance of drugs

The use of drugs has grown since they were introduced in the 1940s. A wide variety of drugs are now available for a range of purposes. Whereas in the earlier days drugs would only be used for therapeutic purposes at suitable dosage, they are now widely used routinely at low dosage for prophylactic or disease prevention purposes, or indeed purely for growth promotion. This prophylactic usage has developed as production methods have intensified. Large areas of the poultry industry with its highly intensive methods fall into this category.

Nature of drugs

The main categories of drugs used in poultry production are antibiotics, coccidiostats and anthelmintics. In the past hormones have been used for 'caponization', and with present interest in the beta-agonist compounds some rogue producers may be tempted to experiment, although evidence is that clenbuterol is not effective in poultry (6, 7). Both hormones and beta-agonists are banned substances in respect of their growth-promoting potential.

- The antibiotics cover a wide spectrum of substances, from the early drugs such as penicillins, tetracyclines, aminoglycosides and sulphonamides, to more modern drugs such as the fluoroquinolones, e.g. enrofloxacin and ciprofloxacin. Within each of these categories there are often many different drugs.
- Several different coccidiostats are available, and because of drug resistance problems poultry producers employ a policy of changing regularly from one drug to another.
- Anthelmintic (deworming) drugs include piperazine, a range of benzimidazoles and other potential drugs.

The most commonly used caponizing agent used was the synthetic substance diethylstilboestrol (DES), an oestrogen which used to be implanted in the neck of the bird so that after slaughter the remains of the DES pellet could be disposed of with the neck.

Testing for drug residues

The methodology used for drug residue analysis is variable both in terms of degree of sophistication and procedure. This is because of the wide variation in drug chemical structure and the matrices from which the drugs may be extracted. Unlike sports drug testing which relies on urine samples, or forensic alcohol analysis which deals with blood or urine, drug residues in animal tissues may come from blood or urine but more often from edible tissues (muscle, offal) or sometimes bile. The subject is reviewed in references 8 and 9. In poultry, blood, muscle, liver and occasionally bile are the target tissues, and testing of eggs is also performed.

Methodology can vary from the simple to the sophisticated. The skills of the analysts and their equipment may be tested to the full as concentrations involved are often less than 1 part per million, and sometimes even lower than 1 part per billion. The main approach relies on partitioning or chromatographic procedures after the drug residue has been extracted from the chicken tissue by aqueous or organic solvents. This partitioning can be between immiscible liquids, e.g. water and petrol, or between solid and liquid. A simple example of chromatography is the separation of an inkspot on a wetted piece of newspaper into its constituent coloured dyes. This is an example of liquid chromatography (LC) where a mobile liquid is passed over a stationary solid matrix and substances in the liquid partition between the liquid and solid phases. Those substances preferring the liquid phase pass through the solid quickly, while the substances that have greater affinity for the solid pass more slowly. A similar effect occurs if the mobile phase is a gas and the stationary phase is a solid (more often a solid with a liquid coated on or tightly bound to the solid surface); this is the basis of the procedure known as gas–liquid chromatography (GLC) where the partitioning effects of the separating substances depend on their volatility as well as their affinity for the gaseous and liquid phases. Techniques for LC and GLC have been greatly refined and are now an extremely powerful tool for analysts.

Methodology can be simplified into three stages: extraction, clean-up and determination.

- Extraction involves homogenization of the tissue with water or more often an organic solvent. This should remove the drug along with a wide variety of co-extractives from which the drug has to be separated.
- The clean-up stage normally involves a variety of crude chromatographic fractionations aimed at separation of the drug from the co-extractives.
- The drug is often subjected to refined chromatographic separation and determination using procedures such as LC or GLC.

Pressure is growing upon the analyst to confirm any positive findings by either using a totally different method or using a technique such as mass spectrometry (MS) which gives a unique 'fingerprint' of the drug. This 'fingerprint' arises from subjecting the drug molecule to high energy bombardment by electrons which causes the molecule to disintegrate into characteristic subsidiary pieces which are separated by size and which are unique for every molecule. Often this technique can be performed by linking the LC or GC to the MS, with the latter acting as a sophisticated detector. Typical analytical flow processes are shown in Table 11.2, as well as a

Table 11.2   General stages in analytical procedure for determination of drug residues.

General stage	General procedures
1. Extraction	Homogenization of samples with aqueous or organic solvent AND
↓	Separation by filtration or centrifugation
2. Clean-up	Liquid–liquid partition AND/OR
↓	Solid–liquid partition
3 Determination	Gas–liquid chromatography OR
	High-performance liquid chromatography Thin layer chromatography

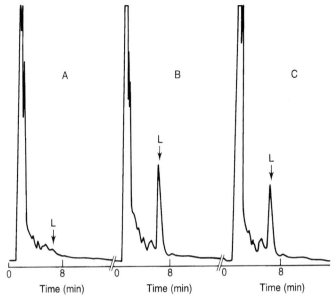

Figure 11.1 Typical LC chromatogram for lasalocid: (A) blank poultry muscle extract; (B) blank poultry muscle extract plus lasalocid standard (0.010 mg/kg); (C) spiked poultry muscle extract (0.010 mg/kg).

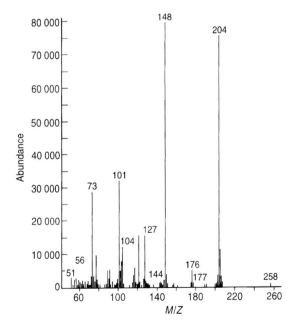

Figure 11.2 Typical mass spectrum of levamisole.

typical LC trace for lasalocid (Figure 11.1) and an MS spectrum for levamisole (Figure 11.2).

In addition to the above, antibiotics can be detected using microbiological inhibition tests. There are a whole gamut of such tests but the one widely used within the EU is the method described by Bogaerts and Wolf (10) and is known as the four plate test (FPT). Here a core of meat is taken from the sample, from which a number of small discs are cut. These are placed on four separate media plates and their juices are allowed to diffuse into the media for about 3 hours before the micro-organisms seeded in the plates are allowed to grow in an incubator. Three of the plates have different pH levels and the fourth contains a different micro-organism; this ensures that an antibiotic will affect at least one plate, although the test is relatively insensitive to sulphonamides. Where antibiotic has leached from the meat disc, growth is inhibited and a clear zone around the disc is observed. Provided this is greater than 2 mm in width the sample is regarded as antibiotic positive. A representative plate is shown in Figure 11.3 and some indication of the sensitivity to a range of drugs given in Table 11.3. This type of testing is easy and cheap to perform and can be applied to many samples, although it neither identifies the antibiotic nor allows a concentration to be determined. This is in contrast to the chromatographic procedures described above which do identify and quantify the drug, but are expensive and have low sample throughput.

The cheaper procedures can be used to screen many samples for potential positives which can subsequently be tested by the more sophisticated methods for positive identification and quantification.

Immunochemical procedures may become important in poultry residue work in the future. These techniques can be used at the 'clean-up' stage of a chemical assay or at the 'determination' stage. They depend on a specific

Table 11.3 Minimum inhibitory concentrations of antibiotics by the four plate test.

Antibiotic	Lower limit of sensitivity (μg/g tissue)
Penicillin	0.03
Neomycin	0.2
Chloramphenicol	10
Chlortetracycline	0.1
Oxytetracycline	0.5
Erythromycin	0.1
Bacitracin	0.2
Sulphadimidine	0.5
Streptomycin	0.5
Trimethoprim	2

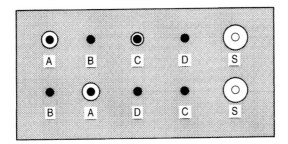

Figure 11.3 Representative four-plate test. Discs of meat 0.5 cm in diameter (dark circles) are placed on a plate of medium covered by growing micro-organism. A standard antibiotic absorbed onto a disc of filter paper (clear circle) is run as a check of the method. Sample A is positive, shown by the surrounding clear zone of growth inhibition produced by diffused antibiotic; samples B and D are negative and sample C is doubtful and needs to be re-run. Sample S is the standard antibiotic control.

antibody being produced to a drug and this antibody having the ability to recognize the drug in a complex mixture of other substances. Antibody and analyte have been likened to a lock and key. At the 'clean-up' stage the analyte in an aqueous mixture is passed over the antibody immobilized in a stationary substance. The analyte is specifically removed from the mixture and, after disengagement from the antibody, analysed. This is known as immunoaffinity chromatography.

A similar principle of antibody–analyte interaction may be employed to allow an assay to be developed where the quantity of analyte present may be determined enzymically (enzyme-linked immunosorbent assay, ELISA) or radiochemically (radioimmunoassay, RIA).

Surveillance requirements and results

Drug residues

The European Union Directive 86/496/EEC (11) lists the classes of drugs to be tested (Table 11.4) and requires each member state to submit a plan of how they intend to test their animal production for the presence of drug residues. This directive applies to red meat only, but it is the intention to extend it to cover poultry as well, by means of another directive.

Because there has been no need for routine surveillance of poultry to date within the EU, information about the occurrence of drug residues is limited. The UK Ministry of Agriculture, Fisheries and Food has undertaken some

Table 11.4 Annex 1 of European Union Directive 86/469/EEC lists the groups of residues that require tests in the EU.

Groups common to all member states

Group I	Stilbenes, stilbene derivatives, their salts and esters
	Thyreostatic substances
	Other substances with oestrogenic, androgenic or gestagenic action
Group II	Authorized substances
	Natural (endogenous) hormones
Group III	Inhibitors: antibiotics, sulphonamides and similar antimicrobial substances
	Chloramphenicol

Specific groups

Group I	Other medicines
	Endoparasitic and ectoparasitic substances
	Tranquillizers and beta-blockers
	Beta-agonists
	Other veterinary medicines
Group II	Other residues
	Contaminants present in feeding stuffs
	Contaminants present in the environment
	Other substances

work as part of its consumer protection activities and limited studies have been made elsewhere. Some results are shown in Table 11.5 (12, 13)

There does not appear to be a major problem with drug residues in poultry and what there is, is at a low incidence. There are occasional examples of antibiotic residues being detected, but it has been many years since a hormone residue has been found and that only at a period when stilbenes were permitted for caponization. The picture is similar for coccidiostatic drugs in poultry meat, but there does seem to be a limited problem with residues of these substances appearing in eggs. Why this occurs is not clear, but residues of lasalocid and nicarbazin have been observed in eggs. As these drugs should not be used in laying birds, it is assumed that the drug is lodged in the oviduct prior to the birds coming into lay, or the drug is being inadvertently supplied to the laying birds in some way. Whether a similar problem exists with other coccidiostats will doubtless be investigated.

Pesticide residues

Pesticides, like drugs, come in many chemical forms but there are two broad groupings, the organochlorine (OC) and the organophosphorus (OP) compounds, with many members in each group. There are other classes but these are for more specific uses. The OP group tend to be unstable and hydrolyse to relatively harmless metabolites, whereas the OCs tend to be very stable chemically and also to accumulate in the fat of animals. Therefore poultry ingesting OC pesticides from feed may over their lifespan accumulate notable levels of these compounds.

Another source of residues in poultry was recognized in the 1980s. This was the wood preservative pentachlorophenol (PCP), which is very widely used. Poultry units often use wood shavings in litter and for a time residues of PCP occurred in poultry. This problem was circumvented by insisting

Table 11.5 Surveillance results for drug residues in poultry and eggs.

Year	Residue	Matrix	Positives	Sample numbers
1985	Stilbenes	Poultry muscle	0	38
1986	Stilbenes	Poultry bile	0	205
1987	Stilbenes	Poultry bile	0	127
1990	Stilbenes	Poultry bile	0	84
1989	Sulphaquinoxaline	Poultry muscle	2	102
		Eggs	0	205
1989	Monensin	Eggs	0	205
	Narasin	Chicken muscle	0	100
	Salinomycin	Turkey muscle	0	103
1989	Lasalocid	Chicken muscle	1	100
		Turkey muscle	0	103
		Eggs	1	100
1993	Lasalocid	Turkey muscle	0	109
		Chicken muscle	0	217
		Chicken liver	0	199
		Eggs (free range)	16	213
		Eggs (other)	14	213
1993	Nicarbazin	Eggs (free range)	3	213
		Eggs (other)	3	213
1993	Sulphonamides	Turkey muscle	1	109
		Chicken muscle	2	216
		Chicken liver	1	198
		Eggs (free range)	3	213
		Eggs (other)	3	213
1993	Tetracycline	Chicken muscle	0	214
		Chicken liver	0	196
		Turkey muscle	0	107

Results for years 1985–90 are taken from reference 12; results for 1993 are from reference 13.

that all shavings for litter had to be certified as arising from non-preserved timber. This approach removed the problem through the cooperation of both the timber supplying industry and the poultry industry.

The Ministry of Agriculture, Fisheries and Food in England and Wales in its consumer protection role has for years run surveillance programmes for

Table 11.6   Pesticide residues in poultry.

Year	Material analysed	Pesticide	Residue detected	Sample numbers	MRL (mg/kg) (Sample numbers above MRL)
1987	Poultry feed	α-HCH	10	31	0.2 (2 of 31)
		Dieldrin	1	31	0.01 (1 of 31)
		DDT	1	31	0.05 (1 of 31)
1988	Poultry feed	α-HCH	5	29	0.2 (3 of 29)
	Pheasant	α-HCH	4	15	1 (0)
		DDE	5	15	1 (0)
		Dieldrin	1	15	0.2 (0)
		DDT	1	15	1 (0)
1989	UK chicken	α-HCH	22	90	1 (0)
		Dieldrin	2	90	0.2 (0)
		DDT	3	90	1 (0)
	Imported chicken	α-HCH	1	7	1 (0)
		Dieldrin	1	7	0.2 (0)
	UK turkey	α-HCH	12	49	1 (0)
		Hexachlorobenzene	1	49	0.2 (0)
		Dieldrin	1	49	0.2 (0)
		DDT	2	49	1 (0)
		Chlordane	1	48	0.05 (0)
1991	Pheasant	α-HCH	7	22	1 (0)
1992	UK chicken	α-HCH	21	68	1 (0)
		Dieldrin	2	68	0.2 (0)
		DDT	6	68	1 (0)

DDT, dichloro diphenyl trichloroethane; DDE, bis chlorophenyl dichloroethylene; α-HCH, hexachloro cyclohexane
Pesticides analysed in addition to above: β-HCH, bromphos, carbophenthion, chlorfenvinphos, chlorpyrifos, diazinon, endrin, heptachlor, propetamphos

pesticides in a wide range of foodstuffs including poultry meat and eggs. No serious problem has been revealed; the few positive samples had pesticide levels well below the MRLs (Table 11.6).

METHODOLOGY

There are well-established methodologies for OC(14) and OP(15) analysis. These are multiresidue procedures based on final determination using gas chromatography. As with veterinary drugs, determination of pesticides at trace level (from parts per million to parts per billion) requires meticulous care and attention in order to obtain good identification and quantification over the range of pesticides covered. The general approach is similar, with extraction, clean-up and determination steps involved.

Also as for veterinary drugs the analyst is being required to confirm positive findings and it is becoming routine in the better laboratories to use mass spectrometry as the detection method for the gas chromatography. Analytical laboratories are also under pressure to have their procedures and analytical methods accredited to international standards or equivalent and to participate in analytical assessment programmes.

Checks for residues

Checks have to be carried out at the farm, at the slaughterhouse and (for imported meat) at the port of entry. Some countries also monitor shops by taking samples of a whole range of foods. Checks also have to be made during the production and sale of drugs, and on the accuracy of records of distribution and sales.

The collection of samples for testing has to be random and usually without prior notice, and the responsibility for this is normally placed with the central authority of each country. This authority also has to decide the frequency of testing, which depends to some extent on the pattern of drug use in the country. In the EU, directives lay down the method of operation of these checks for the whole Community, which ensures that trade can be carried on in the knowledge that all the member countries are operating to the same standards, although poultry have not yet been included in official plans.

Poultry sampling is different from sampling of other farm animals where individually identified animals are tested. For poultry a group of birds of the same species, age range, on the same farm and reared under the same conditions may be classed as a batch, and the sampling may be carried out on a batch rather than individual animals. An advantage of the batch requirement is that samples from a number of birds may be pooled to provide enough material for testing. In the slaughterhouse it may be possible to obtain the samples from the birds that are considered unfit for human consumption, so avoiding the risk of downgrading other birds by taking samples.

The frequency of testing must be related to the results of previous samples; if the vast majority of tests are negative then a more infrequent regimen may be introduced.

Farmers are expected to keep records of the use of drugs on their farms; for example, each time a load of food that includes medicinal substances or other drugs is delivered to the farm, details of the delivery should be recorded, as should the dates when the food is given to the birds. Regular checks on these records have to be made, and sampling of water and feedstuff is necessary to confirm that the withdrawal periods of the drugs have been complied with. Samples may also be taken from culled birds.

Sampling at the slaughterhouse consists of collecting the various parts of the animal required for a particular test. The birds are frequently too small to permit the required amount of material to be collected from one bird, so normally pooled samples are collected from six domestic fowls or ducks, or from two turkeys from the same batch. The samples can be of skin, liver, kidney, bile or muscle, depending on the requirements for the test, which in turn depends on the substance being investigated. Most tests are for antibiotics including sulphonamides, hormones, cocciodiostats, and possible contaminants of the feed or the environment.

When samples are taken by a member of the official inspection service the samples must be marked in such a way that birds that have been sampled can be traced if this proves to be necessary. The samples are normally hard frozen and then sent as quickly as possible to the laboratory for testing, and the record of the action taken should be retained by the inspection service.

Where positive results are obtained tracing must be carried out from the slaughterhouse back to the farm of origin. If the substance is an illegal substance in the country, e.g. stilbene in the EU, then further tracing may be necessary to find out where the farmer obtained it, to investigate other possible sales and where it might have been used to treat other poultry. If the residue is environmental then an investigation on the farm will be necessary.

If the residues are above the MRL of a licensed medicine, it is likely that the withdrawal period of the drug has not been observed. This could be intentional or it could be that there has been a mistake with the feed, e.g. the wrong feed has been given to the birds. If it seems as if other poultry which are still on the farm and are going for slaughter have also not completed the necessary withdrawal period, then the farmer should not send them until the full withdrawal period has been completed.

If the residue is found in imported poultry meat that has been sampled at the port, then the exporting country's competent authority has to be informed and in most cases the meat destroyed.

Conclusion

Residues in poultry meat are generally very well under control as far as can be seen. Pesticide surveillance over a considerable time has shown the problem to be minimal. Veterinary drug residue surveillance will acquire greater significance when the EU include poultry in their national surveillance schemes. How large the schemes are likely to be has yet to be decided and which drugs will be included is still unknown. Limited non-statutory surveillance has identified a few antibiotic residues, no hormones, but some coccidiostat residues, particularly in eggs. The source of these latter residues is still a matter of conjecture but experience suggests that they will be removed. The level at which these coccidiostats occurs varies and since no MRL has been deduced, the residues may be shown to be of little significance.

References

1. Kidd ARM. The potential risk of effects of antimicrobial residues in human gastro-intestinal microflora. Discussion document. Brussels: FEDESA, 1994.
2. Evaluation of certain veterinary drug residues in food. 34th Report of JECFA. Technical Report Series 788. Geneva: WHO, 1989.
3. Woodward KN. Use and regulatory control of veterinary drugs in food production. In: Creaser CS, Purchase R (eds) Food contaminants: sources and surveillance. Cambridge: Royal Society of Chemistry, 1991: Chapter 7, p 99.
4. Code of practice for category A registered manufacturers of medicated animal feedingstuffs. Alnwick: Ministry of Agriculture, Fisheries and Food, 1987.
5. Code of practice for category B registered manufacturers of medicated animal feedingstuffs. Alnwick: Ministry of Agriculture, Fisheries and Food, 1987.
6. Muramatsu T, Kakita M, Aoyagi Y, Okumura J. β-adrenergic agonist effects in liver and breast muscle protein synthesis in female chicks. *Poult Sci* 1991: 70: 1630–32.
7. Buyse J, Decuyfere E, Huyghebaert G, Horremans, M. The effect of clenbuterol supplementation on growth performance and on plasma hormone and metabolite levels of broilers. *Poult Sci* 1991; 70: 993–1002.
8. Crosby NT. Determination of veterinary residues in food. Ellis Horwood, London: 1991.
9. Shepherd MJ. Analysis of veterinary drug residues in edible animal products. See also Chapter 8, reference 3.

10. Bogaerts R, Wolf F. Fleischwirtsch 1980; **60**: 672–3.
11. EC Directive 86/469/EEC. Offic J European Comm L275. 1986; 36–45.
12. Veterinary residues in animal products 1986 to 1990. Food Surveillance Paper 33. London: HMSO, 1992.
13. Medicines Act Veterinary Information Service, July 1994. VMD, Addlestone, Surrey KJ15 3NB.
14. Telling GM, Sissons DJ, Brinkman HW. Determination of organochlorine insecticide residues in fatty foodstuffs using a clean up technique based on a single column of activated alumina. *J Chromatog* 1977; **137**: 405–23.
15. Verlagsgesellschaft VCH, Weinstein FRG Manual of pesticide residue analysis. Method S19 in Vol. 1, 1987: p 383 and Vol. 2, 1992: p 317.

CHAPTER 12

The Manufacture of Poultry Meat Products

Introduction

Poultry meat products are not easy to define because of the great variety which are manufactured. Some countries specify, in their legislation, the requirements for particular named products, e.g. cooked poultry, breaded poultry, or canned poultry. Others define "a product". The European Union in its Directive 92/5/EEC (as amended) states that a poultry meat product is prepared from or with poultry meat which has undergone treatment such that the cut surface shows that the product no longer has the characteristics of fresh poultry meat. This definition also causes problems because breaded, flash-fried poultry meat can contain raw meat (as only the surface is heated to a high temperature) but it is difficult to distinguish whether the poultry meat throughout the product has the appearance of fresh meat or not. This is even more of a problem if minced poultry meat or mechanically recovered meat is used in the product. For the purpose of this chapter, if the meat has been heated throughout, fully cured with a brine solution, or smoked, then it becomes a poultry meat product.

Poultry meat can be mixed with other foodstuffs to form named products such as pizza or chicken salad. If the meat is not fully processed but other foodstuffs are added, it is known as a poultry meat preparation. The requirements for buildings and for monitoring the processing will normally be the same whether the product is a meat preparation or a poultry meat product, except that where the product can be eaten by the consumer without any further processing such as heating, more stringent standards have to be applied. The label on the final product should indicate whether the product has to be cooked before being eaten or whether it is safe to eat without further processing.

Historically, meat products were first used as a way of storing meat so that it remained fit for human consumption by controlling bacterial growth. Pork was put into a mixture of salt, sodium nitrate and nitrite before being suspended from the kitchen ceiling where it was dried. In hot countries meat was cut into strips and put out to dry, again reducing the growth of bacteria by reducing the amount of available water. Later canned food was produced, although in home canning the technology used was not always correct – with disastrous consequences if botulism occurred. However, as refrigeration technology came into common use in homes and shops, temperature control became the preferred way of reducing bacterial growth for many products, and allowed many more types of products to come onto the market. In the early days of refrigeration, meat products were frozen, but once a refrigerated storage and distribution system was introduced which guaranteed temperature-controlled conditions from the meat products factory, through intermediate storage to the supermarket or shop, the chilled poultry meat product became a possibility. Chilled products have some advantages as some foods do not freeze well. An example of this is the sandwiches sold in many shops: a frozen cooked chicken and salad sandwich would not be very appetizing. However, the shelf-life of chilled products is shorter than that of the frozen product so that the shop or supermarket must ensure a fast turnover of the chilled product. The temperature control throughout the life of a chilled product is also more critical because an increase of a few degrees can allow a rapid increase in the number of bacteria present.

The rapid expansion of the poultry industry in the 1940s and 1950s used refrigeration technology to market frozen, and later chilled, carcases and portions. In the 1960s prepared ready-cooked poultry carcases and portions were marketed and this quickly expanded into ready meals where cooked poultry was prepared with other foods. The change in the lifestyle of society has affected the growth of the 'ready meal'. More working women and single person households means that the recipe dish and the quickly prepared meal are very useful as they can be ready for eating in a few minutes.

Managers of shops are always looking for something new to sell and the producers of poultry meat products have responded by manufacturing a large variety of new products. Sometimes changes are made to the ingredients. Some changes may appear small, like adding or removing one ingredient, but in all cases where a new product is being considered the process must be thoroughly reassessed from the food safety aspect. Any new procedure, or addition or removal of an ingredient, particularly where there is no experience of a similar product being sold, should be submitted to a risk assessment. Risk assessment is defined as a scientific process of identifying hazards and estimating risk, both quantitative and qualitative, of an adverse health effect on the consumer of the product. Changes to the process or recipe may be necessary to reduce or remove the risk. An example of a new procedure is the 'sous vide' process, where vacuum-packed food is heated to a temperature that does not destroy bacterial spores. If the subsequent handling and chilling does not prevent the growth of (for example) *Clostridium botulinum*, there is a risk that food poisoning may occur. Reduction of salt or sugar levels in processed food can also pose a risk of food poisoning because the water activity in the product may increase, permitting bacterial growth.

Codes of practice are available for some products and standards are laid down for the bacteriological status of some final products. Where standards have been set for the product, they should be complied with. There are some products, however, where a balance has to be made between spoiling the product (for instance by overcooking) and accepting that with some foods there will be a public health risk, however slight. This is where the risk assessment procedure is important. Some foods are considered too much of a risk for pregnant women, and food for people who are old or in hospital, particularly those whose immune system is not functioning properly, has to be very carefully processed to ensure it is safe for the patients to eat. The risk to any staff in the meat products plant from the ingredients or the processing must also be considered and their health and safety taken into account at all stages of the process. Any new product has, normally, to be tested initially by taste panels and by test marketing in a few shops.

The manufacturing premises must be specifically designed for the type of product which is to be produced, and the appearance of both the inside and the outside of the premises must be clean, neat and tidy. Inspectors would be unlikely to conclude that food production is being carried out hygienically in a factory where the amenity areas are dirty and cramped.

Any assessment of the process in the factory must start with a check on the status of the food entering the factory and the guarantee that the standards of these ingredients can be consistently maintained. Each process must then be investigated to ensure that the public health risk is minimized. Temperature control in particular is critical in the processing of most poultry meat products, and this includes the temperature of the poultry meat on arrival, the heating processes and the subsequent cooling. Temperature control in storage, distribution and exposure for sale is equally important. Wrapping and packaging also play a part. Vacuum packaging reduces the rate of growth of some micro-organisms. Modified atmosphere packaging where gases with a low oxygen content are introduced into the pack also reduces the growth of some spoilage bacteria. These may help to maintain the safety and shelf-life of the product, although there are public health risks if storage temperatures are not maintained, because bacterial spores will survive most cooking processes and toxins of *Clostridium botulinum*, for example, can be formed in anaerobic conditions.

Most processors pass the final wrapped product through a metal detector to ensure that there is no metal foreign body in the product. Finally, the shelf-life must be considered, bearing in mind the lack of control once the product has left the refrigerated cabinet in the shop.

A detailed record is required of the source and batch numbers of the ingredients which go into each batch of products and the results of the monitoring of the processes that have been carried out, from arrival on the premises to dispatch in a lorry or van. This ensures that records can be consulted if there is any concern about the product.

Plant construction and equipment

The site

The site of a poultry meat products plant has to be carefully considered. It should be large enough for modern transport lorries to manoeuvre easily into the reception and dispatch bays. It should have good road access, and in some countries rail access is useful. A supply of electricity is needed, together with gas, oil or solid fuel to heat the hot water and a plentiful supply of potable water, preferably from an official water supply. There should be access to a waste and sewerage system to remove waste solids and waste water. In most urban areas there are plots of land designated for industrial use and a large site on one of these is often suitable for a meat products premises. Buses usually run to these sites, enabling workers to reach the factory. Car parking space is also a requirement.

The site for the processing premises should not be near to another factory or a dumping area if either could cause contamination of the food by pollution or smell, or where vermin like rats or flies are likely to breed. The site should be surrounded by a fence or wall to prevent unauthorized access of animals or people and there should be a controlled entrance and exit to the premises. The raw materials for the process should be delivered and waste removed from one side of the factory and the products should be loaded on the other side, to ensure separation. The roadways and the surround to the premises should be constructed of concrete, with falls to drains to take away surface water and to ensure these areas can be kept clean. A lorry wash should be provided which should consist of a sloped and drained concrete area supplied with a water supply, a hose pipe and disinfectant. In countries that have a cold climate, warm water should be provided to prevent the water from freezing, and the washing area should be covered.

Staff entering the premises should be able to go directly to their changing rooms and canteen without entering any workrooms or storage areas. They should also be able to go directly to their work stations from the changing rooms, without having to go outside where their protective clothing could become contaminated with dust or mud. The outside of the premises should be kept neat and tidy so that staff and visitors recognize that this is a food factory that maintains high standards.

Most companies find that eventually they want to expand their product range, their throughput, or both. If possible the site should be large enough to take this into consideration and the building placed within the site to allow for these additions and alterations.

WATER SUPPLY

If there is any doubt about a continuous supply of water, a water storage tank capable of holding a day's supply should be provided on site. It should be covered and be capable of being cleaned on a regular basis.

In some countries the bacterial status of the water is not always up to the required internationally acceptable standard, and some treatment of the water may be necessary on the site, particularly if the product is to be exported. The most common method of treating water is by chlorination, although other methods can be used such as ultraviolet light. Chlorination does not work if there is organic material in the water, which necessitates some form of preliminary filtration. If the water is from a source that is not potable, full treatment of the water will be necessary. This normally consists of sedimentation, flocculation, filtration and finally chlorination.

In plants where retorting of hermetically sealed containers takes place, the cooling water for the heated containers may be recirculated to save water. It is vital that this water is of a potable standard before being re-used and this is normally guaranteed by chlorinating the water again. Chlorine when added to water must have a contact time of at least 20 minutes for it to be effective, and residual free chlorine should be detectable in the water after the completion of the cooling treatment. Where water treatment is necessary the site must be large enough to accommodate any necessary water treatment plant and equipment.

WASTE WATER

There must be facilities for the adequate disposal of waste water as well as surface water. The waste water should, where possible, enter the sewerage system provided for the area. Sometimes fat removal equipment may be required, and gross dirt may have to be removed by screening the waste water before releasing it to the sewerage system. In some countries treatment to reduce the biochemical oxygen demand (BOD) of the waste water may be required, although careful control within the plant can usually maintain a BOD that is acceptable to most official sewerage treatment plants. Traps in drains and the removal of scraps from the floor rather than washing them down the drain help to control the BOD. Whether any treatment of the waste water is required at the factory will depend on the standard required before the water can be discharged into the sewer. Treatment can be by several methods and can include aeration to activate the bacteria, where mechanical agitation of the waste water takes place in large tanks, or by filtration in towers where bacteria also act on the waste. If waste water has to be treated on the premises then the equipment must be positioned far enough away from the food factory so that contamination by droplets in the air or by personnel movements is kept to a minimum. Pipes carrying sewage from the toilets must be enclosed and should not be joined to the waste water pipes from the factory, to ensure that there is no risk of raw sewage backing up into the food premises.

Design of the processing premises

The design of the premises must be based around the processes that are to be carried out in the building. It is not always possible to convert an existing factory without major structural alterations, and if any changes are made to the products, particularly in product type, extensive changes may be required to the design of the premises. It would be impossible, for instance, to produce canned chicken soup in premises that were designed to produce a chicken pizza. The design of the premises should be 'tailormade' for the product, taking into account the machinery required for the process.

RECEPTION AREA

All premises must have provision for the arrival and reception of the raw materials and ingredients. The lorry or van bringing these foods needs to be able to draw up to a sealed or air-locked reception bay from which the food can be moved as quickly as possible into the storage rooms. These rooms must be capable of storing the food at the desired temperatures or humidity and away from any other food that could cause contamination either by bacteria or by smell. Some ingredients, e.g. flour, can be stored in special containers such as a silo, and provision must be made for this on the site. Boxed ingredients and boxed meat should not be held in the same store as meat or food that is not boxed, so separate stores may be required.

Boxed ingredients must be unpacked in a special room or area so that neither the box contents nor the product are put at risk. The used empty boxes must be removed hygienically without passing through other workrooms. If the poultry meat is frozen on arrival, an area or room is required where thawing can take place under controlled temperature conditions.

PROCESSING ROOMS

The processing rooms have to be designed specifically for the processes carried out at the premises. The criteria for the design must be to ensure that there is minimal risk of the final product being contaminated, and that the storage rooms control any deterioration of the product caused by bacterial growth or any form of contamination. Movement of raw material through processing to the final product stage must take place without crossing of product lines or movement of product back into areas containing raw ingredients.

DISPATCH

A sealed or air-locked dispatch bay must be placed adjacent to the final refrigerated storage rooms. Sometimes a refrigerated area for sorting the products into loads for dispatch will be required in the refrigerated storage rooms.

ANCILLARY ROOMS

Office accommodation is required, including an office for the official inspector. Storage space must be provided for dry goods, boxes and wrapping materials. There should normally be a laboratory on the site, preferably in a separate building not connected to the main building so that there is no risk of contamination to the product from the work carried out in the laboratory. Engineers also need a room with easy access to the workrooms and with space to mend and store equipment. Changing rooms with toilets and showers for the staff are also required; as well as separate rooms for men and women, there is some advantage in having separate rooms for staff working on raw materials and those working on the products.

TEMPERATURE CONTROL

Temperature control is very important. The temperature of the poultry carcases or meat must not be allowed to rise above 4 °C during any storage or cutting prior to processing. After any heating the product must be cooled to the storage temperature for the product, which is usually 3 °C or lower, and thereafter the temperature of the product must not be allowed to rise above this temperature. The refrigeration equipment must be capable of ensuring that the temperature of the heated product does not exceed 7 °C for longer than 2 hours (except for specially controlled conditions) and preferably for as short a time as possible. Thereafter the cooling process should continue until the storage temperature is reached. Some wrapped heated products may be initially cooled by showering with cold water. The shower room used for this must be well drained to remove the water used in the chilling process. Air conditioning may be needed in some workrooms where the cooked product is processed after cooling to at least 7 °C (e.g. rooms where the product is sliced and wrapped), to ensure that the temperature of the product does not rise.

Control of condensation by ventilation and insulation of the structure is important during these cooling and further processing stages. The ventilation must be balanced by introducing filtered air to compensate for the air that is extracted, although a slight reduction of air pressure in cooking rooms is an advantage as this prevents warm air passing into other parts of the premises. In air-conditioned rooms the cold air should not cause draughts, and one way of overcoming this problem is to have large cylindrical sleeves of material attached to the ceiling, through which the cold air is blown. All temperature-controlled rooms or areas must be fitted with temperature monitoring and recording devices, as well as an alarm in the stores to indicate when the temperature rises above an acceptable level.

ROOM SEPARATION

The decision about the number of processing rooms that are required depends on three main factors.

- To ensure temperature control of the ingredients or the product, temperature-controlled workrooms, refrigerated storage rooms and rooms where heating takes place will all need to be separated.
- The second factor is the risk of physical, chemical or bacteriological contamination of the ingredients or products. Procedures such as the smoking of meat and washing raw vegetables should have their own separate rooms. Some ingredients could taint other foods, e.g. fish could taint a poultry meat product, and so these must be processed in separate rooms.
- Thirdly, certain processes are continuous and the product is fully protected by the machinery during processing, so that it is acceptable to combine these processes in a single room (Figure 12.1). Some moving ovens are well insulated and will not affect the temperature of the room; in this case the remainder of the room could be used for forming foods which would pass through the moving oven to exit into another room for chilling and further processing.

Occasionally during processing the poultry meat and other ingredients which need to be temperature controlled have to be stored while awaiting the next process, and this should take place in refrigerated storage rooms, adjacent to the workrooms. At least one of these storage rooms will be required on the 'raw' side of the premises and another on the 'processed' side. These storage areas should also be available in case there is a breakdown in the processing.

In most processing premises, there is a point in the process at which the raw materials become a meat product. This point is usually the heat treatment, and in some cases the final product is then ready for eating without any further heat treatment. At this point in the process, when the heating is finished, there must be a complete separation of rooms used for subsequent processing from those where the raw materials are handled. The rooms used for further processing such as cooling, cutting, mixing and wrapping is sometimes called the 'higher risk' rooms. It is also necessary to control the movement of staff and equipment to prevent cross-contamination from the raw material area to the processed product area by ensuring there is no direct access between the rooms. Frequently equipment has to be moved from processing rooms to an equipment cleansing and disinfection room, and this too should be fitted into the design so that dirty equipment does not have to pass through other workrooms on its way to the cleaning room.

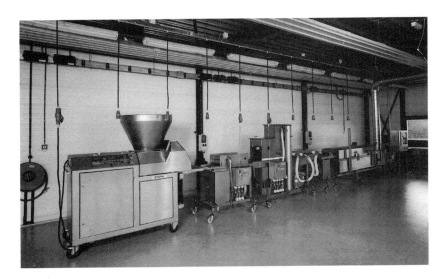

Figure 12.1 A continuous processing unit for pressure-forming a product which is coated with breadcrumbs and heated in fat. (With kind permission of Stork PMT.)

COOKING

Ovens can operate by dry or wet heat, or by smoking; they should preferably have an entrance at the front and an exit door at the back of the oven. This helps to form the separation between the raw ingredients and the cooked product, the latter passing into a separate part of the premises. If there is only one door to the oven, space must be provided to keep the uncooked food away from the oven, so that the cooked product can be taken through this space to the chillers. A barrier in front of the ovens to keep an area free from equipment can be a help.

PACKING AND DISPATCH

Boxing should be done in a separate room and a box store should be provided adjacent to or above this room. Boxes should normally be made up before being brought into the boxing room. If the packaging is a plastic crate this must be cleaned, disinfected and dried in a separate room and may then be brought into the room where wrapping is taking place. A dispatch bay is normally required, and these should be sealed so that the contents for dispatch do not come into contact with the outside air. The bays may be air-conditioned to maintain the temperature of the materials being handled, and an air lock can be provided.

STORES

Stores are required for the materials used in wrapping and packaging, as well as a separate store for ingredients that can be stored at room temperature. The amount of storage space required is often underestimated when designing a poultry meat product plant. Some ingredients that have to be carefully controlled, like spices used in marinades, should be stored in a lockable room and carefully controlled during processing, being weighed in a separate room adjacent to the store. In some premises solutions are injected into the meat or the meat is tumbled with a solution of phosphates or salts. A separate room is required for making up these solutions. Stores are also required for cleaning materials and equipment.

OTHER CRITERIA

Once the flow of the process and the requirement for rooms have been decided, other factors have to be taken into account. The first is the route taken by the staff from their changing rooms and canteen to the workrooms. It is preferable that members of staff enter the room in which they are to work from a corridor; they must certainly not pass through rooms where there are raw materials on their way to rooms where there are processed products. Where the food is intended for human consumption without any further heat treatment, an extra room where the staff can change into protective clothing adjacent to the workroom for that product is sometimes provided.

Secondly, the route taken by waste materials or contaminated products must be considered. Waste should go directly in watertight bins to a holding room, which has direct access to the outside of the premises so that it can be removed easily from the premises. This waste collection exit should not be near to the reception or dispatch bay.

The third criterion is the route taken by moveable equipment which has to go for cleaning, e.g. bins, which should go to a dedicated room to be cleansed and disinfected. The design of this cleaning room is also important to ensure that equipment does not become recontaminated once it has been cleaned. This room must be ventilated to the outside to ensure no steam or water droplets can enter workrooms. It must also have smooth, light-coloured, impervious walls, ceilings that are waterproof with no ledges for lodgement of dirt or water, and floors that are impervious, rotproof, and slope to grated and trapped drains.

The changing rooms must be light and spacious with facilities for staff to change into their protective clothing and leave their outside clothing. Storage for the protective clothing must ensure that it is not contaminated before the workers put it on. Lockers should have sloping tops to prevent things being stored on the top, and either be joined to the floor or raised off the floor so that the area underneath can be cleaned. Flush toilets, wash-hand basins and showers must be provided. Some countries lay down in legislation the number of toilets and wash-hand basins to be provided for the staff; in any case, there must be a sufficient number to allow the staff to go to the toilet and to wash their hands before starting work at the beginning of a shift. Taps for the wash-hand basins should not be capable of being operated by hand or elbow, i.e. they can be operated by knee, foot or photoelectric cell. Towels may be used only once and a container for dirty towels must be provided near to the wash-hand basins. Some countries permit the use of hot-air hand dryers provided they are not operated by pushing a button by hand; other countries do not permit their use as there is some evidence that these dryers contaminate hands with bacteria. Showers for staff to use before putting on their work clothes should also be provided. Staff should be able to enter workrooms from their changing rooms without their protective clothing becoming contaminated. Facilities should be provided where staff can wash their boots and aprons and there should be a dry, clean area where this protective clothing can be stored.

STRUCTURAL STANDARDS

Wash-hand basins, again with taps which cannot be operated by hand or arm, and provided with disinfectant soap and a hygienic method of drying hands, should be provided at the entrance to all workrooms; if staff cannot leave their position during the working period, the basins should be placed near to the work stations. If implements are used in workrooms, 'sterilizers' should be provided for them. The 'sterilizer' should operate with hot water at a minimum temperature of 82 °C, have a continuous overflow of water, and be designed for the implements in use. A sterilizer for a knife, for example, should be able to hold the knife so that during working times only the blade and the lower part of the handle is disinfected, but the whole knife can be immersed at break periods. The waste water from the sterilizer and basins must be connected to the floor drain so that waste water does not flow across the floor.

Workrooms, food storage rooms and corridors where food is transported must be light and spacious, providing staff with good working conditions. The walls, pillars and partitions must have smooth, impervious and light-coloured surfaces, with rounded corners and angles. Protection of exposed corners by stainless steel inset into the surface of the wall, will help to prevent damage to the wall. Doors, doorways and window frames should be covered with a light-coloured, smooth, durable and impervious surface which will not taint the product, and doors should be self-closing, and closely fitting to exclude vermin. Plastic strip curtains are not acceptable in rooms where there are any exposed products or ingredients. The ceilings must be constructed and finished to minimize condensation, mould development, flaking paint or rust and the lodgement of dirt, and be capable of being kept clean. Floors must be durable, impervious, non-slip, capable of being cleaned and, except in rooms where frozen food is stored, sloped to drains. It is difficult, however, to ensure that the floor is both non-slip and smooth, and therefore a compromise has to be reached to ensure that there is no risk to the staff working in the premises. In premises where food and meat is transported in bins, the bin wheels can be very rough on the floor which should be hard-wearing enough to take this abuse. Drains in the floor must be fitted with traps and gratings; floor drains must be designed to be easily cleaned and have a fall so that water is not retained within the channels. The channels should be covered with gratings where personnel and equipment are likely to cross over them.

Lighting must be provided: if windows are necessary they should not be capable of being opened, and should be in the upper part of the walls, with sloped sills. Lighting at work stations should be at an intensity of around 220 lux, and lights should be shatterproof or protected by shatterproof lamp shades.

Ventilation should be very carefully controlled. The ventilators, with filters that can be cleaned, should bring clean filtered air into the rooms, and the air pressure within the rooms must be balanced to ensure that contamination is not carried by air from one room to another, particularly from an area where raw materials are handled to one where exposed final product is present. Air conditioning will also be required in rooms where work is carried out on poultry products.

EQUIPMENT

Equipment used in processing must be designed to comply with several different and sometimes conflicting requirements. It must perform the tasks which it is designed to do efficiently and consistently. It must be easy to monitor the processing the machine carries out, and monitors should be built into the equipment wherever possible. A cooker, for example, should have a way of recording the internal temperature of the product, the oven temperature and the length of time for which it has been heated. Other machines incorporate a system of allowing the staff to visually inspect the product, e.g. by conveying the products past a person who assesses whether they comply with the required specification. With most machines there is some involvement of staff either manually, e.g. by feeding in ingredients, or for monitoring. This must be easy to do so that staff can continue to carry out the task efficiently without physical strain.

All equipment must be capable of being satisfactorily cleansed and disinfected. Big machinery that cannot be moved must either be installed off the floor to allow cleaning underneath or placed on the floor with a waterproof seal round the base. However, a machine (like one that straps boxes) operating in a room where the only food is already wrapped and boxed does not require the same standard of cleanliness as the machine operating in a room where there is exposed food or ingredients. Manufacturers must, during the design stage of the equipment, consider how their machines are to be cleansed and disinfected. All surfaces that come into contact with ingredients or the product must be made of high-grade stainless steel, or in some cases smooth, light-coloured, strong plastic. Particular attention should be paid to joins in the materials to ensure they are smooth and not pitted or cracked.

Electrical and technical parts which operate and control the machines are becoming more complicated as technology improves. However, they are not always easy to keep clean. They should, where possible, be situated away from the machines, or enclosed in a sealed container that can be kept clean. They should not be positioned above the place where food is likely to be present. The machine must be capable of being stripped down for thorough cleaning and disinfection at the end of the working day, and the product contact surfaces and the parts in the area where the food is present must be capable of frequent cleansing and disinfection during breaks in processing. Other parts of the equipment must be made of smooth, impervious material which is corrosion resistant, with no flaking paint, and which can be cleansed and disinfected by food-standard detergents and disinfectants. The supply of services to these machines should enter the workroom as close as possible to the machines, and, where possible through the ceiling immediately above the machine to be supplied.

Processing

Once it has been decided to manufacture a poultry meat product, the process must be carefully investigated to ensure that the product will be safe to eat, provided it is properly treated after it leaves the factory. Codes of practice are available which cover many types of meat products, and should be carefully implemented. However, it is likely that in many premises there will be some variations in processing because of the design of the premises, because the ingredients are slightly different, or because the equipment is of a different specification. Each process has therefore to be investigated for each individual product.

Ingredients

A specification must be laid down for each of the ingredients on arrival and their subsequent storage conditions. This specification (e.g. for poultry carcases, flour or milk) should be agreed with the supplier and samples can be tested on arrival to ensure they are up to these standards. Quality is one standard that must be checked to see that the ingredients conform to the requirements of the processing plant. Other tests that can be carried out are a bacteriological assessment, and the temperature of the sample. It is good manufacturing practice to visit the premises where the ingredients are produced to check the standards of production. When the ingredients arrive at the premises, they must be placed in their storage place, which may have to be refrigerated, and used within the stated time scale, normally using the longest stored material first.

Examination of the process

Every process that is carried out within the premises should be examined. Each separate process in the manufacturing of the product, as well as the cleansing and disinfection of the premises and the responsibilities and duties of the staff carrying out the processing, has to be considered, and written down. The bacterial status of the ingredients or products should be assessed at each stage in the process, which will indicate whether the raw materials and the processing are satisfactory. Consideration should be given to checking if there is any risk of physical contamination, e.g. a splinter of bone in deboned chicken meat, or of chemical contamination from the use of materials such as disinfectants, and also where these checks should be carried out.

Each process should be examined to determine what hazards are associated with it and what risk they pose to the customer. The possibility of a piece of bone being present in some cuts of meat is high, and there is a risk that people may choke on it, if it is present in the product. This becomes a hazard which needs to be carefully monitored. In contrast, if raw poultry meat is contaminated with *Salmonella*, but the meat is going to be cooked, then, provided the temperature is adequate to kill the bacteria and there is no possibility of recontamination, the risk is small. Nevertheless, if the poultry meat is not contaminated with *Salmonella* this would ensure that the slight risk did not occur. The results obtained during the bacteriological assessment of each process have to be considered in relation to the results for the final product. If the final product has a high bacteriological count or there is evidence of contamination, it is possible by looking at the results from samples obtained during processing to find where the problem has arisen and to identify what corrective action is necessary.

At the same time, other steps in the manufacturing process need to be carefully assessed to ascertain the limits of the variations, if any, that can be allowed. Each step should be examined to assess what problems would arise if any deviations were to occur from the standard processing. If a deviation would result in a significant risk to the consumer, then the hazard has to be monitored to ensure that an unacceptable risk does not occur.

PHYSICAL AND CHEMICAL RISKS

Physical and chemical risks should be dealt with by determining where the problem could arise and taking appropriate measures at the relevant places. Pieces of bone should be removed and the meat checked during the stages of cutting and deboning of the poultry meat. If there is any risk of contamination of the product with minute pieces of metal from implements or equipment, a metal detector can be placed near the end of the wrapping process to reject any contaminated product.

Temperature control

Temperature control of poultry meat is most important. Bacteria associated with human food poisoning may grow if the temperature of the raw poultry meat is allowed to rise, and could contaminate the environment of the factory or form heat-resistant toxins which can cause food poisoning. If the poultry meat is allowed to spoil it will never be satisfactory even if cooked.

If cooking forms part of the process, the deep muscle tissue should reach a specified temperature which should be above 172 °C for at least 2 minutes, or an equivalent degree of heating, to ensure that vegetative forms of bacteria that can cause food poisoning, including *Listeria*, are destroyed. However, poultry is usually cooked to a higher temperature, which for broiler carcases can reach 90 °C. The size of the pieces of meat or of the carcases to be cooked should be laid down so that all the meat in the oven is cooked consistently. If the cooking temperature rises a degree or so above the set temperature, this may be allowed, so a range rather than a specific temperature may be laid down. The time and temperature graph of the oven should be monitored, and a probe thermometer should be used to monitor the temperature of the product, which should also be recorded.

After processing, the product has to be cooled in a chiller which allows air to circulate round the product to ensure even cooling; if the product is sealed in a wrapper, a water shower may be used for the initial cooling. To control bacterial growth, the product should be retained for as short a time as possible – and certainly no longer than 2 hours – within the temperature range 63 °C to 7 °C, and cooled as quickly as possible thereafter to storage temperature. Records of time and temperature should be maintained.

It is preferable not to have to cool large pieces of meat as this can take too long, so a large turkey should be portioned prior to cooking. When the product is cooled sufficiently, it may be taken into the further processing room (sometimes known as the 'high risk' room) where a separate team using separate utensils and equipment carry out any further assembly or cutting of the product prior to wrapping. Ventilation and air conditioning of this room should provide clean, preferably filtered air at positive pressure to ensure a low humidity and a temperature of 12 °C or lower. The ventilation should not cause draughts which could chill the staff working in the room. The temperature of the room and of samples of the product should be taken and recorded to ensure that the critical points are being complied with. Recording thermometers with temperature probes placed in the warmest part of the room should supply a continuous record of the room temperature. Any product surplus to requirements should be stored in a dedicated chiller which can hold the material at the appropriate temperature.

If the product is to be frozen it should be moved into the freezer as quickly as possible. This can be a blast freezer or a tunnel filled with nitrogen at a low temperature.

Wrapping and packaging

The specification and storage of the wrapping and packaging material should ensure that the product is not contaminated and is adequately protected during storage, loading and subsequent sales. Boxing should take place in a separate room. Most poultry products are stored either frozen at minus 18 °C or lower, or chilled to less than 3 °C. Loading can be into a clean insulated vehicle, if the journey is short, or, preferably, into a clean refrigerated lorry which is cooled to the storage temperature of the product before loading commences. A record of the temperature in the van or lorry should be maintained when food is present.

Monitoring the product

Investigating the final product for bacteria can be a way of assessing the processing, and it is possible to identify weaknesses in the process from these results. However, management should not depend on the bacteriological testing of the final product to see whether the process has been carried out satisfactorily but rather on controlling the process as it is taking place. However, in the case of product processed as a shelf-stable one, in a hermetically sealed container, some of the containers have to be incubated and monitored prior to dispatch of the batch, in which case storage has to be provided to hold the products until the results are known. This does not always happen, in which case there has to be a recall procedure if the results are unsatisfactory.

One method of monitoring the process is the Hazard Analysis Critical Control Point (HACCP) system (Table 12.1, Figure 12.2). This has been accepted by some countries as a means of controlling the safety of food. However, any system can only be as effective as its weakest link, and therefore the right professional help must be obtained when planning to introduce an HACCP system. There has to be a team effort by key personnel which should include the management of the factory, the processing manager and an engineer. A bacteriologist experienced in HACCP is a vital member of the team; this is not necessarily the plant bacteriologist, although this person also has a part to play. The official inspector for the premises should also be involved. The team has to examine the processes, identify the hazards and then assess these in relation to risk. The process is then examined again to identify where these hazards can be controlled. A

Table 12.1 HACCP guidelines.

Principles

HACCP is a system which identifies specific hazard(s) and preventative measures for their control. The system consists of the following seven principles:

Principle 1
Identify the potential hazard(s) associated with food production at all stages, from growth, processing, manufacture and distribution, until the point of consumption. Assess the likelihood of occurrence of the hazard(s) and identify the preventative measures for their control.

Principle 2
Determine the points/procedures/operational steps that can be controlled to eliminate the hazard(s) or minimize its likelihood of occurrence – (Critical Control Point (CCP)). A 'step' means any stage in food production and/or manufacture including raw materials, their receipt and/or production, harvesting, transport, formulation, processing, storage, etc.

Principle 3
Establish critical limit(s) which must be met to ensure the CCP is under control.

Principle 4
Establish a system to monitor control of the CCP by scheduled testing or observations.

Principle 5
Establish the corrective action to be taken when monitoring indicates that a particular CCP is not under control.

Principle 6
Establish procedures for verification which include supplementary tests and procedures to confirm that the HACCP system is working effectively.

Principle 7
Establish documentation concerning all procedures and records appropriate to these principles and their application.

Application of the principles of HACCP
During the hazard analysis and subsequent operations in designing and applying HACCP systems, consideration must be given to the impact of raw materials, ingredients, food manufacturing practices, role of manufacturing processes to control hazards, likely end-use of the product, consumer populations at risk and epidemiological evidence relative to food safety.

The intent of the HACCP system is to focus control at CCPs. Redesign of the operation should be considered if a hazard is identified but no CCPs are found.

From reference 1, with kind permission of the Food and Agriculture Organization of the United Nations.

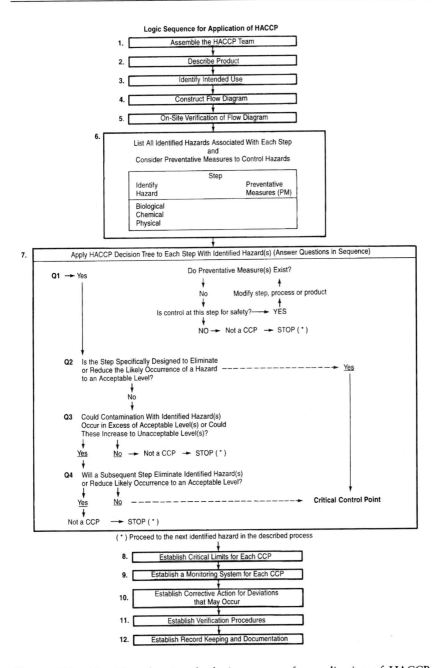

Figure 12.2 Algorithm showing the logic sequence for application of HACCP. (From reference 2, with kind permission of the Food and Agriculture Organization of the United Nations.)

control programme is produced indicating what monitoring is required, how the results are to be recorded and what action is to be taken when the set limits have been exceeded or not reached. It may, for instance, be necessary to take the temperatures of the products, in which case monitoring equipment will be necessary at many of the control points. The responsible staff should be aware of what action to take if the set parameters are not achieved.

A programme detailing the protective clothing to be worn, how hands and boots are to be cleaned and how illnesses have to be reported, should be provided for the people who are working in the plant and for any visitors.

Details should also be provided for the cleansing and disinfection of the premises during the breaks in production and at the end of the day. This should be checked visually and bacteriologically and the results recorded.

The results of the monitoring should also be recorded in relation to the batch being processed so that the full history of the ingredients and the processing is available for each batch. These records can be checked if there is any subsequent problem and should be retained for a period of time, depending on the type of product. The results of all the records taken over a period should also be examined to see whether there is evidence of trends which indicate that something is gradually going wrong. It may be noticed, for instance, that the cooking is taking slightly longer, in which case the ovens should be checked.

If any equipment or the ingredients or processing are changed, a new assessment should be made of the process and it is necessary to re-assess the process at regular intervals to ensure that the monitoring programme is still satisfactory.

Requirements for staff

The role of staff in maintaining food hygiene is discussed in Chapter 7. Staff working on the product may contaminate it with micro-organisms which can cause food poisoning, particularly if they suffer from diarrhoea or vomiting. Sore throats can be caused by staphylococci, and cuts or abrasions on the skin can also become infected. Staff with any of these complaints should not work on food, although small cuts, etc. which are not infected may be covered with a waterproof covering. The covering should be a distinctive colour such as blue, so that if it inadvertently becomes loose, it can easily be detected. The covering may also have a metal thread running through it so that it can be detected by the metal detector at the end of the line, if it has fallen into a product. Legislation in some countries requires that a person taking on work in a food factory must have a medical certificate stating that there is no impediment to this person working with food. Some countries require this to be renewed annually, although it is more satisfactory to have a system of staff reporting to management, if they suffer an illness or return from a holiday in a country where food hygiene standards are not high. The company doctor can then decide whether to request a medical examination of the person.

Cleansing and disinfection

Cleansing and disinfection of the equipment, including the refrigeration equipment, and the premises must be carried out on a daily basis at the end of the working day (see also Chapter 7). Some cleansing and disinfection should also be carried out at break times in the production cycle. The daily cleaning must be carefully planned and the staff doing the work must have precise instructions. Ceilings are not always cleaned every day but they must be remembered in the programme. Some production rooms need to be dry when they are manufacturing product and so a time for drying may need to be built into the programme; machines that both wash the floor and suck up the dirty water may also prove useful. Although in some factories the whole premises is given the same cleaning treatment, this may not be the most satisfactory way of doing it because different rooms have different requirements. Some dry areas where damp would cause problems may need vacuum cleaners, whereas other rooms can be washed down with water. During the design of the premises consideration should be given to putting in a centralized cleaning pipe system which goes to all rooms. A supply of hot water, cold water, detergent and disinfectant will be required. Some companies sell products which carry out two or more of these processes at once, but care must be taken to ensure that the disinfectant is not used where there is visible dirt on the surface to be disinfected. The cleaning equipment itself and the room in which the equipment and materials are stored must also be kept clean.

Monitoring of the cleansing and disinfection should be carried out. A visual assessment is useful, but just because the area looks clean does not mean that it is properly disinfected. Bacteriological testing either of the surfaces or of some of the contact surfaces of the products can be carried out. Smooth surfaces are the easiest to clean so nooks and crannies should also be examined, although if the premises is properly constructed there should be few of these.

Vermin control

Although the buildings should be constructed to prevent the entry of vermin, a routine for controlling vermin, particularly rats and mice, should be introduced. The poisoned bait and rooms should be checked regularly to see if there is any evidence of activity of vermin, which can be detected by the presence of droppings or disturbance of the bait. If there is any evidence of infestation then an inspection should be made to see if there are any ways of preventing entry and destroying breeding sites, and the number of baiting sites should be increased. Care must be taken to ensure that the bait cannot contaminate any food. A report should be kept of each check and inspection that is made. In storage rooms, there should be space between the wall and the items being stored so that the presence of vermin can be detected more easily.

Water

The standard of the water supplied within the premises is most important, as contaminated water can result in food poisoning in the consumer of the product. Water also contains spoilage organisms so a high count of these bacteria may cause contamination of the product. If the water comes from an official water supply to the area, in most industrialized countries it can be assumed that the toxicological, physical and chemical standards are acceptable, although the water company's reports on these substances should be reviewed annually. The standards for potable water used within the EU are contained in Directive 80/778/EEC.

To ensure a constant supply of water it is normal to store at least the equivalent of a 12-hour supply on the premises so that even if the supply of water is cut off, the factory would still be able to function for this time. Storage tanks must be covered with sealed lids to prevent dirt or dust contaminating the water, and must be emptied and cleaned as part of the regular cleaning schedule of the premises.

When plumbers make alterations to the water pipes they may close off a portion of a pipe which although full of water does not have a flow of water through it. Bacteria will grow in this 'dead end' water and subsequently may filter into the mains water. Such 'dead ends' of pipes must therefore not be permitted.

Back siphonage may be a problem, particularly if hose pipes are used to fill up tanks of water and the pipe extends into the water. If this is possible a vacuum breaker should be installed in the system so that if there is loss of pressure in the water system, air and not dirty water is sucked back into the water supply.

TESTING THE WATER

Water samples should be tested on a regular basis to check that both the incoming water and the water coming from the taps within the premises are up to the required standard. A sampler tap is normally placed in the pipe near to the point where the water enters the premises.

Prior to collecting the samples the taps should be sterilized either by heating with a blow torch or by using a hypochlorite solution. The tap should then be left running for about 5 minutes and should not be turned off again before sampling. The water is collected into a sterilized plastic bottle, avoiding splashing, and if the water is chlorinated the sample bottle should contain sodium thiosulphate to neutralize the chlorine. This substance should also be included if the tap is sterilized with hypochlorite solution.

Water entering the premises must be sampled at least once a year. In the workrooms cold-water taps or mixer taps, which mix both hot and cold water, should be sampled on a regular basis (usually monthly) and each tap should be tested at least once a year. A plan of the premises with the positions of the cold-water and mixer taps marked and numbered on it, is useful for recording on the sample bottle the number of the tap as well as the date of collection, so that if the results are unsatisfactory the source can be easily investigated. Contact must be maintained with the water company to be sure that the management of the food factory and the inspection team are alerted if there are any lowering of standards, especially increasing bacteriological counts.

The sample collected from the tap should be cooled and taken quickly to a laboratory for testing for bacteria. In hot climates the water should be kept cold during transport, e.g. by immersing the bottle in ice in a cool-box. Total viable counts at 22 °C after 72 hours incubation and at 37 °C after 48 hours incubation should be recorded. Testing should also be carried out for coliform bacteria, *Escherichia coli*, and less frequently for faecal streptococci and sulphite-reducing clostridia.

Guidelines are suggested for the total viable counts of 100 at 22 °C and 10 at 37 °C, but what is more relevant is a significant rise in these numbers which indicates the water is unsatisfactory. Records of the results should be retained for several years so that a 'normal' pattern can be recognized. Coliforms may be found; if they occur infrequently in very small numbers this may not be significant, but several coliforms in a sample or in several samples, or the presence of *E. coli*, faecal streptococci or sulphite-reducing clostridia indicates that the water is not acceptable.

If the results indicate that the source of water is unsatisfactory then processing should stop. If a single tap has a poor result it should be isolated and not used, and any storage tanks supplying the tap should be cleaned out and water pipes checked for any dead ends. The tap and the washer should be cleaned and perhaps the washer replaced, and then the tap can be resampled.

Private water supplies must be tested for toxicological, physical and chemical aspects at least once a year, and for bacteria on a regular basis at least once a month. Any unsatisfactory results in the water entering the premises must lead to the immediate closure of the factory.

Satisfactory water from a borehole, well or spring should normally bechlorinated by a drip feed of hypochlorate solution to ensure a residual level of about 0.5 parts per million of free chlorine at the end of the treatment, which involves holding water in a tank or tanks to ensure that there is a 20-minute contact time for the chlorine before the water is used. This ensures that any slight problem with bacteria in the water can be overcome. The water may also pass through ultraviolet light treatment which kills bacteria but has no residual effect. The covering of the borehole, well or spring must be watertight and capable of being kept clean, and concreted round in a way that diverts surface water away from the water source.

Hermetically sealed containers

Hermetically sealed containers include two- or three-piece cans, glass jars, or rigid, semi-rigid and flexible containers which protect the contents against entry of micro-organisms during and after heat processing. The seals for plastic containers are formed by pressure and heat. In premises where cans and glass jars are processed, more storage space is required both for empty and processed containers.

The empty containers and the lids (or 'ends') of cans, when delivered to the factory, must be up to the standards laid down by the factory management and a sample from each batch should be checked visually. Samples of the seams of the manufacturer's end of cans (Figure 12.3) and of the body of three-piece cans should be checked by tearing down and carrying out section checks (see below). The seam made by the processer end is tested by the same method used for the maker's end seam; samples are taken after the can has been filled and the lid fitted.

The containers must be conveyed hygienically to the workrooms; cans can be moved on magnetic or belt conveyors, or in channels of metal tubes leading to the filling machines. If the cans are stored on the top storey of the building, they can be fed by gravity to the workrooms. The empty cans must be cleaned by jets of air, steam or water being forced into the inverted can. The water must drain out of the inverted cans before they are put the right way up for filling. The cans can be filled either manually or by machine; a space should be left at the top as overfilling may damage the seals of the cans during heating in the retort. Preparation of the filling material normally

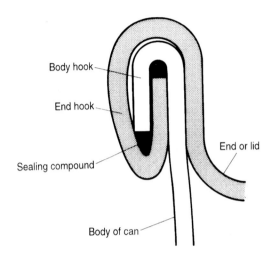

Body hook

End hook

End or lid

Sealing compound

Body of can

Figure 12.3   Cross-section of can seam.

involves heating, so that the food is still warm when filled into the containers. If the filling is cold, a partial vacuum has to be applied during the sealing process. Care must be taken when filling all types of containers to ensure that the seal is not contaminated with food. After filling the cans go through the seaming machines which in two operations seal the end to the can. The cans should be washed in warm water after sealing to remove any food from the outside of the can.

Glass containers should also be inverted for cleaning by compressed air, water jets or suction to ensure there is no broken glass or dirt in the containers, before filling.

Constant checks should be made on the filled and sealed containers. Technology has advanced such that a comprehensive account is beyond the scope of this book. However, serious faults can be detected by visual and tactile inspection.

Seam checks must be carried out on the sealed containers. Plastic containers can be tested by injecting compressed air into the container until either the seam or the material bursts. The pressure required for this must be recorded and checked against the manufacturer's recommendation. The seal thickness can also be measured using a micrometer and checked against the manufacturer's recommended thickness.

The variation in cans now available on the market makes it difficult to set precise standards for can seam testing. The aim of tearing down and assessing and measuring the seam of the cans is to monitor the overall standard of the seaming process and enable corrective action to be taken when results are abnormal. Some manufacturers of cans set standards for their products, but others do not. There are debates about what testing is necessary, particularly when new equipment of a high standard is being used. However, there should be no relaxation of the historical standards. Testing the seam involves section checks and the seam being torn down and measured, usually by micrometer although a seam projector may be used. Measurements should be made at different points on the seam depending on the can's shape and size. A cylindrical can is normally tested at three points. The manufacturer of the can should set the acceptable levels for the results from the tests, although these are laid down in codes of practice for standard cans.

The frequency of testing of hermetically sealed containers varies in different countries, but the seams should always be tested when the machines start up after a significant break and then after every 3 or 4 hours of production, at the least.

Retorting in steam under pressure is the next step after filling. The food can either be pasteurized, in which case it has to be stored under refrigeration, or retorted to a temperature that achieves commercial sterilization, in which case it is normally shelf-stable. For most foods, a process which is adequate to ensure destruction of all the spores of thermophilic organisms results in a deterioration of quality through overcooking which is unacceptable to the consumer. A compromise, therefore, has to be reached between killing all the spores and the palatability of the food. Experience has shown that this compromise, called commercial sterilization, is both safe for the consumer and the food remains palatable. If commercially sterilized products are held at very high temperatures, such as may be found in tropical climates, some spoilage may occur, but this happens very infrequently in countries with temperate climates.

The aim for the manufacturer of commercially sterilized products is the virtual destruction of the spores of *Clostridium botulinum*. The sterilizing procedure is calculated using information recorded during laboratory testing from thermocouples placed in the food at the coldest point in the container, while the container is heated. A time and temperature programme for heating the containers is then defined to ensure that the product is safe to eat. These programmes are unique to the food and the container tested.

Retorts are either batch cookers or continuous. Time and temperature, and time and steam pressure are the important criteria to be monitored, using calibrated recording equipment. The cooking pressure retorts must be fitted with calibrated recording thermometers and steam pressure gauges. Continuous hydrostatic retorts should be fitted with calibrated thermometers just above the steam and water interface and at the base of the steam chamber. The length of time the product is heated must also be recorded unless the containers travel through the retort at a set speed.

Flexible pouches and glass containers, in particular, must be protected from large changes in pressure during heating and subsequent cooling in the retort.

The water used in the cooling process must be of the highest bacteriological standard, as this water may enter some of the containers through minute holes in the seams. After leaving the retort the containers must be taken to a special clean area or room which is ventilated with filtered air, and they must not be handled until they are cool and dry. Some continuous retorts have a drying stage built into the retort, from which the cans are collected in a basket and then conveyed to a cooling area. It is important to know which containers have been processed and in which retort. Each basket of containers should carry a mark giving this information. Markers can be put on baskets for batch retorting which change colour on heating. Records of the heating process should be retained for 3 years.

After heating, any rough handling or abuse of the containers must be avoided as temporary or permanent leakage through small holes in the containers may occur. Bacteria may enter through these holes, particularly when the container is cooling and wet. The method of conveying containers must ensure that the containers do not knock against and damage each other, and the conveyor systems must be kept clean and dry.

Samples of the shelf-stable products should be incubated out at temperatures usually laid down by national legislation, and any gas formation in the containers should be investigated to detect faults in the process.

Training of all staff working with hermetically sealed containers is very important as visual and tactile monitoring is required at all stages in the process, with appropriate action being taken as soon as any abnormalities are detected. The staff controlling the retorts also have a very important job. An expert in hermetically sealed containers should always be on site as a consultant and training officer.

References

1. FAO. Codex Alimentarius. 1993:**1** (suppl.1):98.
2. FAO. Codex Alimentarius. 1993:**1** (suppl.1):102.

Index

Page numbers in *italic* refer to illustrations or tables; numbers in **bold** refer to main references

W. BIRD   INSP.

FST   SEPTIC
FEM   EMAC
FSk   SKIN LES.
FAs   ASCITIES
FMD   MACHINE DAM
FCO   CONTAM

FTA   TRAUMA
FAB   COLOUR/SMELL AB COLOUR
FOV   OVERSCALD
FTU   TUMOUR
FOR   DRAGON

STUNNER   SETTINGS   S VAL

Px   AMPS   402 - 456
      VOLTS   35 - 36

Cx   AMPS   524 - 582
      VOLTS   33 - 35

LINE SPEED ♂ Cx 110/MIN = 6,600/hr   100,000/SHF?
            ♀ Px 125/MIN = 7,500/hr   200,000/day

HANG ON   ♀ 1½ MIN ♂ 30-45 SEC (L. REQ 3MIN MAX)

BATH STUNNER

NECK CUTTER
   BLOOD SAMPLES TAKEN FOR LAB. (HELEN)
   BACK UP STUN
   MISSED. BIRD 100% (BONUS PAYMENT) MISSED W/ISSUE)
   NECK PULLER   GUIDE BARS ONLY.

PM FGM RM (H+I) REGS 1995 AS AMM

SCH 8 P11

IMMERSION CHILLERS

COUNTER FLOW SYSTEM

CHICKEN IN   AUGER SYSTEM FOR   CHICKEN OUT
WATER OUT   CONTINUOUS MOVEMENT (CARCASES)   WATER IN

+16°C   OVERFLOW SYSTEM   +4°C

PADDLES   4' — 12' FT   TEMP AS PER SCH 12
                         ACHIEVED IN SHORTEST PASS TIME

PRE-WASH

    < 2.5 kg   1.5 LTR/ CARCASE
    2.5 kg - 5 kg   2.5 LTR/ CARCASE
    > 5 kg   3.5 LTR/ CARCASE   MONITORING
                                           OF WATER

WATER FLOW (EXC AMOUNT TO FILL TANK)   FLOW THROUGH.

    < 2.5 kg   2.5 LTR/ CARCASE
    2.5 kg - 5 kg   4 LTR / CARCASE
    > 5 kg   6 LTR / CARCASE

TIME LIMITS

    MAX 30 MIN IN 1ST CHILL
    OTHERS (NO) "LONGER THAN STRICTLY NECESSARY"

EMPTIED/ CLEANED - AS NEC - AT LEAST 1 PER DAY

INSIDE / OUTSIDE CARCASE WASH
    NOT LEGAL REQ FOR AIR CHILLING

HIGH FREQUENCY STUNNING

MAINS 50 MHZ - PRIME FOR INDUCING SPASM
- (WILL KILL BIRDS - AORTIC
RUPTURE) ie SPASM IN HEART

INC FREQUENCY (>1000 MHZ (1400 BRANDON MHZ APP)))

NORMAL ELEC SIGN WAVE ∿∿

H.F. SQUARED SIGN WAVE ⊓⊔⊓⊔⊔

= DOESN'T INDUCE MUSCLE SPASM SO
CAN RECOVER ∴ BOTH CAROTID ARTERIES
MUST BE CUT AS BIRDS CAN RECOVER
RESTORATION OF BRAIN STEM ACTIVITY

BIRD ON FLOOR RAISE NECK NO RESISTANCE AFTER
15SEC (APPROX) SOME RESISTANCE IN NECK, (ALSO
. WAY OF TELLING EFFECTIVE STUN AS BIRDS
WILL FLAP (DIE FROM BLOODLOSS)

IN NORMAL STUN
CHECK STUN - NICTATATING MEMBRANE - REFLEX &
PINCH COMB - PAIN REFLEX
VISUAL HAND TO EYE REFLEX